SAMUEL, KINGS, CHRONICLES, EZRA-NEHEMIAH, II

Texts@Contexts

Series Editors

Athalya Brenner-Idan
Archie C. C. Lee
Gale A. Yee

SAMUEL, KINGS, CHRONICLES, EZRA-NEHEMIAH, II

Texts@Contexts

Edited by
Athalya Brenner-Idan and Gale A. Yee

LONDON • NEW YORK • OXFORD • NEW DELHI • SYDNEY

T&T CLARK
Bloomsbury Publishing Plc
50 Bedford Square, London, WC1B 3DP, UK
1385 Broadway, New York, NY 10018, USA
29 Earlsfort Terrace, Dublin 2, Ireland

BLOOMSBURY, T&T CLARK and the T&T Clark logo are trademarks of
Bloomsbury Publishing Plc

First published in Great Britain 2021
This paperback edition published 2023

Copyright © Athalya Brenn-Idan, Gale A. Yee and contributors, 2021

Athalya Brenner-Idan and Gale A. Yee have asserted their right under the Copyright,
Designs and Patents Act, 1988, to be identified as Editors of this work.

Cover design: Charlotte Design
Cover image © Jean-Philippe Tournut/Getty Images

All rights reserved. No part of this publication may be reproduced or transmitted
in any form or by any means, electronic or mechanical, including photocopying,
recording, or any information storage or retrieval system, without prior
permission in writing from the publishers.

Bloomsbury Publishing Plc does not have any control over, or responsibility for,
any third-party websites referred to or in this book. All internet addresses given
in this book were correct at the time of going to press. The author and publisher
regret any inconvenience caused if addresses have changed or sites have
ceased to exist, but can accept no responsibility for any such changes.

A catalogue record for this book is available from the British Library.

A catalog record for this book is available from the Library of Congress.

ISBN: HB: 978-0-5677-0115-2
       PB: 978-0-5677-0119-0
       ePDF: 978-0-5677-0116-9
       ePUB: 978-0-5677-0118-3

Series: Texts@Contexts, volume 8

Typeset by RefineCatch Limited, Bungay, Suffolk

CONTENTS

Series Preface	vii
List of Contributors	xiii
Abbreviations	xiv

INTRODUCTION   1
   Athalya Brenner-Idan

Part I
SAMUEL

'DAVID HATES THE LAME AND THE BLIND': TOWARDS AN
INTER(CON)TEXTUAL READING OF 2 SAMUEL 5.6-9   9
   Dominic S. Irudayaraj

'WHO CAN SPEAK FOR ME?' DAVID'S TEN CONCUBINES AND THE
CASE FOR COMFORT WOMEN   31
   Hyun Ho Park

THE POLITICS OF ANCIENT AND MODERN BURIAL: REVISITING THE
CASE OF RIZPAH   43
   Talia Sutskover

RIZPAH (RE)MEMBERED   57
   Athalya Brenner-Idan

Intermezzo
ON (HEROIC) DEATH BEYOND THE HEBREW BIBLE

COMMEMORATING FIRST WORLD WAR SOLDIERS AS MARTYRS   83
   Jan Willem van Henten

Part II
KINGS

THE TWO WOMEN IN SOLOMON'S JUDGEMENT: READING CROSS-
TEXTUALLY WITH CHINESE SOURCES   109
   Wei Huang

THE GOLDEN AGE OF ELIJAH THE PROPHET AS CULTURE
HERO IN ZIONIST EDUCATION   119
    Tamar Lammfromm

SANCTIFIED ASSASSINATIONS – QUEEN ATHALIAH OF JUDAH
AND ISRAEL'S PRIME MINISTER RABIN: A COMPARISON OF
TWO POLITICAL-RELIGIOUS MURDERS   139
    Ora Brison

Part III
CHRONICLES-EZRA-NEHEMIAH

MANASSEH AS PERPETRATOR IN KINGS AND CHRONICLES:
A VIEW ON VULNERABILITY   163
    Gerrie F. Snyman

PLUS ÇA CHANGE, PLUS C'EST LA MÊME CHOSE: RABBINIC
INTERPRETATIONS OF DEUTERONOMY FROM EZRA-NEHEMIAH TO
CONTEMPORARY ISRAEL'S CONVERSION CONTROVERSY   175
    Atar Hadari

SUKKOT AS RESISTANCE IN THE DAYS OF NEHEMIAH   191
    Lisbeth S. Fried

READING THE BIBLE REPATRIATELY: EZRA-NEHEMIAH, A CASE STUDY   203
    Roger S. Nam

Index of Biblical References   221
Index of Authors   225

SERIES PREFACE

> Myth cannot be defined but as an empty screen, a structure ...
> A myth is but an empty screen for transference.
> — Mieke Bal (1993)

'The Torah has seventy faces' (שבעים פנים לתורה)[1]

The discipline of biblical studies emerged from a particular cultural context; it is profoundly influenced by the assumptions and values of the Western European and North Atlantic, male-dominated, and largely Protestant environment in which it was born. Yet like the religions with which it is involved, the critical study of the Bible has traveled beyond its original context. Its presence in a diversity of academic settings around the globe has been experienced as both liberative and imperialist, sometimes simultaneously. Like many travelers, biblical scholars become aware of their own cultural rootedness only in contact with, and through the eyes of, people in other cultures.

The way any one of us closes a door seems in Philadelphia nothing at all remarkable, but in Chiang Mai, it seems overly loud and emphatic – so very typically American. In the same way, Western biblical interpretation did not seem tied to any specific context when only Westerners were reading and writing it. Since so much economic, military, and consequently cultural power has been vested in the West, the West has had the privilege of maintaining this cultural closure for two centuries. Those who engaged in biblical studies – even when they were women or men from Africa, Asia, and Latin America – nevertheless had to take on the Western context along with the discipline.

But much of recent Bible scholarship has moved toward the recognition that considerations not only of the contexts of assumed, or implied, biblical authors but also the contexts of the interpreters are valid and legitimate in an inquiry into biblical literature. We use *contexts* here as an umbrella term covering a wide range of issues: on the one hand, social factors (such as location, economic situation,

---

1. This saying indicates, through its usage of the stereotypic number 70, that the Torah – and, by extension, the whole Bible – intrinsically has many meanings. It is therefore often used to indicate the multivalence and variability of biblical interpretation, and does not appear in this formulation in traditional Jewish biblical interpretation before the middle of the first millennium CE. Its most known appearances are in the medieval commentator Ibn Ezra's introduction to his commentary on the Torah, toward the introduction's end (as in printed versions), in midrash *Numbers Rabbah* (13.15-16), and in later Jewish mystical literature.

gender, age, class, ethnicity, color, and things pertaining to personal biography) and, on the other hand, ideological factors (such as faith, beliefs, practiced norms, and personal politics).

Contextual readings of the Bible are an attempt to redress the previous longstanding, and grave imbalance that says that there is a kind of 'plain' unaligned biblical criticism that is somehow 'normative', and that there is another, distinct kind of biblical criticism aligned with some social location: the writing of Latina/o scholars advocating liberation, the writing of feminist scholars emphasizing gender as a cultural factor, the writings of African scholars pointing out the text's and the readers' imperialism, the writing of Jews and Muslims, and so on. The project of recognizing and emphasizing the role of context in reading freely admits that we all come from somewhere: no one is native to the biblical text, no one reads only in the interests of the text itself. North Atlantic and Western European scholarship has focused on the Bible's characters as individuals, has read past its miracles and stories of spiritual manifestations, or 'translated' them into other categories. These results of Euro-American contextual reading would be no problem if they were seen as such; but they have become a chain to be broken when they have been held up as the one and only 'objective', plain truth of the text itself.

The biblical text, as we have come to understand in the postmodern world and as pre-Enlightenment interpreters perhaps understood more clearly, does not speak in its own voice. It cannot read itself. *We* must read it, and in reading it, we must acknowledge that our own voice's particular pitch and timbre and inflection affect the meaning that emerges. Biblical scholars usually read the text in the voice of a Western Protestant male. When interpreters in the Southern Hemisphere and in Asia have assumed ownership of the Bible, it has meant a recognition that this Euro-American male voice is not the voice of the text itself; it is only one reader's voice, or rather, the voice of one context – however familiar and authoritative it may seem to all who have been affected by Western political and economic power. Needless to say, it is not a voice suited to bring out the best meaning for every reading community. Indeed, as biblical studies tended for so long to speak in this one particular voice, it may be the case that that voice has outlived its meaning-producing usefulness: we may have heard all that this voice has to say, at least for now. Nevertheless we have included that voice in this series, in part in an effort to hear it as emerging from its specific context, in order to put that previously authoritative voice quite literally in its place.

The trend of acknowledging readers' contexts as meaningful is already, *inter alia*, recognizable in the pioneering volumes of *Reading from This Place* (Segovia and Tolbert 1995, 2000, 2004), which indeed move from the center to the margins and back and from the United States to the rest of the world. More recent publications along this line also include *Her Master's Tools?* (Vander Stichele and Penner 2005), *From Every People and Nation: The Book of Revelation in Intercultural Perspective* (Rhoads *et al.* 2005), *From Every People and Nation: A Biblical Theology of Race* (Hays and Carson 2003), and the *Global Bible Commentary* (*GBC*; Patte *et al.* 2004).

The editors of the *GBC* have gone a long way toward this shift by soliciting and admitting contributions from so-called Third, Fourth, and Fifth World scholars alongside First and Second World scholars, thus attempting to usher the former and their perspectives into the *center* of biblical discussion. Contributors to the *GBC* were asked to begin by clearly stating their context before proceeding. The result was a collection of short introductions to the books of the Bible (Hebrew Bible/Old Testament and New Testament), each introduction from one specific context and, perforce, limited in scope. At the Society of Biblical Literature's annual meeting in Philadelphia in 2005, during the two *GBC* sessions and especially in the session devoted to pedagogical implications, it became clear that this project should be continued, albeit articulated further and redirected.

On methodological grounds, the paradox of a deliberately inclusive policy that foregrounds differences in the interpretation of the Bible could not be addressed in a single- or double-volume format because in most instances, those formats would allow for only one viewpoint for each biblical issue or passage (as in previous publications) or biblical book (as in the *GBC*) to be articulated. The acceptance of such a limit may indeed lead to a decentering of traditional scholarship but it would definitely not usher in multivocality on any single topic. It is true that, for pedagogical reasons, a teacher might achieve multivocality of scholarship by using various specialized scholarship types together; for instance, the *GBC* has been used side by side on a course with historical introductions to the Bible and other focused introductions, such as the *Women's Bible Commentary* (Newsom and Ringe 1998). But research and classes focused on a single biblical book or biblical corpus need another kind of resource: volumes exemplifying a broad multivocality in themselves, varied enough in contexts from various shades of the confessional to various degrees of the secular, especially since in most previous publications the contexts of communities of faith overrode all other contexts.

On the practical level, then, we found that we could address some of these methodological, pedagogical, and representational limitations evident in previous projects in contextual interpretation through a book series in which each volume introduces multiple contextual readings of the same biblical texts. This is what the Society of Biblical Literature's (SBL) Contextual Biblical Interpretation Consultation has already been promoting since 2005 during the American Annual Meeting; and since 2011 also at the annual International SBL conference. The Consultation serves as a testing ground for a multiplicity of readings of the same biblical texts by scholars from different contexts.[2]

---

2. Since 2010, when this book series was started and the first volume published with this Preface, interest in contextual interpretation has grown considerably. Worth noting is the SBL Press series *International Voices in Biblical Studies (IVBS)*. As can be seen from the website (http://www.sbl-site.org/publications/Books_IVBS.aspx), seven volumes have been published since 2010. However, the *IVBS* mission is different from ours, although two of the volumes (Vaka'uta 2011 on Ezra-Nehemiah 9–10 and Havea and Lau [eds.] 2015 on Ruth) do discuss specific texts against contextual, geographical-cultural perspectives. Worth noting too in this connection is the SBL series Global Perspectives on Biblical Scholarship (https://www.sbl-site.org/publications/Books_GPBS.aspx), and especially the 2012 volume on postcolonial African interpretation, edited by Musa W. Dube, Andrew M. Mbuvi, and Dora R. Mbuwayesango,

These considerations led us to believe that a book series focusing specifically on contextual multiple readings for specific topics, of specific biblical books, would be timely. We decided to construct a series, including at least eight to ten volumes, divided between the Hebrew Bible (HB/OT) and the New Testament (NT). Each of the planned volumes would focus on one or two biblical books: Genesis, Exodus and Deuteronomy, Leviticus and Numbers, Joshua and Judges, the so-called History books and later books for the HB/OT; Mark, Luke-Acts, John, and Paul's letters for the NT.[3] The general HB/OT editor is Athalya Brenner, with Archie Lee and Gale Yee as associate editors. The first general NT editor was Nicole Duran and is now James Grimshaw, with Daniel Patte, Teresa Okure as associate editors. Other colleagues have joined as editors for specific volumes.

Each volume focuses on clusters of contexts and of issues or themes, as determined by the editors in consultation with potential contributors. A combination of topics or themes, texts, and interpretive contexts seems better for our purpose than a text-only focus. In this way, more viewpoints on specific issues will be presented, with the hope of gaining a grid of interests and understanding. The interpreters' contexts will be allowed to play a central role in choosing a theme: we do not want to impose our choice of themes upon others, but as the contributions emerge, we will collect themes for each volume under several headings.

While we were soliciting articles for the first volumes (and continue to solicit contributions for future volumes), each contributor was and is asked to foreground her or his own multiple 'contexts' while presenting her or his interpretation of a given issue pertaining to the relevant biblical book(s). We asked that the interpretation be firmly grounded in those contexts and sharply focused on the specific theme, as well as in dialogue with 'classical' informed biblical scholarship. Finally, we asked for a concluding assessment of the significance of this interpretation for the contributor's contexts (whether secular or in the framework of a faith community).

Our main interest in this series is to examine how formulating the content-specific, ideological, and thematic questions from life contexts will focus the reading of the biblical texts. The result is a two-way process of reading that (1) considers the contemporary life context from the perspective of the chosen themes in the given biblical book as corrective lenses, pointing out specific problems and issues in that context as highlighted by the themes in the biblical book; and (2) conversely, considers the given biblical book and the chosen theme from the perspective of the life context.

The word *contexts*, like *identity*, is a blanket term covering many components. For some, their geographical context is uppermost; for others, the dominant factor may be gender, faith, membership in a certain community, class, and so forth. The balance is personal and not always conscious; it does, however, dictate choices of interpretation. One of our interests as editors is to present the personal beyond the

---

3. At this time, no volume on Revelation is planned, since Rhoads's volume, *From Every People and Nation: The Book of Revelation in Intercultural Perspective* (2005) is readily available, with a concept similar to ours.

autobiographical as pertinent to the wider scholarly endeavor, especially but not only when *grids of consent* emerge that supersede divergence. Consent is no guarantee of Truthspeak; neither does it necessarily point at a sure recognition of the biblical authors' elusive contexts and intentions. It does, however, have cultural and political implications.

Globalization promotes uniformity but also diversity, by shortening distances, enabling dissemination of information, and exchanging resources. This is an opportunity for modifying traditional power hierarchies and reallocating knowledge, for upsetting hegemonies, and for combining the old with the new, the familiar with the unknown – in short, for a fresh mutuality. This series, then, consciously promotes the revision of biblical myths into new reread and rewritten versions that hang on many threads of welcome transference. Our contributors were asked, decidedly, to be responsibly nonobjective and to represent only themselves on the biblical screen. Paradoxically, we hope, the readings here offered will form a new tapestry or, changing the metaphor, new metaphorical screens on which contemporary life contexts and the life of biblical texts in those contexts may be reflected and refracted.

The Editors

Bibliography

Bal, Mieke (1993), 'Myth à la Lettre: Freud, Mann, Genesis and Rembrandt, and the Story of the Son', repr. in *A Feminist Companion to Genesis*, edited by A. Brenner; Sheffield: Sheffield Academic Press, 343–78. Originally in *Discourse in Psychoanalysis and Literature*, ed. S. Rimon-Kenan, London: Methuen, 1987: 57–89.

Dube, Musa W., Andrew M. Mbuvi, and Dora R. Mbuwayesango (eds.) (2012), *Postcolonial Perspectives in African Biblical Interpretations*, Global Perspectives on Biblical Scholarship, 13, Atlanta: SBL Press.

Havea, Jione, and Peter H.W. Lau (eds.) (2015), *Reading Ruth in Asia*, IVBS; Atlanta: SBL Press.

Hays, J. Daniel, and Donald A. Carson (2003), *From Every People and Nation: A Biblical Theology of Race*, New Studies in Biblical Theology; Downers Grove, IL: InterVarsity Press.

Newsom, Carol A., and Sharon H. Ringe (eds.) (1992, 1998), *The Women's Bible Commentary*, Louisville, KY: Westminster/John Knox Press.

Patte, Daniel et al. (eds.) (2004), *The Global Bible Commentary*, Nashville: Abingdon Press.

Penner, Todd, and Caroline Vander Stichele (eds.) (2005), *Her Master's Tools? Feminist and Postcolonial Engagements of Historical-Critical Discourse*, Global Perspectives on Biblical Scholarship; Atlanta: SBL Press.

Rhoads, David et al. (eds.) (2005), *From Every People and Nation: The Book of Revelation in Intercultural Perspective*, Minneapolis: Augsburg Fortress Press.

Segovia, Fernando F. (ed.) (1995), *Reading from This Place*. Vol.1, *Social Location and Biblical Interpretation in the United States*, Minneapolis: Augsburg Fortress Press.

Segovia, Fernando F., and Mary Ann Tolbert (eds) (2000), *Reading from This Place*. Vol. 2, *Social Location and Biblical Interpretation in Global Perspective*, repr., Minneapolis: Augsburg Fortress; originally published 1995.

Segovia, Fernando F., and Mary Ann Tolbert (eds) (2004), *Teaching the Bible: The Discourses and Politics of Biblical Pedagogy*, repr., Eugene, OR: Wipf & Stock; originally published 1997.

Vaka'uta, Nasili (2011), *Reading Ezra 9–10 Tu'a-Wise: Rethinking Biblical Interpretation in Oceania*, IVBS; Atlanta: SBL Press.

LIST OF CONTRIBUTORS

Gale A. Yee
Emerita
Episcopal Divinity School
Boston
USA

Athalya Brenner-Idan
Emerita
Universiteit van Amsterdam
The Netherlands
& University of the Free State
South Africa

Dominic S. Irudayaraj
Pontifical Biblical Institute
Rome
Italy
& University of Pretoria
South Africa

Hyun Ho Park
Pastor, Grace United Methodist Church
San Ramon, CA
USA

Talia Sutskover
Tel Aviv University
Israel

Jan Willem van Henten
Universiteit van Amsterdam
The Netherlands
& Stellenbosch University
South Africa

Wei Huang
Shanghai University
China

Tamar Lammfromm
David Yellin College
Jerusalem
Israel

Ora Brison
Independent scholar
Tel Aviv
Israel

Gerrie F. Snyman
University of South Africa
South Africa

Atar Hadari
Poet, writer and translator
Liverpool Hope University
UK

Lisbeth S. Fried
University of Michigan-Ann Arbor
USA

Roger Nam
Emory University
Atlanta
USA

ABBREVIATIONS

11Q19	The Temple Scroll, 11QTemple Scrolla
AB	Anchor Bible series
ABD	Anchor Bible Dictionary
AJSL	American Journal of Semitic Languages
BibInt	Biblical Interpretation
ANE	Ancient Near East
BDB	Francis Brown, S. R. Driver and Charles A. Briggs (eds), *A Hebrew and English Lexicon of the Old Testament*, Oxford: Clarendon Press, 1907
CBQ	Catholic Biblical Quarterly
HALOT	Ludwig Koehler and Walter Baumgartner (eds), *The Hebrew and Aramaic Lexicon of the Old Testament* (trans. M. E. J. Richardson; rev. W. Baumgartner and J. J. Stamm). Leiden: E. J. Brill, 1994–1999
HB	Hebrew Bible (*TaNaKh*)
JBL	Journal of Biblical Literature
JPS	*Tanakh: A New Translation of the Holy Scriptures according to the traditional Hebrew Text,* Philadelphia & Jerusalem: Jewish Publication Society, 1985.
JSOT	Journal fort the Study of the Old Testament
JSS	Journal of Semitic Studies
KJV	King James Version
LXX	Septuagint, Greek Old Testament
m.	Mishna
NETS	*A New English Translation of the Septuagint*
NH	New Historicism
NKJV	New King James Version
NRSV	New Revised Standard Version
NT	New Testament
NTS	New Testament Studies
RSV	Revised Standard Version
Tal.	Talmud (*b.*, Babylonian Talmud; *Jer.*, Jerusalem Talmud)
VDK	Association for the Care of the German Military Cemeteries (*Volksbund Deutsche Kriegsgräberfürsorge*)
VT	Vetus Testament
ZAW	Zeitschrift für die AlttestamentlicheWissenschaft

INTRODUCTION

Athalya Brenner-Idan

This seventh volume in the T@C series is a companion to Volume 5 of the series on the Hebrew Bible's so-called 'historical books', *Samuel, Kings and Chronicles, Volume I* (2017), including essays on Ezra-Nehemiah, which pick up historically after the period depicted in Chronicles. Like other volumes in the series, its aim is to bring together disparate views about biblical texts and their influence in the life of contemporary communities, and conversely, to demonstrate how today's environments and disorders help readers to acquire new insights into such texts.

The contributing scholars hail from different continents, from East Asia to the United States to Europe to Africa and Israel, and count themselves as members of various Jewish and Christian traditions or secularist ways of life. But, in spite of their differences in location and community membership, and perhaps in the spirit of the times (2020 and its global discontents), they share preoccupations with questions of ethics in politics and life, 'proper' death, violence and social exclusion or inclusion. Perhaps one of the main insights of this volume, as a whole, is a better understanding of how politics and faith are melded, then and by implication now, to serve the interests of certain classes and societies, at the expense of social entities considered as Others to the culture the biblical texts promote.

The volume contains twelve essays. They are partly arranged in the order of the relevant books in the Hebrew Bible, and then in the historical order of events: that is, essays pertaining to Samuel-Kings first, then Chronicles, then Ezra-Nehemiah. An exception is essay number 5, which basically deals more with the New Testament than with the Hebrew Bible; and see below for the reasons for its inclusion in this collection.

On the Books of Samuel

Dominic S. Irudayaraj rereads the hate attributed to King David against physically challenged individuals (2 Sam 5.6-9). Going back and forth between the Bible and his present reality, his reading is motivated by current Hindu–Muslim clashes in his Indian context, and religio-political conflicts of in- and out-groups, majorities and minorities, and societal identity forming. In so doing, Irudayaraj introduces a theme that is truly intercultural and therefore recurrent in this collection of essays: the interlocking of religious and political explanations, and propaganda, as motives for social behaviour across global boundaries.

Hyun Ho Park looks at the information about David's 'concubines' who are sexually violated by Absalom as a political act of rebellion against his father David (2 Sam. 15.16, 16.21-22, 20.3). This is done through the prism of Korean women who were forced into prostitution for Japanese soldiers in the Second World War. Although they were recognized politically by Japan and South Korea in 2015, it was in an unsatisfactory manner and without suitable rectification. Park attempts to give the so called Korean 'comfort women' and the biblical women a voice that will – at the very least – manifest their suffering.[1]

Talia Sutskover and Athalya Brenner-Idan look at the story of Rizpah daughter of Aiah (2 Sam. 21.1-14) from a shared perspective, but in different directions. Jewish and Israeli cultures are certainly not unique in requiring proper burial as part of a person's proper death.[2] Not to be buried properly, or at all, implies an ignoble death. This is exemplified by the compact Rizpah story (as well as by contemporary practice). Sutskover takes the story in the direction of other Ancient Near East cultures; Brenner-Idan traces Rizpah burial ideology in Western cultures, especially as recorded on the internet.

Intermezzo

Jan Willem van Henten writes about First World War soldiers as martyrs, declared as such by religious (Christian) authorities in burial places while mainly relying on the New Testament (and especially Revelation). On the face of it, then, this essay does not belong here, especially since 'The concept of heroic death is conspicuously absent in Bible. This sharply contrasts with ancient Near Eastern and Greek tropes, as well as with the First book of Maccabees and modern-day commemorations … How should we understand this difference?'[3] And yet, the promotion of heroic, violent [military] death into martyrdom is claimed to derive

---

1. The 'comfort women' issue continues to be relevant. Recently (beginning 2021) a Harvard professor named Ramseyer claimed in a scholarly article that Korean women forced into sex slavery in WWII did so 'voluntarily': https://www.cnn.com/2021/03/10/us/comfort-women-ramseyer-article-trnd/index.html Now he's facing a backlash. See for a press release and one petition at https://sites.google.com/view/feministsonramseyer/press-release?authuser=0, which Gale Yee, the co-editor of this volume, signed.

2. On 'proper' death in juxtaposed Dutch/South American contexts, and from a different perspective, see also Klaas Spronk's essay on Qoheleth in the *Five Scrolls* volume of this series (Spronk 2018: 145-55).

3. Jacob L. Wright, 'Honoring the Death of Soldiers'. TheTorah.com (2018). https://thetorah.com/article/honoring-the-death-of-soldiers

from the Hebrew Bible, although developed later to it in both Christian and Jewish sources; and this promotion or glorification of dead soldiers into martyrs at time displaces or augments proper burial.[4] At times, a flimsy connection with a Hebrew Bible text out of context is sufficient to start the process or advance it.

Such a process of after-death elevation into martyrdom, especially as death is the result of war or religious, ethnic and political (such as a terrorist) opposition, has become widespread in today's cultures, on all continents and in many religions. This is a disturbing popular trend, a battle cry that takes the original martyrdom definitions out of contexts. Because of this topic's importance, we decided to include this essay here, as a complement to the previous essays about proper burial in the Hebrew Bible and beyond it in Jewish culture, as well as a bridge to Brison's essay further in this volume.

On the Books of Kings

Wei Huang rereads the story of the two women and Solomon's judgement (1 Kgs 3.16-28) in the light of Chinese Buddhist scriptures and in Chinese secular writings. In her own words, 'The juxtaposition of the Hebrew and Chinese sources will reveal how cultural contexts produce variants. At the same time, it will be seen how the female characters are maneuvered to support the social norms and customs in both contexts'. In addition, how the story came back to Western culture in a different format and modified ideology will be delineated.

In modern day Israel, Hebrew Bible classes are integral to school education, even in secular state schools and at all levels, from primary education to high school. As a result of this and other processes, biblical figures may be updated into useful, contemporary cultural heroes – and then lose their newly acquired status as fashions and ideologies change. In her case study, Tamar Lammfromm charts the journey of one such figure, the rise and fall of the prophet Elijah, in non-observant schools in Israeli pre-state and state formal education.

Ora Brison juxtaposes the murder of Queen Athaliah (2 Kgs 11.13–16; 2 Chron. 23.12–15) to the murder of Yitzhak Rabin, Israel's prime minister who actively sought peace with Palestinians at the time of his murder (1995). Athaliah's murder is presented in the biblical text as positive, a religious necessity as well as a political one. Rabin's murder was politically motivated, as well as supported and even incited by religious-orthodox authorities. Brison examines the interplay of religious and political ideologies in both cases, as they shed light one upon the other.

On the books of Chronicles-Ezra-Nehemiah

King Manasseh of Judah is depicted in 2 Kgs 21.1-18 in the most negative terms, as a perpetrator, idolator and unethical ruler similar to kings of the Northern

---

4. On the concept of 'martyrdom' see for instance in van Henten 2020: 72–87.

Kingdom and responsible for the later destruction of Judah. And yet, he reigned for 55 years, which must mean that he governed wisely or at least effectively. Gerrie F. Snyman shows how Chronicles (2 Chron. 33.1-20) solves this apparent contradiction by attributing to Manasseh exile, repentance and remorse that changed his initial behaviour and made his continued rule possible. Against his own (White) South African context, Snyman shows how Chronicles adds an element of vulnerability and remorse to Manasseh, thus turning him from a perpetrator into a better ruler and person.

Atar Hadari looks at the issue of conversion into Judaism, tracing the attitudes towards foreigners who wish to join the Hebrew, then Jewish, communities' in relevant biblical texts, then moves beyond those into past and contemporary rabbinic judicial decisions. Such attitudes are potentially ambivalent: joining Judaism is either condemned as unwished for, or else encouraged. Hadari shows through a case study how conversion decisions according to the halakhah can be lenient, although the orthodox establishment mostly chooses the other existing option, severity, over moderation and compassion, to the cost of individuals and groups. Once again, as in Irudayaraj's essay, the issue of the societal 'other' and societal identity looms large here.

Lisbeth S. Fried surveys the different prescriptions for the Sukkot festival in the Torah – in Exodus, Numbers, Deuteronomy and Leviticus. In view of the differences among the sources, her questions are: What does the call to celebrate Sukkot in Nehemiah 8 actually mean, and which Torah sources are implied? And then, using extrabiblical sources, she asks: How was Sukkot celebrated in Second Temple times, and what external influences are implicit in the celebration? Having done these surveys she analyses the Sukkot celebration in Nehemiah against the political background of the times as practice of religious and political resistance, which is certainly applicable to today's practices too.

Roger Nam critiques mainstream, modern biblical studies (read: mainly Protestant, Euro-American) and the place of minoritized scholarship in it from the viewpoint of a Korean-American. To rectify the situation and following recommendations by other scholars from the margin, he suggests that a new fusion of historical criticism and minoritized criticisms is in order, with a new balance introduced between texts and readers and relevance to the community as well as to the academy, so as to create an inclusive circle of learning to the benefit of all. His case study is a reading of Ezra-Nehemiah for power, trauma, identity and hope.

Afterword

Some editorial notes seem to be in order here.

Six out of the twelve articles in this volume (in order of appearance: by Sutskover, Brenner-Idan, Lammfromm, Brison, Hadari and Fried) are written from an Israeli/Jewish contributor context. This certainly makes for lack of balance in an anthology that aims at presenting as many scholarly viewpoints, from varied geography/faith backgrounds, as possible. To an extent, this is the result of works by scholars who openly engage in the mutual interaction between study and social reality that was available to us at the time of editing this collection. However, another major aim is thus preserved: bringing to the fore elements of a contemporary culture in its interplay with the Hebrew Bible that remains by and large either unknown or else marginal for out-group readers.

This book does not make for comfortable reading. At least seven of the articles (by Irudayaraj, Park, Suskover, Brenner-Idan, van Henten, Brison and Snyman) focus on social violence and its results. Justice and its lack, as linked to social boundaries and their formation, are central to the discourse in other essays. A back-and-forth studying of the past and present texts in their mutual light is beneficial for obtaining insights into both. But in today's world, can the Bible be looked to as a source of consolation, a therapeutic text, at least at times? This is a key question that arises from this collection too, a question that will be especially important for members of faith communities, albeit not only to them. Whom to believe? What to believe? What is fake, what is true?

And yet. Both Irudayaraj (the first essay here) and Nam (the last essay) nevertheless end their studies on a notion of hope and at least guarded optimism. In this difficult time (March 2021) of Coronavirus, global upheavals, race and ethnic conflicts and the collapse of democracy in many places, even the ideas of an open global world, some consolation and reconciliation are sorely needed. Let us end, then, on a notion of humanist hope.

The poem 'Creed' ('I believe') was written in Hebrew by the Jewish, later Israeli, medical doctor and poet Shaul Tchernichovsky (b. 1875, Ukraine; d. 1943, Jerusalem) in 1892. It is addressed, grammatically, to an unspecified second-person feminine listener.[5] The first two stanzas, and the fifth, are here reproduced in English translation.[6] The translation presented here is, however, a fresh one.

Creed (I Believe)
Mock, mock at the dreams
I the dreamer recount.
Mock that in man[7] I believe,
I even believe in you lot.

---

5. For readers of modern Hebrew: the original lyrics, and more information about the poem and poet, can be found, for instance, in http://www.yekum.org from 2017/11 or https://web.nli.org.il/sites/nlis/he/song/pages/song.aspx?songid=4336#133,60,8094,1759 (also with links to recorded performances of the poem set to music).

6. There are quite a few translations into English, most of them quite free translations; see for instance the one from the PoemHunter site, https://www.poemhunter.com/poems/creed/page-2/25030419/. Other English renditions can be readily obtained on the Internet.

7. The Hebrew here, as in line 7 below, has *ba-'adam* in the sense also sometimes used in the Hebrew Bible as gender inclusive 'humans', 'humankind' or 'humanity'. Since the poem was written at the end of the nineteenth century, it was decided not to update it to present-day gender expression.

For my soul still longs for liberty
I've not sold it for a golden calf,
for I still believe in man
and his spirit, his spirit tough.

...

I believe even in what's to come
though the day may be far off
but come it will – peace will be waged
and blessings passed, state to state.[8]

Amen to hope and change.

Bibliography

Henten, Jan Willem van (2020). 'Early Jewish and Christian Martyrdom', in Paul Middleton, ed., *The Wiley Blackwell Companion to Christian Martyrdom*. Chichester: Wiley-Blackwell, 72–87.

Spronk, Klaas (2018). 'Dealing with Death: Reading Qoheleth in Different Contexts', in *The Five Scrolls: T@C*. Edited by Athalya Brenner-Idan, Gale A. Yee and Archie C. C. Lee. London: Bloomsbury, 145–55.

Wright, Jacob L. (2018). 'Honoring the Death of Soldiers', in TheTorah.com (2018). https://thetorah.com/article/honoring-the-death-of-soldiers.

---

8. © Atar Hadari 2020. Our thanks to Hadari, who is a contributor to this volume, for making this translation especially for this volume.

Part I

SAMUEL

'DAVID HATES THE LAME AND THE BLIND': TOWARDS AN INTER(CON)TEXTUAL READING OF 2 SAMUEL 5.6-9*

Dominic S. Irudayaraj

The king and his men marched to Jerusalem against the Jebusites, the inhabitants of the land, who said to David, 'You will not come in here, even the blind and the lame will turn you back' – thinking, 'David cannot come in here.' Nevertheless, David took the stronghold of Zion, which is now the city of David. David had said on that day, 'Whoever wishes to strike down the Jebusites, let him get up the water shaft to attack the lame and the blind, those whom David hates.' Therefore it is said, 'The blind and the lame shall not come into the house.' David occupied the stronghold, and named it the city of David. David built the city all around from the Millo inwards.

(2 Sam. 5.6-9, NRSV)

1. Introduction

Double Trouble. Hate rhetoric hurts. And when hateful words are hurled out by persons of prominent profile, they are all the more appalling. Two instances of hate rhetoric are the focus of this essay: one ancient, the other current. The current one was unveiled when Mr Yogi Adithyanath (hereafter, the Yogi) – the political head of Uttar Pradesh, the most populous state in India – was addressing a public gathering. With an oratory that is characteristic of the Yogi, he declared: *'If they* [the Muslims] *kill even one Hindu, we will kill* [he paused and cried out] . . . *101!*' (Crabtree 2017).[1]

---

* My grateful acknowledgments are due to Professors Athalya Brenner-Idan and Gale Yee and the co-chairs of the session on 'Contextual Interpretation of the Bible' (ISBL 2017, Berlin) where an earlier version of this chapter was presented; and to Prof. Steven Pisano (1946–2019) of good memories for his helpful comments on the pre-conference draft.

1. See https://foreignpolicy.com/2017/03/30/if-they-kill-even-one-hindu-we-will-kill-100-india-muslims-nationalism-modi/.

That this unrestrained 'call to kill' could be uttered in 2017 makes it all the more ominous, as the said year marked the twenty-fifth anniversary of the infamous incident of the destruction of Babri Masjid (a sixteenth-century mosque) by a Hindu right-wing group, which led to nationwide riots and the merciless murdering of over 2,000 people both Hindus and Muslims.[2] The Yogi's outburst is not an exception in the current socio-political context of India where increasing instances of anti-Muslim, anti-Christian and anti-Minority atrocities are amply attested.[3] As a Christian from India, when I hear these words of the Yogi, they constitute the first trouble.

The second trouble stems from the very pages of the book that is normative to me and my faith community: the Bible. It concerns an event in David's life, which records that 'David hates (שׂנא) the lame and the blind' (2 Sam. 5.8).[4] When such hate words are heard from David, whose centrality in the Bible can hardly be missed by even a cursory reader, they present a formidable problem.[5] This essay aims to undertake an inter(con)textual reading[6] of these two cases of hate rhetoric. Following this reading strategy, I as 'contextualized' reader, who is baffled by the *excess* in the Yogi's calumnious call, endeavour to read the biblical instance of hatred for any *excess* therein by situating the text in its literary 'context'. In order to cull out such *excess*es, the findings of New Historicism function here as methodological guideposts.

Accordingly, I will proceed as follows: (i) retracing the dominant storyline of David's Jerusalem takeover, where his hatred for the lame and the blind is hinted at; (ii) informed by New Historicism insights, will attempt a rereading of the same pericope with a view to elucidating the *excess* in it; (iii) will glean the findings around a heuristic term: *proximate 'other'*; and (iv) finally, informed by these findings of a 'contextualized' text, an interpretive ramification for the chosen text and a pastoral significance for my Indian 'context' are indicated.

---

2. For an appraisal of Babri Masjid issue, see Jaishankar 2009: 26.

3. See, for example, 'India's Turn toward Intolerance', *The New York Times*, July 17, 2017, sec. Opinion, https://www.nytimes.com/2017/07/17/opinion/indias-turn-toward-intolerance.html.

5. The MT (*Qere*) can be understood as 'those whom David hates'; the LXX (and MT *Ketib*), on the contrary, read as 'those who hate David'. Campbell (2005: 54) suggests that 'Those who hate David' would refer to the defenders' boast in v. 6'. The root שׂנא Qal does not occur in 1 Samuel. Of its eight occurrences in 2 Samuel (5.8; 13.15 [*2]; 22; 19.7 [*2]; 22.18, 41), only in the chosen text and in a direct discourse is David the subject of this verb.

5. As Kirsch exclaims: 'What, after all, are we to make of the fact that God's chosen king declares his hatred for "the lame and the blind" with such callousness and cruelty?' (Kirsch 2000: 151).

6. An inter(con)textual reading 'involves a bringing together ... of the contextualized text and the contextualized reader, yielding analysis of both by way of close and sustained interweaving' (Segovia 2009: 354). On 'inter(con)textuality' and its relevance as a reading strategy, see Liew 1999: 22–45 (33, 39), Yamada 2009: 97–117.

2. David's Jerusalem Takeover: The Narrative Portrayal

Commenting on the biblical portrayal of David, Walter Brueggemann exclaims: 'The literature and the faith of Israel are endlessly fascinated with David' (Brueggemann 1985:113), as abounding references to his name[7] amply attest. Equally exalted is Jerusalem,[8] together with its synonymous poetic name, Zion.[9] The chosen text (2 Sam. 5.6-9)[10] paints in broad strokes how this central figure of Israel's historiographical memories comes to possess the religiously noteworthy locus.[11] Given this double importance of David and Jerusalem, it is hardly surprising that much scholarly ink has been spent on the motive(s) behind David's choice of Jerusalem: could it be because of its geographical, strategic location? Or, is it due to David's political savviness, as Jerusalem belonged to neither the southerners nor the northerners?[12] Or, is it on account of the historical importance that is accorded to this city?[13] Or, finally and in a proleptic sense, is it due to the

---

7. Of 1073 occurrences of 'David' in the Hebrew Bible, about 788 instances have 'the standard three-letter orthography (*dwd*) while the remainder (c. 285) are spelled with four letters (*dwyd*)'. See Freedman 1983: 89.

8. While 'Jerusalem' occurs 633 times, Zion has 154 entries (Nelson 2004: 131). 'Jerusalem is mentioned ... more often than any other. Geographically and theologically it is located "in the center of the nations" (Ezek. 5.5)' (Youngblood 1992: 853).

9. With Jon Levenson (1992: 1098–1102), Arnold (2003: 454) avers that 'the etymological meaning of Zion is unclear'. 'Zion ... probably denotes the hill on which the fortress stood, though it has also been suggested that it originally referred to the fortress itself. It is the south-east hill of Jerusalem; the modern "Mount Zion" in the south-west of the city perpetuates a centuries-old misunderstanding' (Gordon 1986: 226).

10. Drawing on Anderson, this essay treats verses 6-9 as a meaningful literary unit. Verses 10 and 12 'are in the nature of short theological comments which may have been intended to tone down any undue emphasis on any human achievement, and to point to Yahweh as the real source of success' (Anderson 1989: 80). From a literary perspective, the Jerusalem takeover signals the conclusion of the so-called 'History of David's Rise (HDR)' which begins from 1 Sam. 16. Some deem HDR 'an original narrative source' (Arnold 2003: 450). Others see it as a hypothetical construction (for instance Morrison 2013: 5). Even on the delimitations of HDR, debates continue: see for instance Yoon 2014.

11. For Payne, two of the most significant events in Israel's religious history include David becoming the king of a united Israel and making Jerusalem the capital (Payne 1982: 177–8).

12. 'David was convinced the way to union lay within the gates of Jerusalem' (Landay 1988: 82). See also Chafin 1989: 270 and McCarter 1984: 141.

13. Jerusalem is 'mentioned in the Ebla archives (c. 2500 BCE), in the Egyptian Execration Texts of the nineteenth (?) century BCE ... and the Amarna Letters ... of the fourteenth century BCE'. For details on relevant resources, see Anderson 1989: 82. Also, Jerusalem (meaning, 'the foundation of the god Salem, or Prosperor') was a legendary place and the city figures prominently in Patriarchal narratives. See Landay 1988: 82–3.

future religious significance that this city would garner? Proposals are many and so consensus is hard to come by. As with David's motives, scholarly efforts have also been spent in searching for the details of the takeover. But such ventures have been vexed by both the brevity[14] and obscurity[15] of the text. Despite the said paucity and obscurity, the takeover incident still leaves a number of notable features that are pertinent for the present discussion.

'His Men'. A key feature concerns David's accompanying forces. David marches into Jerusalem with 'his men' (אנשיו, v. 6). By relying neither on the Judahite base nor on the northern tribes, David's choice of his 'personal army' – to borrow Gordon's phrase (Gordon 1986: 226) – may indicate that the credit of the takeover would solely rest with him. And this is made all the more clear when David calls the city after his name (v. 9; cf. v. 7). In other words, as Albrecht Alt avers, 'Jerusalem became David's own property'.[16]

The King's Activities. Another notable feature concerns the occupants of Jerusalem. 'Jebusites (היבסי)'[17] is their name. And they are described as 'the inhabitants' (יושב)[18] of the land. Both details are significant. In the Pentateuch, the Jebusites typically feature in the litany of the nations that inhabited the land of Canaan whom the Israelites were directed to dispossess.[19] However, the books of Joshua (15.63) and Judges (1.21) recount how Israel could not conquer Jerusalem.[20] Against this

---

14. And so, scholars feel impelled to supply probable explanations. For example, see Chafin 1989: 271, Anderson 1989: 80.

15. For example, the meaning of צנור (v. 8) has remained a perennial challenge to exegetes. Jones, for instance, suggests 'water supply' or 'overflow' (Jones 1990: 122). See also Gordon 1986: 227, Holm-Nielsen 1993: 42. Other difficult words include: נכה, נגע (v. 8), מצדה, מלוא (v. 9).

16. Alt also suggests that the city thus 'retained its previous status of a sovereign city-state now ruled by David, but independent of Israel and Judah'. Alt's position (Alt 1953: 45–46), though widely accepted, is nonetheless disputed. See Anderson 1989: 81.

17. *Contra* the Syriac translation that renders the following verb in the pl. (cf. also 1 Chron. 11.5) and *pace* Anderson, היבסי is to be taken as a collective noun, matching the MT's sg. verb.

18. Based on the Hurrian name Abdi-ḥepa, who was the governor of Jerusalem, Jones argues 'that the Jebusite settlement in Jerusalem had a long history going back to the Amarna period [1400–1350 BCE]' (Jones 1990:122).

19. Cf. Exod. 3.8, 17; 13.5; 23.23; 33.2; 34.14; Deut. 7.1; 20.17.

20. However, Judg. 1.8 claims that the Judahites fought against Jerusalem, put it to the sword, and set the city on fire. These contradictory claims (Judg. 1.8 vs Josh. 15.63 and Judg. 1.21) are solved by some scholars by a two-site proposal. Accordingly, 'Jerusalem' comprised a fortified city on the south-east and an open country on the south-west. David took over the city on the south-east. Following this proposal, Jones suggests that the information in 2 Sam. 5.6 is correct. All the same, the text suffers from lack of precision as it 'uses the name of the whole for the part and does not specify that, when David went up to Jerusalem, he was going to attack the fortress on the south-eastern hill'. Even the name of the city '*yᵉrûšāla[y]im*' (lit., 'Two Jerusalems') is indicative of two distinct sites. See Jones 1990: 125–26, as cited in Youngblood 1992: 854. However, for a counter view, see Anderson 1989: 81.

backdrop, David's 'capture represented ... the sweeping away of the last vestiges of Canaanite resistance to domination by the Israelites'.[21] And, as the last of the Canaanite strongholds falls to David, a dramatic transposition of description is recorded. Whereas the text begins by describing the Jebusites as 'the inhabitants', the closing verse culminates in attributing that key description ('dwelling', וישב) to David (v. 9). Added to this act of 'dwelling', David is credited with two other activities: The king 'names' (ויקרא) the city after himself[22] and 'builds' (ויבן) it all around from the Millo (v. 9).[23] Taken together, verses 6a and 9 show in substantial strokes the singularity of David's role in the Jerusalem takeover.

Discursive 'Takeover'. Right in the midst of these two verses (verses 6a and 9), a discursive duel between the Jebusites and David is documented. On learning David's intention to take hold of Jerusalem, the Jebusites respond: 'Even the blind and the lame will turn you back' (2 Sam. 5.6). Although the exact meaning of this expression has baffled many, a sizeable number of scholars have pointed to the taunting tone[24] as well as the confident boasting[25] of the Jebusites. Challenged by this Jebusite jibe, David's response is not so much in words as in decisive action, delineated in powerful pithiness: 'Nevertheless David took the stronghold of Zion'[26] (v. 7). It is a short but telling description. And it could have very well functioned as a fitting conclusion to the whole episode, had the focus of the text been merely the takeover of the city. But the narrative goes on to supply more details. The text, as though in a narrative 'rewind' mode, pauses, goes back in time, and documents David's verbal response to the Jebusite taunt – a befitting as well as an expected response in the ANE context.

---

21. An observation that is further supported by the fact that the Jebusites occupy 'the rear in the list of Canaanite tribes ... [who] were to come under the sway of Abraham's descendants' (Gordon 1986: 226).

22. 'The expression ["city of David"] in 2 Sam. 5.7 is a marginal gloss anticipating its occurrence in v. 9' (Robinson 1993: 175).

23. V. 9 and also v. 11 give 'the only record of David's building projects. Such accounts are often associated with various kings of the ancient Near East, and their function is to stress the wealth, power, and greatness of the rulers concerned' (Anderson 1989: 81). Arnold draws on Kegler 1977: 218-32.

24. For example, Glück sees it as an 'epitome of the terminology used in pre-battle taunting and reviling' (Glück 1966, as cited in Anderson 1989: 82). Morrison suggests that 'the "blind and lame" served as metaphor to amplify the Jebusites' battle rhetoric ... a hyperbole ... to ridicule their aggressor' (Morrison 2013: 74). But Chafin suggests that it was 'probably a proverb indicating that the city was so well located that it could even be defended by the blind and the lame in the city' (Chafin 1989: 270).

25. Anderson, for instance, observes from the choice of the grammatical tense: 'One would expect impf [here] ... but the pf may indicate the speaker's certainty and self-confidence' (Anderson 1989: 80 n6e). The suggestion is supported by the following explanatory note: 'David cannot enter here' (Anderson 1989: 80 n6f).

26. The contrastive *waw* is perceptibly rendered as 'Nevertheless' in the NRSV.

Scholars have noted that, in ANE contexts where honour plays a significant role, verbal contestations are attempts at occupying the discursive space of the opponent, thus undermining the latter's honour. The opponent is expected to retort in kind in order to not merely reclaim the lost honour, but also dent the proponent's honour.[27] Perceived against this backdrop, the Jebusites' taunt can be counted as their attempt at undermining the honour of the approaching David. And, as expected, the king responds in kind[28] and in a remarkable crescendo. David, in a rhetorical spur that is characteristic of him,[29] calls out: 'Whoever would strike down (כל־מכה) the Jebusites, let him get up the water shaft (צנור)' (v. 8). He then adds force to it with a further summons: 'to attack (ויגע) the lame and the blind',[30] together with an accompanying explanation 'the blind and the lame whom David hates (שׂנא)' (v. 8). Finally, the crescendo reaches its climax in the aetiological narrative note: 'Therefore, it is said that "the blind and the lame shall not enter into the house (הבית)"' (v. 8).

To sum up, while the activities such as 'taking over', 'naming' and 'building' paint a formidable picture of the king of all Israel *in deeds*, David's counter-taunt that comes in a crescendo adds to that dominant depiction. Arnold summarizes it succinctly: 'This text establishes both the king and his royal city firmly in the psyche of Israel for the rest of biblical history' (Arnold 2003: 450). Despite such a singular significance accorded to David, other details of the same text, when situated within its larger literary setting and sifted through New Historicism findings, point to a different portrait of the king. But, before proceeding with the proposed New Historical sifting, a short overview of New Historicism is in order.

3. New Historicism: Clarifying the Guideposts

As ample scholarship on New Historicism (NH) is readily available[31] and also given the limited space here, the present discussion focuses only on a few New Historical findings that are pertinent for this essay.

27. On honour and shame in the ANE and its interpretive relevance, see Esler 2001: 64-101.

28. '[T]he lame and the blind ... in the mouth of the Jebusites ... is a taunt reflecting their confidence in their stronghold and in the mouth of David it is a reply *in kind* that he will take the city' (Jones 1990: 124; emphasis added).

29. Such a spur can be found in David's wish for 'a drink of water from the well of Bethlehem' in 2 Sam. 23.13-17. See Poirier 2006: 28-9.

30. The Jebusites taunt David but the latter focuses on 'the blind and the lame', which does not seem to follow logically from 5.6. See Morrison 2013: 74. However, *pace* Anderson, David's reply in a similar vein makes 'the "Jebusites" and "the blind and the lame" synonymous' (Anderson 1989: 82). Cf. Table 1 below on the use of opponents' words.

31. For an introduction to New Historicism, see Hens-Piazza 2002. On NH's assumptions, strategies and techniques, see Erisman 2014: 71-80. For a case study, see Sherwood 1997: 364-402. For my recent comments on and the use of NH, see Irudayaraj 2017: 99-124.

'Interested' texts. The NH asserts that 'words can be understood only against the background of their own times' (Barton 2013: 121) because texts 'are caught up in the *social processes* and *contexts* out of which they emerge' (Hens-Piazza 2002: 6, emphasis added). As a result, NH does not expend its energy in searching for nonbiased data in the texts, which are nonexistent, but pays particular attention to the purpose or the 'interest' that a text is produced to serve (Carvalho 2006: 197).

Multiplicity of Voices. On account of the said 'interested' nature, every piece of literature has an agenda which it belabours to assert either overtly or covertly. Even as it does so, the text leaves behind other minor voices – voices that oppose and critique the dominant one (on this, see Sharpe 2009: 1). As a result, 'mainstream ideologies are formed by dominant and emergent forces, but mixing with, and possibly subverting them, are residual elements' (Sherwood 1997: 368). Such elements are often on 'the margins of dominant hegemonic discourse'.[32]

'Decentred' Characters. Due to this coalescence of various and often dichotomous voices, textual characters turn out to be complex. If earlier methods granted standalone existence to textual characters, NH lays them bare 'as decentered, fashioned, and compromised in a complex of relation to social forces' (Sherwood 1997: 368-9).

NH Reading Strategy. Guided by the 'interested' nature of the texts, the multiplicity of voices therein, and so the resulting 'decentred' characters, NH invites its adherents to train their eyes to perceive any text – including biblical ones – as 'ideologically plotted, crafted, and designed, and how the 'confidently plotted storyline' inevitably represents a 'sentimentality, an excess, an exaggeration'.[33] And, in order to unearth the *excess*, the 'New Historicist hunts for the marginal, the curious and bizarre' (Sherwood 1997: 367). As such, New Historical reading strategy involves:

1. Reading a text: paying attention to the plotted storyline.
2. Rereading the text for any 'excess': hearing the dominant voice for any instances of excess.
3. Hearing other 'voices': 'voices' that have hitherto been unheard or treated as unimportant.
4. Describing the 'decentred' character: the dominant voice vis-à-vis other subversive voices.
5. Gleaning some findings: by listing interpretive as well as pastoral significances.

Earlier, in subsection 2 here, I dwelt at length on the dominant depiction of David as narrated in the Jerusalem takeover, which fulfils the first step of the NH reading strategy. The following subsection, therefore, rereads the same text for some instances of *excess*, exaggeration, subverting voices and, as a result, the decentred protagonist.

---

32. For an illustrative case from the Talmud, see Hens-Piazza 2002: 57-60.

33. Even while quoting this idea of Hoffman, Sherwood is quick to acknowledge that not all biblical texts fall into this naïve outline. See Sherwood 1997: 374.

4. A NH Rereading of the Jerusalem Takeover

Commenting on our text, Morrison perceptively observes: 'David seizes his future capital in three biblical verses' (Morrison 2013: 70). Despite its brevity, the text is not without its notable features as it was underscored in 'The dominant portrayal' (Subsection 2). It is to this confidently constructed dominant portrayal that we turn now in order to sift it through NH findings. For this purpose, the Jerusalem-takeover text is situated in its larger literary context in order to highlight some common as well as contrasting features. Again, due to the limited space, the proposed comparison is limited mainly to two other texts: The Goliath-slaying episode (1 Sam. 17) and the purchase story of Araunah's threshing floor (2 Sam. 24). The reasons for the choice of these two texts need mentioning here. The first and perhaps the most obvious reason is the reference to 'Jerusalem' in all three episodes: (i) in 1 Samuel, 'Jerusalem' makes its entry – in fact, its only occurrence[34] – in the Goliath episode (1 Sam. 17.54); (ii) the city's ultimate occurrence is in the context of Araunah's threshing floor (2 Sam. 24.16); (iii) in between these two instances is the depiction of the takeover of this very city in 2 Sam. 5. Reference to 'Jerusalem', however, is not the only rationale for the proposed comparison, as there are other relevant points of contact between the three texts (cf. Tables 1 and 2).

4.1. Common Features

Table 1 Goliath-episode and Jerusalem Takeover: A Comparison

Themes / words	Goliath Episode (1 Sam. 17)	Jerusalem Takeover (2 Sam. 5)
Jerusalem	The first occurrence in the books of Samuel	The depiction of this very city's takeover
Invincibility of the opponent	Saul tells David: 'You are not able to go against this Philistine' (v. 33)	Jebusites' declaration: 'You will not come in here' (v. 6)
Taunting tone	Goliath 'disdained him' (v. 42), cursed David.	Jebusites' jibe (cf. n. 25 above)
Using opponent's words; and, even reversing[35]	Goliath: 'I will feed your flesh to *the birds of the air and the wild animals of the field*' (v. 44)	Jebusites: '*the blind and the lame* will turn you back' (v. 6) David: 'attack *the lame and the blind*, those whom David hates' (v. 8).

---

34. However, scholars suggest that the reference to Jerusalem in this text could be a case of anachronism or proleptical history writing. For details, see Tsumura 2007: 468.

35. The repetition of a speech, 'including any alternations or deviation from the original speech, is often thought to be an important part of how a character is being portrayed as well as differing points of view that may emerge within a narrative' (Cook 2017: 1). Cook here draws on R. Alter and A. Berlin. For relevant resources, see Cook 2017: 1 n.3.

Themes / words	Goliath Episode (1 Sam. 17)	Jerusalem Takeover (2 Sam. 5)
	David: 'I will strike you down … cut off your head and … give the dead bodies of the Philistine army … to *the birds of the air and to the wild animals of the earth*' (v. 46)	Reversal: Jebusites say, 'the blind and the lame' (v. 6); David responds, 'the lame and the blind' (v. 8a)[36]
Striking (נכה)	David 'struck' (ויך) the Philistine on the forehead … and he fell' (v. 49)[37]	'Whoever would strike down (מכה) the Jebusites …' (v. 8)[38]
Excess	Goliath threatens to feed the flesh of *only* David to the birds and the animals (v. 44). But David retorts by including the entire Philistine army as his object of attack and later as food to the birds and the animals (v. 46).	While the Jebusites say, 'the blind and the lame will turn you back' (v. 6), David calls for attacking 'the lame and the blind' and adds a note of 'hatred'. And the explanatory note (forbidding entrance into the house) enhances that excess.
Take away (סור Hif.)	Of its three occurrences (verses 26, 39, 46), when the object is a human person, it refers to a violent removal of that person's head (v. 46)	If read with Goliath's story, the words of Jebusites that 'the blind and the lame will *turn you back*' (הסירך) would sound ominous (v. 6)

Table 2 Jerusalem Takeover and the Purchase of Araunah's Threshing Floor: A Comparison

Common themes	Jerusalem Takeover (2 Sam. 5)	Threshing Floor Purchase (2 Sam. 24)
Jerusalem	The very takeover of city.	Purchase of a threshing floor for building an altar in order to avert the impending destruction of Jerusalem (v. 16)
David's title	'The king' (המלך, cf. v. 6)	'The king' (המלך, cf. v. 20; see also verses 22, 23 [*3], 24)
Accompaniment	'The king and his men' (v. 6).	'King and his servants' (v. 20)
'Jebusite' presence	'The Jebusites (היבסי), the inhabitants of the land' (v. 6)	'Araunah, the Jebusite (היבסי)' (v. 18)
David's post-event activity	After the takeover, David is portrayed as 'building' (ויבן) the city (v. 9)	After the purchase of the threshing floor, David is depicted as 'building' (ויבן) an altar (v. 25)

36. The explanatory (aetiological) note in v. 8b, however, switches back to 'the blind and the lame'.

37. The root נכה (in the Hif.) occurs 12 time in the Goliath episode (17.9 (*2), 25, 26, 27, 35 (*2), 36, 46, 49, 50, 57). In all these instances it connotes 'killing' or 'striking that ends in killing'. Verse 50 uses both 'to strike' and 'to kill'.

38. Although the root נכה in this text has perplexed scholars, its occurrence can still argue for the comparison of these two pericopes.

Whereas the details listed in Tables 1 and 2 grant a reasonable basis for a comparison of the takeover episode with the other two selected events, the contrasts between them can help underscore the *excess* in 2 Samuel 5.6-9, and also reassess the singular prominence that is given to David.

4.2. Contrasting Details

4.2.1. Contra *the Goliath Episode*

Single combat vs combat in company   The Goliath episode powerfully portrays the single combat between the Philistine champion and David, in which a swift decimation of a formidable foe is achieved by means of a single shot from David's sling. The Jerusalem takeover matches the Goliath episode – but only in swiftness; not in singularity, as the text attests to David's accompaniment ('his men', v. 6). Further, in David's pre-combat boast we hear that, even as a peasant 'boy', David could deal deadly blows to wild animals and so claims that he could do the same to Goliath. He then matches his words with action as he quickly sinks a stone in Goliath's forehead. The takeover text, on the other hand, presents some curious contrasts: despite his elevated status as 'the king' (*contra* a shepherd boy), the takeover credit is distributed between David and his men, which appears to make the first 'dent' in David's portrayed prowess. The 'dent' gets deeper when David, after matching the Jebusites in words, leaves takeover action to an unspecified audience as the call to strike is given to a general addressees: 'whoever' (כל-).

Excess in word and action   In situations of contestation and combat, excessive words and exaggerated actions are not uncommon phenomena. Often, the purpose is to undercut the opponent's challenge. The Goliath episode is an illustrative instance. David's words in *excess* of and his actions in *exaggeration* to Goliath's (cf. Table 1) considerably enhance the depiction of David. Along similar lines, in the Jerusalem-takeover, the Jebusite taunt is not only matched by David's call to strike them but also receives a touch of *excess* in the addition of the 'hatred' clause. The same *excess* is given further emphasis when the narrator adds the prohibition of the blind and the lame from entering the house (cf. Table 1).

However, these instances of *excess* in words miss the usually accompanying, commensurate *exaggerated* actions. First of all, the actual takeover is not recounted.[39] Further, rare words, odd expressions, and enigmatic references in the

---

39. This is particularly odd in a book which is otherwise noted for its inclusion of 'minutiae'. Such examples include (i) the buildup to Tamar's rape; and (ii) the lengthy conversation between a bogus widow and a beguiled king (14.4-20). See Morrison 2013: 2–3.

text make the takeover all the more obscure.[40] Also, if the call to 'strike' the Jebusites is read against the backdrop of the Goliath episode, it would sound ominous (cf. Table 1), but no such death-dealing 'strike down' of Jebusites is reported. In fact, as one reads along, the next 'Jebusite' reference in the book of Samuel is a powerful attestation to the continued presence of this supposedly 'hated' lot.

4.2.2. Contra the Araunah Episode   The preceding discussion pointed out how the many contrasts between David in the Jerusalem-takeover vis-à-vis his image in the surrounding texts help highlight David's *excess* and *exaggeration*, hence the *de-centred* picture of David. A similar juxtaposition with David's purchase of Araunah's threshing floor can contribute further to David's compromised character.

The 'lingering' Jebusite   Earlier, our discussion dwelt on the dramatic transposition of the term 'inhabit'. The initial descriptive note assigns it to the Jebusites (v. 6). However, it gets transposed to David by the end of the pericope (v. 9). Such a transposition can be suggestive of an interpretive option that the Jebusites were driven out after the takeover. In fact, some choose to tread such an interpretive path. And others go as far as to propose that, in a literal adherence to David's call (cf. v. 8), the Jebusites were 'struck down' (cf. Morrison 2013: 8). Such suggestions are indicative of an interpretive desire to grant closure to the persisting Jebusite presence. But the book of Samuel defies any such easy closure. On the contrary: the closing words of the book record an event which attests to a lingering Jebusite presence – David's purchase of the threshing floor of Araunah, a Jebusite.

Despite the fact that a victorious king of David's time could take over the land of the conquered people at will, the king is shown as paying – in fact, insisting on paying – for Araunah's threshing floor. Herein lie some significant specifics: (i) 'the Jebusite' continues to co-exist;[41] (ii) owns a threshing floor; (iii) most likely, Araunah is a person of importance, deserving the visit of a victorious king who comes with his servants; (iv) the Jebusite's generosity is boundless in proposing to give away the floor for no charge, together with the other requirements for sacrifice (v. 22), and topping it with an unsolicited benediction (v. 23). Thus, David's encounter with Araunah depicts not merely a 'lingering' Jebusite but a prominent one, as we

---

40. On the obscurity as well as brevity of this passage, see Arnold 2003: 454, Campbell 2005: 54, Anderson 1989: 80. Given this obscurity, interpreters have always felt the need to supply explanations. Such elucidations are as old as the Bible itself. For example, the Chronicler's version includes: (i) Joab's role in the takeover, (ii) without retaining the enigmatic reference to 'the blind and the lame' (cf. 1 Chron. 11.4-9). Among the later examples, Josephus suggests that (i) the Jebusites placed blind and lame on the wall; and that (ii) David expelled the Jebusites from the city (cf. *Ant.* 7.65, 67), see Avioz 2015: 104. In rabbinic tradition 'the blind and the lame' are understood as Canaanite idols (Anderson 1989: 82).

41. The continued Jebusite existence with Israel is attested as late as post-exilic times (2 Chron. 8.7; Ezra 9.1; Neh. 9.8): Merrill 1995: 299.

shall shortly see. And Araunah was not the only indication of a continued 'Jebusite' presence. Scholars have shown a number of other Jebusite references in Samuel, a few of which deserve mentioning.

In David's personal life One of the post-events of David's Jerusalem takeover includes the king taking wives and concubines from Jerusalem (מירושלם). Andrew Hill suggests that the preposition /מ/ in the phrase מירושלם, when read in a *locative* or a *partitive* sense, may imply that the 'concubines and wives [were] from the resident population of Jerusalem. Stated more directly, at least some of these women added to David's harem were local Jebusites!' (Hill 2006: 131).[42] If so, this marks an important Jebusite 'presence' in David's family space. Further and along the same line, the names of David's children present pertinent information. Georg Hentschel highlights that 'the theophoric names of the children born to David in Jerusalem (2 Sam. 5.14-16) incorporate the divine name "El" not "Yah/weh", presumably because the mothers who named them were Jebusite women – not Hebrew women from Israel or Judah'.[43] This too contributes to an increased Jebusite 'presence' in David's personal life.

In David's political arena The takeover pericope begins by describing David as 'the king', which echoes back to the event that immediately precedes it, namely David's anointing as 'king' over Israel at Hebron (2 Sam. 5.3c). In fact, even before the anointing, David is described with the epithet 'king' twice (verses 3a, 3b). The text then presents in summary form the total length of the king's reign: David ruled from Hebron over Judah for seven years and six months; and from Jerusalem, over all Israel and Judah, for thirty-three years, making the total about forty years – a number quite significant for a Hebrew mind.[44] The repeated epithet 'king', together with the symbolically significant number of years of David's reign, clearly establishes his royal role. However, other elements in the Araunah episode cast a different light on David's kingship.

In the Araunah episode, a pericope of just eight verses (2 Sam. 24.18-25), the title 'king' appears eight times (verses 20 [*2], 21, 22, 23 [*3], 24) and in almost all cases as designation of David – but with one exception! The epithet appears twice in v. 23a: הכל נתן ארונה המלך למלך. While some choose to translate המלך in a vocative sense ('All this, O king, Araunah gives to the king', cf. NRSV), the same word can also be taken in an appositive sense ('All these things did Araunah, as a king, give

---

42. Hill draws on Hertzberg's proposal (Hertzberg 1976: 271).

43. Hentschel 1994: 22, 66, as cited in Hill 2006: 131 n. 7. In a similar vein, Jones (1990: 127) suggests a Jebusite connection in the names Absalom and Solomon (although the former was born in Hebron while the latter has an alternative name, Jedidiah).

44. As such, the exact total exceeds the symbolic number 'forty' by six months. The books of Kings (cf. 1 Kgs 2.11) and Chronicles (1 Chron. 29.27) get around this discrepancy and even place such summary statements at the end of David's reign. For details, see Pisano 1984: 100.

unto the king', cf. KJV). Supporting this second possibility, Lester Grabbe argues that the threshing floor must have been owned by Araunah, the king. Further, Grabbe underscores that 'The word "Araunah" is curious. It does not look like a typical Hebrew name, and in part of the episode the word occurs with the article which is not normal with names. It has been explained as a Hittite word meaning "aristocrat" or a Hurrian word meaning "lord"'.[45] If this suggestion is accepted, the name and the title are evidence for a Jebusite's commensurate importance with David; and this, in turn, points to a Jebusite 'presence' in David's royal arena as well.

Several of David's officials have names that are further pointers in this regard. In the appointment of Shausha the scribe, Ahithophel the king's counsellor, Jehoshaphat son of Ahilud the recorder, and Ittai the Gittite, Jones perceives that '[t]he sap of Canaanite culture was absorbed and assimilated through trained scribes and craftsmen, legislators, archivists' (Jones 1990: 136). If so, Araunah is not without company in the post-takeover scenario where not only the presence, but also the prominence, of non-Israelites is granted by the narrative traces that the narrative of 2 Samuel leaves behind.

In David's religious sphere Even in David's religious sphere, the Jebusite presence makes some perceivable inroads. David's priest Zadok is a case in point. Scholars suggest that he may have been 'the former Jebusite king-priest of Jerusalem' (Landay 1988: 88; cf. Ahlström 1980: 287). Jones, even while conceding that the evidence is indirect, grants such a possibility.[46] Based on the meaning of his name ('dedicated to Ṣedeq'), Grabbe suggests that Zadok may have 'belonged to the pre-Davidic shrine in Jerusalem' (Grabbe 2004: 153). Accepting this suggestion may contribute further to the Jebusite presence in the worship circles around David – and in an all-important priestly role.

The purchase of the threshing floor[47] was occasioned by David's encounter with the 'destroying' angel whose outstretched arm was extended against Jerusalem (2 Sam 24.16). On account of David's census, the LORD's judgement broke out in a devastating pestilence that took a toll of seven thousand people. Now, David encounters the smiting (מכה) angel at Araunah's threshing floor. So the king makes a passionate entreaty to the LORD. In response, the LORD relents and restrains the angel. David is then directed to build an altar at that site and offer sacrifices which he faithfully follows and thus averting the plague (verses 17–19). Here, it pays to point out a contrast. In the Jerusalem takeover, David's call to 'strike down' (מכה)

---

45. For details, see Grabbe 2004: 153. Along similar lines, Nelson Jr. observes that Araunah is 'both a title ("lord") in Hittite and a personal name in Ugaritic' (Nelson Jr. 2004: 128).

46. Zadok's support of Solomon and the priest's absence in the genealogies are some of the supporting reasons (Jones 1990: 132).

47. Jones observes that 'receiving divine messages and altars are frequently associated with threshing-floors both in biblical and Ugaritic literature'. For details as well as relevant resources, see Jones 1990: 129.

presents a possibility of obliterating the Jebusites. But, as already noted, no such action is reported. On the other hand, as part of the final act of 2 Samuel, in the appearance of the 'striking' (מכה) angel, it is Jerusalem's obliteration that seems imminent. At this poignant moment, the instruction that the disaster can be averted only through offerings at a site[48] that belongs to none other than a Jebusite is powerful attestation to Jebusite presence and prominence. Further and as noted earlier, whereas the LORD's presence and role is notably absent in the takeover narrative, the Araunah episode records the LORD's explicit mandate to David, mediated through the prophet Gad (2 Sam. 24.18). The mandate unambiguously stipulates the threshing floor's ownership as well as Araunah's Jebusite lineage. Thus, the presence of a Jebusite in divine speech is further attestation to Jebusite inroads into David's religious sphere.

The discussion thus far compared and contrasted the takeover text with other relevant texts from the larger literary context, with the help of some of the NH insights. The next section endeavours to reappropriate these findings around a heuristic term: the proximate 'other'.

5. Gleaning the Findings: Jebusites, the Proximate 'Other'

In the context of inter-group interactions, the term *proximate 'other'* helps highlight three key features:[49] (i) persisting category, (ii) permeable boundary, and (iii) ambivalence. These features underscore that:

1. The 'other' who is perceived as 'proximate' rarely leaves the discursive arena of an in-group, despite the in-group attempts to obliterate the proximate 'other' – discursively or otherwise.
2. Despite the repeated efforts to paint a formidable boundary between an in-group and its proximate out-group, a closer analysis reveals that a projected boundary often is not so much of a dividing barrier as a locus of intense interactions.
3. Due to such intense interactions, the discursive context turns into a contested locus, an agonistic arena.[50]

---

48. On the appropriateness of this location as well as the price, namely, fifty shekels of silver which is 'the assigned value for a sizeable piece of land that was dedicated to God (Lev. 27.16)', see Andrews and Bergen 2009: 369.

49. Drawing upon Jonathan Z. Smith's notion of *proximate 'other'* (Smith 1985: 3-48); and see my comments on Smith in Irudayaraj 2017: 54–61.

50. Drawn from the Greek athletic context, the word *agonistic* points to the fact that, in the *agon*, a keenly engaged contestation is given greater significance than the final outcome (victory/defeat).

Such agonistic traces are borne out in discursive ambiguities and ambivalences. These observations on the proximate 'other' can be used meaningfully for the NH reading of the Jerusalem-takeover text.

Jebusite, a persisting category Commenting on the Jebusite 'presence in the David Narrative', Morrison aptly observes that it 'frames King David's public life in Jerusalem: his first act is to seize the Jebusite city, and his final act is to build the first altar in Jerusalem on a land purchased from Araunah, the Jebusite (2 Sam. 24.21-24)' (Morrison 2013: 73). Thus, Jebusites and Jerusalem appear in some of the key moments in David's life: (i) the taking over of Jerusalem, naming it after himself, and his building activity; (ii) purchasing Araunah's threshing floor. While the first chain of events points to the future capital as well as David's royal role, the latter is suggestive of the future temple. In both – with their allusions to kingship, capital and temple – the Jebusite presence cannot be missed. In fact, the books of Samuel conclude by depicting the very feature which is bemoaned in the book of Joshua: 'so the Jebusites live with the people of Judah in Jerusalem to *this day*' (Josh. 15.63). All these texts argue for the persisting category of the 'Jebusite'.

Permeable boundary The Pentateuch presents a repeated mandate to the Israelites to drive out and decimate the Canaanites, of whom the Jebusites are the last in the list (Exod. 23.23, 33.2, 34.11; Deut. 7.1; and more, also in other biblical books).[51] In other words, the list contains an attempt at keeping the Israelite space 'clean' of any Jebusite element. Stated differently, the stipulation paints an ostensibly insurmountable boundary between the Israelites and the Jebusites. However, the lingering Jebusite presence in David's personal, political, and religious spaces (cf. subsection 4.2.2) is a powerful testimony that the projected boundary was anything but insurmountable. In short, Araunah's presence and prominence, the names of David's officials, the wives and concubines *from* Jerusalem, the names of their children, and the probable Jebusite lineage of Zadok are some of the salient textual traces that point to a boundary that is crisscrossed at multiple levels.

Ambivalence As already observed, a violated boundary constitutes a contested locus. The traces of such contestations frequently show forth in textual ambivalences and ambiguities, because they embody a double vision of an in-group in which the latter simultaneously 'draws close' to as well as 'distantiates' its out-group. For instance, in the Jerusalem-takeover narrative, David's call to 'strike down' the Jebusites could be indicative of the Israelite attempt at distantiating (even decimating) the Jebusites. However, the same short text, ironically, ends up by memorializing the Jebusites as the 'inhabitants' of Jerusalem. And the 'drawing close' reaches its zenith when that Jebusite presence is prominently attested in the closing narrative of the book (the Araunah's episode). In short, the 'Jebusite' as a

---

51. Although, in other texts such as Josh. 3.10 and 24.11, the Jebusites are not the last on the Canaanite nations list, which appears in the Bible about twenty times.

persisting category and the permeable boundary that it shared with David (and therefore Israel) at many levels can help appropriate the ambivalences[52] and ambiguities that attend the text. This observation can point to a pertinent interpretive ramification.

Interpretive ramification The chosen text has remained an interpretive challenge to scholarship mostly due to the obscure words, odd subject-verb combination, and enigmatic expressions with polyvalent significance – to name just a few difficulties. Often, scholarly efforts are spent in collating all possible evidence in support of one possible meaning (and so, to the exclusion of all other options), which is frequently the case in many interpretive endeavours. However, if the proposed category of proximate 'other' and the discursive ambivalences that attend it are accounted for, then the prospect of accommodating more than one possible meaning, particularly for obscure terms, need not necessarily be counter-intuitive. For example, let us consider the case of צנור. Anderson presents the main interpretive options for this perennially perplexing word: (i) weapons such as dagger, trident or pitchfork, grappling-iron; (ii) some form of mutilation; (iii) one's *membrum virile*; and (iv) water-supply.[53] The Jerusalem takeover presents a contested context. And when such a charged event is recorded in a book that is noted for its polyvalent pithiness (Auld 2005), perplexing words with multiple meanings need not always be met with an interpretive choice of *one single* meaning. In fact, such words with their scope for multiple, even contradictory, meanings can pack immense power to the contested event that gets narrated. If so, for ויגע בצנור the translation options as diverse as 'getting up the water shaft' and 'dealing a powerful blow by means of a weapon' need not necessarily be mutually exclusive.

Pastoral pertinence Earlier it was shown how the prominent portrayal of David, when scrutinized through the NH guideposts, reveals the excess in the takeover narrative. The proposed reading is not intended so much to discredit David's dominant depiction as to alert our eyes to the other voices and the textual traces that help situate the troubling details in the text. Whereas the Goliath episode points to David's capacity for *excess* both in words and actions, the Araunah episode attests to the king's *excess* only in words but not in action. If so, David's words that he 'hates' the lame and the blind are merely that – just words! No corresponding action follows. In fact, the opposite gets memorialized. The 'Jebusite' survives and even thrives as 'he' is shown to be owning the threshing floor. And there is more. After David's census, when the continued existence of Israelites in Jerusalem is hanging by a thread as the outstretched arm of the destroying angel is directed towards that city, the king makes a passionate plea. And David's desperate

---

52. In a somewhat similar vein, Jones suggests that one of the reasons for contradictory statements is 'the plurality of boundary traditions' (Jones 1990: 120).

53. Having indicated these options, Anderson eventually settles for 'water supply' (Anderson 1989: 84).

wish for respite receives a positive reply from the LORD, but only with an accompanying reference to a Jebusite! To state it differently, it is in the continued existence of the Jebusite[54] that the very hope of the continued existence of the Israelites rests. Israelite destiny is shown to be inextricably intertwined with that of its proximate 'other', the Jebusite. If so, it would not be an exaggeration to say that the Jebusites will survive as long as the Israelites do.

6. The Pertinent Prospect of the Proximate 'Other': Revisiting the Yogi's Outburst

This essay began by describing a double trouble, namely, two instances of hate rhetoric. A NH rereading of the text has helped to underscore the excess and the exaggeration therein. The insights gleaned suggest the promising possibility of the Jebusites as Israel's proximate 'other'; and that the destinies of the two groups are deeply interconnected. In short, the text is 'contextualized' in its larger literary setting to cull out these findings. Thus, a baffling biblical passage is read for its potential for pointing beyond the 'hate' word that first meets one's eyes.

Turning now to the Yogi's outbursts, the *excess* and exaggeration in his words are well chronicled in numerous reports by leading political analysts. Such analyses show that the dominant picture which he takes pain to construct in his public rhetoric is subverted if it is 'contextualized' in his larger socio-political arena. That *excess* is a common feature in David's as well as the Yogi's instances need no belabouring, though the two events are culturally and chronologically far apart. However, there is one other pertinent – in fact, urgent – point that needs to be underscored.

Inter-group discourses take pains to sketch a formidable boundary between an in-group and its out-group, the proximate 'other'. It takes a NH subversive glance to point to the porousness of such boundaries. This discovery presents a pertinent invitation to myself as a 'contextualized', 'doubly troubled' reader. The Yogi's call pits 'all Hindus' against 'all Muslims'. In other words, it stereotypes both groups. First, it attempts to present all Hindus across the state (and even the country) as a single, undifferentiated entity; and the same is done to other minority groups, including Muslims. In other words, the Yogi's rhetoric endeavours to construct a formidable boundary between the Hindu majority and other, minority groups. Such efforts fly in the face of centuries-old experiences of religious communities living as neighbours.[55]

---

54. Jones, for example, imagines that 'it was a situation in which the new minority Israelite element and the old majority Jebusite element attempted to co-exist in the same city-state' (Jones 1990: 140). Further, Jones observes that 'a policy of outright rejection and obliteration was not pursued, but that there was a process of assimilation and adaption of what was found there' (Jones 1990: 130–31).

55. For a pertinent recent event in this regard, see Paniyadi 2017, http://www.deccanchronicle.com/nation/current-affairs/250617/karnataka-historic-vishwesha-teertha-hosts-iftaar-at-krishna-math.html.

Hence, if one is not vigilant,[56] intoxicating words such as the Yogi's can slowly but subtly instil in people – who have lived as near-neighbours – a divisive idea, leading to a false belief that one's identity has to be constructed in contradistinction to one's religious 'others'.

Finally, I quote the poetic words of the mystic Jalaluddin Rumi: 'Raise your words, not voice. It is rain that grows flowers, not thunder.' If my (Indian) context's tropical downpours are any indication, thunder and rain come in each other's company. While thunder is short-lived, rain lasts; thunder has destructive force, rain is rich with nourishing prospects. Extending this analogy to the trajectory of this essay would highlight the following. It is true that hate rhetoric hurts; but situating it in its larger context points to plentiful prospects of continued and amicable coexistence – both in the case of the ancient instance (namely, the interpretive provision for the Israelite–Jebusite interrelationship) and the current context (the value in the continued neighbourliness of various religious groups in India).

Following Rumi, may our reading choices facilitate many such nourishing rains.

Bibliography

Ahlström, G. W. (1980), 'Was David A Jebusite Subject?' *ZAW* 92: 285–87.
Alt, Albrecht (1953), *Kleine Schriften zur Geschichte des Volkes Israel*, Vol. 2, Münich: Beck'sche.
Anderson, Arnold A. (1989), *2 Samuel*, WBC 11, Dallas, TX: Word.
Andrews, Stephen J., and Robert D. Bergen (2009), *1, 2 Samuel*, Holman Old Testament Commentary, Nashville, TN: Broadman & Holman.
Arnold, Bill T. (2003), *1 and 2 Samuel*, The NIV Application Commentary, Grand Rapids, MI: Zondervan.
Auld, A. Graeme (2005), 'Review of Antony Campbell, *2 Samuel*', *RBL*, http://www.bookreviews.org.
Avioz, Michael (2015), *Josephus' Interpretation of the Books of Samuel*, The Library of Second Temple Studies 86, London: Bloomsbury T&T Clark.
Barton, John (2013), 'The Legacy of the Literary-Critical School and the Growing Opposition to Historico-Critical Bible Studies: The Concept of "History" Revisited – Wirkungsgeschichte and Reception History', 96–124 in *Hebrew Bible / Old Testament: The History of Its Interpretation*, edited by Magne Sæbø, vol. III/2, Göttingen: Vandenhoeck & Ruprecht.
Brueggemann, Walter (1985), *David's Truth in Israel's Imagination & Memory*. Minneapolis, MN: Fortress Press.
Campbell, Antony F. (2005), *2 Samuel*, Vol. VIII, FOTL. Grand Rapids, MI: Wm. B. Eerdmans.

---

56. I borrow here the words of the former president of India, Mr Pranab Mukharjee, when he addressed the nation in the context of 'Cow vigilantism', another case of the Hindu right wing's hit at the business endeavours of minorities. Cf. http://www.tribuneindia.com/news/nation/reject-vigilantism-but-be-vigilant-president-to-people/430266.html.

Carvalho, Corrine L. (2006), *Encountering Ancient Voices: A Guide to Reading the Old Testament*. Winona, MN: Saint Mary's Press.

Chafin, Kenneth (1989), *1, 2 Samuel,* Vol. VIII, The Communicator's Commentary, Dallas, TX: Word.

Cook, Sean E. (2017), *The Solomon Narratives in the Context of the Hebrew Bible: Told and Retold*, LHBOTS 638, London: Bloomsbury T&T Clark.

Crabtree, James (2017), 'If They Kill Even One Hindu, We Will Kill 1001!' *Foreign Policy*, March 30, sec. Argument, https://foreignpolicy.com/2017/03/30/if-they-kill-even-one-hindu-we-will-kill-100-india-muslims-nationalism-modi/.

Erisman, A. Roskop (2014), 'New Historicism, Historical Criticism, and Reading the Pentateuch', *Religion Compass* 8, no. 3: 71–80.

Esler, Philip F. (2001), '"By the Hand of a Woman": Culture, Story and Theology in the Book of Judith', 64–101 in *Social Scientific Models for Interpreting the Bible: Essays by the Context Group in Honor of Bruce J. Malina*, edited by John J. Pilch, Leiden: Brill.

Freedman, David N. (1983), 'The Spelling of the Name "David" in the Hebrew Bible', *Hebrew Annual Review* 7: 89–104.

Glück, J. J. (1966), 'The Conquest of Jerusalem in the Account of II. Sam. 5.6a-8', 98–105 in *Biblical Essays*, Potchefstroom, South Africa: Pro Reg-Pers.

Gordon, Robert P. (1986), *I & II Samuel: A Commentary*, Exeter, UK: The Paternoster Press.

Grabbe, Lester L. (2004), 'Ethnic Groups in Jerusalem', 145–63 in *Jerusalem in Ancient History and Tradition*, edited by Thomas L. Thompson, JSOTSup 381, London: T & T Clark International.

Hens-Piazza, Gina (2002), *The New Historicism*, Guides to Biblical Scholarship: Old Testament Series, Minneapolis, MN: Fortress.

Hentschel, Georg (1994), *2 Samuel*, NEchtB 34, Würzburg: Echter Verlag.

Hertzberg, Hans W. (1976), *I and II Samuel: A Commentary*, OTL, Philadelphia, PA: Westminster John Knox.

Hill, Andrew E. (2006), 'On David's "Taking" and "Leaving" Concubines (2 Samuel 5.13; 15.16)', *JBL* 125.1: 129–39.

Holm-Nielsen, Svend (1993), 'Did Joab Climb "Warren's Shaft"?', 38–49 in *History and Traditions of Early Israel: Studies Presented to Eduard Nielsen, May 8th 1993*, edited by André Lemaire, Benedikt Otzen, and Eduard Nielsen, VTSup 50, Leiden: Brill.

Irudayaraj, Dominic S. (2017), *Violence, Otherness and Identity in Isaiah 63:1-6: The Trampling One Coming from Edom*, LHBOTS 633, London: Bloomsbury T&T Clark.

Irudayaraj, Dominic S. (2017), '"What Is This Evil Thing . . . Profaning the Sabbath?" A New-Historicist Look at the Sabbath Restrictions in Nehemiah 13:15-22', *Conspectus* 23: 99–124.

Jaishankar, K. (2009), 'Communal Violence and Terrorism in India: Issues and Introspections', 21–34 in *The Ethics of Terrorism: Innovative Approaches from an International Perspective (17 Lectures)*, edited by Thomas A. Gilly, Yakov Gilinskiy, and Vladimir Sergevnin, Springfield, IL: Charles C. Thomas.

Jones, Gwilym H. (1990), *The Nathan Narratives*, JSOTSup 80, Sheffield, UK: Sheffield Academic.

Kegler, Jürgen (1977), *Politisches Geschehen und Theologisches Verstehen*, Calwer Theologische Monographien 8, Stuttgart: Calwer Verlag.

Kirsch, Jonathan (2000), *King David: The Real Life of the Man Who Ruled Israel*, New York: Random House.

Landay, Jerry M. (1988), *David: Power, Lust and Betrayal in Biblical Times*. Berkeley, CA: Seastone.

Levenson, Jon D. (1992), 'Zion Tradition', 1098–1102 in *ABD*, Vol. 6, edited by David N. Freedman, New York: Doubleday.

Liew, Tat-Siong B. (1999), *Politics of Parousia: Reading Mark Inter(Con)Textually*, Biblical Interpretation Series 42, Leiden: Brill.

McCarter, P. Kyle (1984), *II Samuel*, AB 9, New York: Doubleday.

Merrill, Eugene (1995), 'Jebusites', 298–99 in *The Complete Who's Who in the Bible*, edited by Paul D. Gardner, London: HarperCollins.

Morrison, Craig E. (2013), *2 Samuel*, edited by Jerome Walsh, BERIT OLAM: Studies in Hebrew Narrative & Poetry, Collegeville, MN: Liturgical Press.

Nelson Jr., William B. (2004), 'Jebusites', 120–21 in *The Oxford Guide to People & Places of the Bible*, edited by Bruce M. Metzger and Michael D. Coogan, New York: Oxford University Press.

New York Times (July 17, 2017), 'India's Turn toward Intolerance', https://www.nytimes.com/2017/07/17/opinion/indias-turn-toward-intolerance.html.

Paniyadi, Gururaj A. (2017), 'Karnataka: Historic! Vishwesha Teertha Hosts Iftaar at Krishna Math', *Deccan Chronicle*, June 25, sec. Nation, http://www.deccanchronicle.com/nation/current-affairs/250617/karnataka-historic-vishwesha-teertha-hosts-iftaar-at-krishna-math.html.

Payne, David F. (1982), *I & II Samuel*, The Daily Study Bible Series, Louisville, KY: Westminster John Knox.

Pisano, Stephen (1984), *Additions or Omissions in the Books of Samuel: The Significant Pluses and Minuses in the Massoretic, LXX and Qumran Texts*, Orbis Biblicus et Orientalis 57, Freiburg: Univ.-Verlag.

Poirier, John C. (2006), 'David's 'Hatred' for the Lame and the Blind (2 Sam. 5.8a)', *Palestine Exploration Quarterly* 138.1: 27–33.

Robinson, Gnana (1993), *Let Us Be Like the Nations: A Commentary on the Books of 1 and 2 Samuel*, International Theological Commentary, Grand Rapids, MI: Wm. B. Eerdmans.

Segovia, Fernando F. (2009), 'Towards Minority Biblical Criticism: A Reflection on Achievements and Lacunae', 365–94 in *They Were All Together in One Place? Toward Minority Biblical Criticism*, edited by Randall C. Bailey, Tat-Siong Benny Liew, and Fernando F. Segovia, Semeia Studies 57, Atlanta, GA: SBL.

Sharp, Carolyn J. (2009), *Irony and Meaning in the Hebrew Bible*, Bloomington, IN: Indiana University Press.

Sherwood, Yvonne (1997), 'Rocking the Boat: Jonah and the New Historicism', *BibInt* 5.4: 364–402.

Smith, Jonathan Z. (1985) 'What A Difference A Difference Makes', 3–48 in *'To See Ourselves As Others See Us': Christians, Jews, 'Others' in Late Antiquity*, edited by Jacob Neusner, Ernest S. Frerichs, and Caroline McCracken-Flesher, Studies in the Humanities, Chico, California: Scholars.

Tribune News (2017), 'Reject Vigilantism, but Be Vigilant: President to People', *Trinuneindia News Service*, July 1, sec. Nation, http://www.tribuneindia.com/news/nation/reject-vigilantism-but-be-vigilant-president-to-people/430266.html.

Tsumura, David T. (2007), *The First Book of Samuel*, The New International Commentary on the Old Testament, Grand Rapids, MI: Wm. B. Eerdmans.

Yamada, Frank M. (2009), 'What Does Manzamar Have to Do with Eden? A Japanese American Interpretation of Genesis 2–3', 97–117 in *They Were All Together in One*

Place? Toward Minority Biblical Criticism, edited by Randall C. Bailey, Tat-Siong Benny Liew, and Fernando F. Segovia, Semeia Studies 57, Atlanta, GA: SBL.

Yoon, Sung-Hee (2014), *The Question of the Beginning and the Ending of the So-Called History of David's Rise: A Methodological Reflection and Its Implications*, BZAW 462, Berlin: Walter de Gruyter.

Youngblood, Ronald F. (1992), '1, 2 Samuel', 551–1104 in *The Expositor's Bible Commentary: Deuteronomy-2 Samuel*, edited by Frank E. Gaebelein, Grand Rapids, MI: Zondervan.

'WHO CAN SPEAK FOR ME?'
DAVID'S TEN CONCUBINES AND THE CASE FOR COMFORT WOMEN

Hyun Ho Park

The Unheard Voices of Comfort Women: 'Are you ignoring us?'

'Who do you think you are? Are you living my life? *Are you ignoring us*, because we are old and ignorant?' Yong-Soo Lee, a former 'comfort woman', said this during a conversation with the vice-minister for foreign affairs of South Korea on 29 December 2015. South Korea and Japan reached an agreement on the 'comfort women' issue on 28 December 2015. On the surface the agreement seems to contain everything Koreans hoped for: a formal apology from the Japanese government and 8.3 million in monetary compensation. At the heart of this diplomatic deal, however, there is a disturbing condition: 'This agreement confirms that this issue is finalized irreversibly, and the Korean government and Japanese government agree to refrain from criticizing each other on this issue in international society including the United Nations'.[1] The Japanese government and the pro-Japanese Korean government attempt to erase one of the most inhumane crimes, sexual slavery, committed by the Japanese military against Korean women during the Second World War.

Apologizing, however, is not enough. Giving money will never cover up the scar that is so deep – especially if an offender demands the victim remain silent. If *that* is the condition of the apology, then it is not an apology but a non-apology, a fake. What if the prime minister of Germany announces an apology with monetary compensation to the victims of the Holocaust, on condition that Jews can never criticize Germany's past war crimes within international society? Would Jewish people, tormented and suffering during the Holocaust, see such an announcement

---

1. 'Korea and Japan agreed to resolve the issue of the Comfort Women,' *Hankyoreh*, December 29, 2015, accessed June 15, 2016, http://www.hani.co.kr/arti/politics/diplomacy/723743.html.

as an apology? Not only is it fake, but it is an insult. On a deeper level, the issue at stake is not just the condition stipulated in Japan's 'apology' and the South Korean government's collaboration with it, but also the actual process of the agreement. Victims' voices were never heard, while the powerful spoke and made a decision. The victims are ignored, not recognized. Furthermore, according to the agreement, victims cannot speak up later, because from now on their voice should not be heard in the international community. They cannot exist in public spheres, because they are not allowed to tell their stories. The history of comfort women is in danger of vanishing.

The Unheard Voice of David's Ten Concubines

Silencing the victim is not a new technique. Korean and Filipino voices were not heard in the making of the Taft-Katsura agreement in 1905, in which Japan and the United States secretly agreed not to question each other's control of – and, thus, colonial expansion to – another country: Korea for Japan, and the Philippines for the United States. Koreans and Filipinos did not even know what was discussed between these two powerful nations, though this agreement determined their own fate. They were not informed and were completely ignored.

In the same vein, the story of David's ten concubines in 2 Samuel seems to provide no alternative reality. Its characters, setting, and plot are quite similar to the story of the comfort women: marginalized women (characters), especially their bodies, are exploited for the benefit of powerful men (plot) during war (setting). David's ten concubines never speak, while the powerful make decisions for them. David orders them to look after his house when he leaves Jerusalem in the face of Absalom's usurpation (2 Sam. 15.16). Following Ahithophel's advice, Absalom violates them sexually (2 Sam. 16.22). As soon as David returns to Jerusalem, he shuts them up until their death (2 Sam. 20.3). In these sporadic scenes the women's existence seems to be disappearing. Their cry is never heard in the midst of David's victory over his enemies. One wonders, 'Is God also ignoring the suffering of the ten concubines? Who can speak for these marginalized women?'

My aim is to speak up for these women by re-examining previous readings of the snippets of story about them (2 Sam. 15.16, 16.21-22, 20.3), reinterpreting those within the narrative context of the book of Samuel, and re-evaluating the implications in current political discourse between South Korea and Japan on the issue of the comfort women. I argue that *major characters in the story abuse power and ignore the suffering of the ten concubines; that the story reveals David as a betrayer, unlike his loyal men; and that it speaks for the faithful ten concubines.* To demonstrate my thesis, I first introduce the concept of unifying plot and episodic plot in the narrative and the practice of speaking for the other in colonial literature. Second, I discuss how these methodologies produce a new way of interpreting the story. Third, I show how major characters in the story abuse power and ignore the suffering of these women in 2 Sam. 16.20-23 and 20.3; and yet how the story portrays David as a betrayer – unlike his loyal men – in chs. 15–20 and speaks up for the faithful ten concubines. Finally, I discuss how this story invites its readers to speak for the comfort women in the South Korean context.

Unifying Plot and Episodic Plot and Speaking for the Other

In order to explore the story of David's ten concubines, I employ two methodologies, the first of which is the distinction between unifying plot and episodic plot. A macro-narrative often contains multiple micro-narratives. Though various components change in a given narrative, such as setting and character, what holds different and/or similar pieces together is the plot. Marguerat and Bourquin differentiate a unifying plot from an episodic plot. They define *unifying plot* as 'the plot of a narrative sequence or macro-narrative which overhangs and encompasses the plots of the episodes which it contains', whereas an *episodic plot* is a plot of the micro-narrative (Marguerat and Bourquin 1999: 56). For example, Jesus' meeting with a blind beggar in Lk. 18.35-43 has its own plot, with causality and sequence. The beggar hears that Jesus is passing by and cries out for help. Jesus comes and heals him, and he follows Jesus. Yet, in a bigger picture the episode is not only contrasted with a rich ruler's rejection of Jesus' invitation to follow him, but also re-emphasizes a thoroughgoing theme of Luke's travel narrative: following Jesus. In short, an episodic plot is related to other episodic plots and, thus, reveals what a unifying plot is up to. Yet, since different themes, not a single theme, penetrate a plot of a given narrative, readers need to be aware of multiple themes. For example, Mary's Magnificat (Lk. 1.46-55) foreshadows a definitive characteristic of Jesus' ministry: the reversal of fortune. God will bring down the rich and powerful and lift up the poor and lowly (v. 52). By the same token, the fortune of a rich ruler and a beggar is reversed in Lk. 18.18-43. A rich ruler fails to follow Jesus, but a blind beggar follows him and, thus, inherits the kingdom of God (cf. Lk. 9.62). Two themes, the following of Jesus and the reversal of fortune, are embedded simultaneously in Lk. 18.18-43.

The second methodology which I employ in the discussion is the practice of speaking for the other from *Orientalism*. For Edward Said, Orientalism is the discourse of the West positioning itself as superior and creating the East as an inferior other. This is possible in Western colonial literature, because it was the West who spoke of and for the East. The East exists only as a *reference*, not as a *voice*, because their actual words are never heard. Said notes:

> There is very little consent to be found, for example, in the fact that Flaubert's encounter with an Egyptian courtesan produced a widely influential model of Oriental woman; she never spoke of herself, she never represented her emotions, presence, or history. *He* spoke for and represented her. He was foreign, comparatively wealthy, male, and these were historical facts of domination that allowed him not only to possess Kuchuk Hanem physically but to speak for her and tell his readers in what way she was 'typically Oriental.' My argument is that Flaubert's situation of strength in relation to Kuchuk Hanem

was not an isolated instance. It fairly stands for the pattern of relative strength between East and West, and the discourse about the Orient that it enabled. (Said 1994b: 133) .

The problem of such colonial discourse is twofold. First, the voice spoken is the distorted voice of the East. The East is not only weak and passive, but also agrees to submit its will to the West. It is a fake. Second, colonial discourse ignores the suffering of the colonized.

The emotion of the East is not represented. From his examination of colonial adventure literatures, Said points out that the West's colonial discourse does not accuse but, on the contrary, serves the imperial undertaking of the West (Said 1994b: 187). Since the voice of the victor, not of the victim, is narrated, exploitation is replaced with exploration and defeat is celebrated for victory. It is not just a fake, but an *insult*. The voice of the exploited should be restored and heard. The story of David's ten concubines seems not to do justice for those women, because they remain silent the entire time. Yet, when readers explore a bigger story (2 Sam. 11–20), the story discloses that the implied author actually reverses the practice of colonial writers. By speaking *of* the marginalized, he speaks *for* them.

David's Ten Concubines Re-examined

There have been three foci of interpretations concerning David's role in this story.

1. David innocently leaves his concubines behind, while Absalom is guilty of having intercourse with his father's concubines. Hertzberg (1960: 341) argues that David left them to keep the house, because he did not imagine them 'to be in any danger'. McCarter (1984: 376) also argues that David is not responsible for his flight from Absalom, yet it is Amnon's rape of Tamar, a 'sacrilege', that brought this calamity on Israel. David's flight from Absalom is a pilgrimage in which he experiences humiliation and restoration for the sin of Israel. In order to be fully restored to his throne, those women illegally claimed by Absalom 'must be put away' (McCarter 1984: 423). Anderson (1989: 214) and Barron (2015: 137-54, 173-78) go further and do not even mention David's shutting the concubines up, while accusing Absalom of publicly and deliberately humiliating David.
2. David is innocent, because he follows the ancient custom of leaving concubines behind. Hill (2006: 129-39) argues that David's concubines are local Jebusites whom David took *from* Jerusalem (2 Sam. 5.13) and it was 'a royal protocol in the Jebusite city-state of Jerusalem' that prohibited Jebusite members of the royal harem from leaving the city.
3. The story of David's ten concubines is a parable signifying David's relationship with the ten northern tribes of Israel. Auld thinks that the concubines' 'confined "widowhood" till their death' can be seen as a 'Davidic perspective of northern Israel after Solomon: spoiled and fruitless till it exists no more'. He

argues that Sheba's calling out of *ten* tribes (2 Sam. 20.1-3) coheres with David's shutting up of *ten* concubines (Auld 2011: 562).

Although these interpretations are valid at some points, they fail to acknowledge how an episodic plot of a micro-narrative (2 Sam. 15.6, 16.21-22, 20.3) contributes to the unifying plots of the macro-narrative (2 Sam. 11.1–20.22). Two unifying plots are worth noting. One is that *David falls* in 2 Sam. 11–20. After David sees Bathsheba bathing on the roof (2 Sam. 11.1-2), he falls miserably. In this macro-narrative David is often depicted as one of the following: a sinner (e.g., the Bathsheba incident in chs. 11–12), an incapable father who does not take care of family conflicts quickly and decisively (e.g., Amnon's rape of Tamar, Absalom's murder of Amnon and usurpation in chs 13–19), and a king who struggles with rebellion (e.g., Revolt of Absalom and Sheba in chs 15–20). He is a man with many flaws and weaknesses.

With this unifying plot in mind, a different way of reading the story of David's ten concubines is possible: David is *not innocent* of Absalom's violation of them. He is guilty of Absalom's usurpation because he fails to punish Amnon who has raped Tamar, Absalom's sister, and thus contributes in a way to Absalom's murder of Amnon, the heir apparent. Thus, Absalom comes a step closer to the throne. This fuels Absalom's ambition to be king. Furthermore, Ahithophel is said to be Bathsheba's grandfather (cf. 2 Sam. 11.3, 23.34). Ahithophel is avenging 'what David has done to his granddaughter and her husband Uriah' (Kim 2008: 127). Nathan announces it explicitly, when he accuses David of taking Bathsheba and murdering Uriah: 'I will raise up trouble against you from within your own house; and I will take your wives before your eyes, and give them to your neighbor, and he shall lie with your wives in the sight of this very sun' (2 Sam. 12.11). David is responsible for Absalom's usurpation and the rape of his ten concubines. Since their violation is the fulfillment of Nathan's prophecy, the story of the ten concubines cannot be read as a parable either. David commits a sin, and others suffer. At his return, he puts the women under house arrest. This episode is a clear indication that he is *still* falling.

David's Ten Concubines Reinterpreted

The second unifying plot, crucial for reinterpreting the story, is that *one's loyalty is tested*. Kim points out that the theme of חסד, loyalty, is prevalent in the story of Absalom's revolt (chs 15–19): 'David encounters several characters in his flight from Jerusalem. Some will show *ḥesed* to him, and others will not' (Kim 2008: 129). I argue that the theme of loyalty is also relevant to ch. 20, because the rebellion of Sheba, a Benjaminite, underscores the same issue: who will remain loyal? Ten northern tribes withdraw their loyalty to David but allude to their loyalty to the fallen house of Saul (verses 1-2). The last snapshot of the ten concubines' story (v. 3) is not an exception. This second unifying plot, the testing of one's loyalty, allows readers to interpret the story of David's ten concubines in a new way.

First, *the major characters of the story abuse power and ignore the suffering of the ten concubines.* There are three major characters involved in this story: David, Ahithophel and Absalom. David decides to leave his concubines as he flees from Absalom. David's taking of ten concubines is likely a political arrangement to strengthen his relationship with powerful families in Jerusalem (Hackett 1998: 98–9). Whether it was a royal protocol to leave royal harems in the city of Jerusalem or not is unclear, because this would provide a usurper with the means to claim his legitimacy by producing a royal heir through sexual intercourse with royal harems (Morrison 2013: 225). Ahithophel is keenly aware of this, thus advises Absalom to do so. David seems unaware of the danger, because the narrator states that David has left his concubines behind to look after the house. Yet, his ignorance is not free from critique, because those women suffer violation and humiliation 'in the sight of all Israel' (2 Sam. 16.22). If David knew what would come upon them, he is guilty of ignoring their suffering in order to keep his selfish interest in keeping the house in order. The narrative alludes to David's awareness, because the narrator acknowledges that his advice is considered to be 'the oracle of God' by David as well as Absalom (v. 23). Therefore, Absalom sexually violates the women without hesitation on the roof where David saw Bathsheba. In so doing, he gains two benefits. Symbolically, his action shows that the king is dead. His concubines are taken over by another man. Usurpation is successful. Since the family tie between David and Absalom is broken, the last thing that remains is to eliminate the old king. Practically, Absalom's action provides him with the validity of his throne. The womb of the former king's harem is now under his control. David must be keenly aware of this, because he himself has taken Saul's wife, Ahinoam, as his wife (cf. 1 Sam. 14.50, 25.43).[2] So, Absalom takes David's. He humiliates them in the sight of all Israel. In this story, women are tools designed to serve strong men's interests: revenge for Ahithophel, usurpation for Absalom, and household business for David. Even people whose hands are strengthened by Absalom's intercourse with them are Absalom's army, mostly men (v. 21). Three men abuse their power, while ignoring the suffering of those women. Like Said's critique of the West's representation of the East, they remain passive, silent and submissive to their masters.

Second, *the story reveals David as a betrayer, unlike his men.* The narrator shows that David's men remain loyal to him during the revolt of Absalom and Sheba. David's encounter with Ittai the Gittite (2 Sam. 15.19-22) is programmatic in the story of Absalom's usurpation. Polzin points out that 'the narrative role of Ittai ...

---

2. There are two Ahinoam[s] in the books of Samuel. One is Saul's wife, Ahinoam, a daughter of Ahimaaz (1 Sam. 14.50). The other is David's wife, Ahinoam of Jezreel (1 Sam. 25.43). Levenson and Halpern argue, based on Nathan's words (2 Sam. 12.8) – 'I gave you your master's house, and your master's wives into your bosom' – that David took Ahinoam from Saul: Halpern 2003: 288; Levenson and Halpern 1980: 507–18. Green points out that David's marriage with Abigail after the death of Nabal who has been 'holding a feast in his house, like the feast of a *king*' (1 Sam. 25.36) and the narrator's introduction of David's wives immediately after Nabal's story (1 Sam. 25.2-44) make David's taking of his master's wife, Ahinoam, plausible (Green 2003: 405).

whose very name suggests "loyalty" or "companion" is *to be with David wherever he goes*'; and furthermore, the word את, 'with', is used in the story of Absalom's revolt (chs 15–19) far more frequently than in other parts of 2 Samuel (Polzin 1993: 151). So Ittai, a foreigner, and his household are with David. Abiathar and Zadok also remain faithful to David, and so does Hushai, while staying in Jerusalem, not to mention that as soon as David says 'Let us flee', his officials follow him. These men's loyalty to David is contrasted with the disloyalty of Shimei, a Benjamite, and Ziba. Seeing David has lost power, Shimei reveals his true loyalty to Saul's house and now Absalom in public: 'Out! Out! Murderer! Scoundrel!' (2 Sam. 16.7).[3] David hears that Mephibosheth has ceased to remain loyal to him and tells Ziba, the servant of Mephibosheth, to take everything that belongs to his master. Yet, the implied author describes that David even in the midst of tribulation is surrounded by those who are loyal to him. Shobi, Machir, and Barzillai provide food for him (2 Sam. 17.27-29). In Sheba's revolt, Joab clearly reveals that David still has his men: 'Whoever favors Joab, and whoever is for David, let him follow Joab' (2 Sam. 20.11).

David's conversations with Mephibosheth and Barzillai especially reveal what kind of loyalty David receives from his cohorts: loyalty without expecting something in return. After Mephibosheth explains how Ziba has mistreated and slandered him during Absalom's revolt, David does not restore his full possessions. He orders him to divide the land with Ziba. He casts doubt on Mephibosheth's loyalty, because he has not come with David. Mephibosheth says in response, 'Let him take it all, since my lord the king has arrived home safely' (2 Sam. 19.30). For him, material possessions are nothing by comparison to the king's safe return. Barzillai too does not expect something in return for the food he has provided to David. As an aged man, he refuses to accept David's material compensation because he does not want to be a burden for the king (verses 32, 35–36). He responds to David's request to feed his troops in the wilderness out of his loyalty and generosity (2 Sam. 17.29). In sum, the implied author shows that David has many loyal cohorts.

Unlike his men, however, David betrays some who have been loyal to him. Ten concubines remain in David's house, as he commanded them. Because of this, their bodies are exploited by another man. Surrounded by Absalom's army, they are too weak to resist or escape. Perhaps their loyalty to David has sustained them in the palace, despite humiliations and violence. They are left there to look after *his* house. Their bodies are tools of strong men, yet their souls remain faithful to David. Upon his return, however, David does not show loyalty to them. He puts them under house arrest, as if they are criminals. David takes care of them, but at the same time shuts them up until their death. For David, their bodies are the sign of rebellion and the symbol of his temporary defeat (Morrison 2013: 267). David can bring them back to his palace after the possibility of pregnancy with Absalom is gone, as he has brought Michal from Palti (2 Sam. 3.13-16). He does not do so. Just as he has

---

3. 'The LORD has avenged on all of you the blood of the house of Saul, in whose place you have reigned; and the LORD has given the kingdom into the hand of your son Absalom. See, disaster has overtaken you; for you are a man of blood' (2 Sam. 16.8).

done to Michal, David has no sexual relations with them 'till the day of their death' (2 Sam. 20.3. Cf. 2 Sam. 6.23). He is disloyal to them, because they are just tools that connect David to something greater for his kingship – his solidarity with Jerusalem. David betrays these women. David's disloyalty or selective loyalty to his people is also demonstrated in his encounter with Mephibosheth. The narrator's portrayal of Mephibosheth as a mourner clearly shows whose side he is on. He is David's man (2 Sam. 19.30). But David seems not to see him (v. 29).

Third, *the story speaks for the faithful ten concubines*. At the surface level, the implied author seems to focus on the weakness of the ten concubines. The women speak no word, passively follow the commands of strong men who decide their fate, and become objects of exploitation. Much like the custom of colonial literature, the author seems to produce an orientalist image of the marginalized women. Yet, below the surface, a radically different truth is found. The storyteller is actually *speaking for* the women. The following evidence supports this argument.

1. The implied author problematizes David's leaving of the ten concubines in his crafting of 2 Sam. 15.16. Everybody in David's house leaves except his concubines. The storyteller places the leaving behind of the ten concubines at the centre of the short episode:

> So the king left, followed by all his household,
>   except ten concubines whom he left behind to look after the house.
> The king left, followed by all the people. (15.16-17a)

According to Morrison (2013: 205), the chiastic structure suggests that 'it should not be overlooked'. It not only marks the beginning of Absalom's revolt[4] but also prepares readers to see what is at stake in the unifying plot of the bigger narrative (chs 15–20): testing of one's loyalty. Based on Berlin's category of David's wives – (1) agent; (2) type; (3) character – David's ten concubines are somewhere between the *agent* 'about whom nothing is known except what is necessary for the plot;' and the *type* 'who represents the class of people' (Berlin 1982: 78). Those women represent the marginalized women in David's palace (type), and the information about them within the plot is limited (agent). David's action toward them will reveal who he is, as his actions related to Bathsheba manifested his fall.[5] David should not have left them there. His selfish choice reveals his disloyalty.

---

4. Morrison argues that the ten concubines function as a literary *inclusio* for the story of Absalom's revolt: 'When David returns to his palace and places these women under house arrest, the curtain drops on Absalom's rebellion (20.3)' (Morrison 2013: 205).

5. Berlin (1982: 79) categorizes David's character in relation to Bathsheba as 'Lust, grasping what is not his'. In light of David's action toward his ten concubines one can add the following: (1) David's women: the ten concubines. (2) David's character: annoyed, abandoning what he dislikes but used to be his. (3) David's stage in life: desire to hold on to his position as a king.

2. The implied author demonstrates that David is a selfish figure. The shutting up of ten concubines is the end of the story of David's Ten Concubines. This cold-blooded treatment by David is different from his heartbreaking mourning for Absalom (2 Sam. 18.33). It is almost shocking. Why so, then? Absalom is *his* own son. By the same token, these concubines are *his* women but violated by another man. *His* masculinity is challenged and humiliated. Therefore, they should remain desolate. David is the centre of his own universe. It is not an accident that the shutting up of ten concubines is the first thing David does upon his return to Jerusalem.
3. The implied author *tells* the story. The narrative flow seems not interrupted without the story of ten concubines (2 Sam. 15.16, 16.21-22, 20.3). David and his officials flee, Absalom seeks advice from Ahithophel, and David subdues two consecutive rebellions. Therefore, some scholars argue that this story is a secondary narrative inserted in the larger narrative of 2 Samuel 15–20.[6] What then does the implied author and/or final editor of Samuel do by inserting this story? First, he *tells* the story, because for him this story is important enough to be included in the bigger narrative. Second, he allows readers to *hear* the voice that is missing: the unspoken voice of women. He reveals that they were *there* and *suffered*. Third, by juxtaposing their loyalty with David's disloyalty, he *speaks for* them. They are the victims who need to be recognized. In so doing, he conveys a profound truth: God too does not ignore the women's existence and their voice.

David's Ten Concubines Re-Evaluated

The story of David's ten concubines has often been interpreted and thus evaluated from the perspective of men. Liberating implications from this story have been scarce, because their fate is determined by others. Likewise, South Korea's President, Geun-Hye Park, announced after the South Korea–Japan agreement on the comfort women issue that the effort is made to ease 'the mental pains of the elderly comfort women'.[7] The South Korean government might think that they are doing the right thing, but they are actually betraying the victims. 'You should have listened to our voice', Bok-Dong Kim, a former comfort woman, said to the vice-minister for foreign affairs of South Korea. Another comfort woman, Yong-Soo Lee, repeated, 'He is ignoring us!' In my ears, their cry is translated thus: 'Where is

---

6. 'Langlamet . . . would strike verses 16b-17a as secondary for two reasons: (1) He does not think the concubine episode in 16:21-22 was an original part of the story of Abishalom's revolt . . ., and (2) he reads the (inferior) text of the received Hebrew (MT) of v. 17a, according to which it was "all the army" that marched out after David in contradiction to v. 16a'. McCarter 1984: 369.

7. 'Japan and South Korea agree WW2 "comfort women" deal'. *BBC*, 28 December 2015, accessed 15 June 2016, http://www.bbc.com/news/world-asia-35188135.

our voice? Who will speak for us?' In the middle of war, they were victims of violence. Their country lost its power. Their men left them on their own because they were unable to fight back their enemy. So, women were abused sexually and suffered humiliation by other men. The women of the colonized nation were the marginalized among the marginalized. Now, their own men along with their former colonizer are telling them to be silent. They are trying to shut them up until their death.

The story of David's ten concubines, however, brings different implications on this issue. It invites us to do the exact opposite of what these men are telling those comfort women to do. *Speak for them*: not in order to close the matter irreversibly but to let the broader public know their stories so that it continues to be remembered throughout the centuries. Sexual slavery during the Second World War was a denial of their *bodies*. Theirs were just tools of pleasure for men. Forcing them not to speak up within the international community is a denial of not only the colonizer's dark past but also the women's very *existence*, because as Hannah Arendt says, 'a life without speech and action . . . is literally dead to the world; it has ceased to be a human life because it is *no longer lived among men*' (Arendt 1998: 176; italics mine). What differentiates humans from other beings is that we can speak and act. In this sense, the world in which we live exists not in physicality only but in relationality. We create and live in this world by telling our own stories to others. No human being can live on an island. Taking away the comfort women's right to speak up is to put them under house arrest. The author of Samuel refuses to do so. Rather, he takes the story of the marginalized women and inserts it in the material he has inherited. The story speaks for the women, so that readers might hear the story of these marginalized women and remember them for centuries to come.

Conclusion

Since the story of the Korean comfort women was told to the public audience for the first time in 1991 by Hak-Soon Kim, a former comfort woman herself, their stories have been recorded and expressed through various means,[8] where they function as spokespersons of their own stories. They are the voice. In Homer's term, they are heroes, because they boldly insert their story into history.[9] Now, their actions invite us to have courage to speak and act for them, so that we may also

---

8. For comfort women's own paintings see Hye-Jin, 2000. For Se-Woon Chung, a former comfort woman's story, watch 'Herstory', last modified 15 January 2014, https://www.youtube.com/watch?v=0CmWdrlv3fI.

9. 'The hero the story discloses needs no heroic qualities; the word "hero" originally, that is, in Homer, was no more than a name given each free man who participated in the Trojan enterprise and about whom a story could be told' (Arendt 1998: 186).

insert our story and become heroes of our time.[10] This act of speaking for those women is not intended to evoke hatred among people, but to remind every human being of who we are – we are humans – just as our fellow Japanese Americans have been speaking of the injustice of internment during the Second World War.[11] The story of David's ten concubines awakens us to the fact that there is always a danger of dehumanizing others and the temptation to make another human being into a tool, an object of exploitation. At the same time, we are called to remember that every human needs to be treated as a human. It is a wakeup call for us to fight against any crime towards fellow humans. The powerful already made decisions for us not to speak up. But, we, humans, will continue to speak for the women. We will not give up being humans, we will not ignore the sufferings of those comfort women, and we will not stop telling their stories, because by keeping silent we collaborate in dehumanizing, controlling and objectifying others. Truly, the biblical story of the ten concubines, and the Korean-Japanese story of the comfort women, put to the test our loyalty not only to fight against any form of power that enslaves us and makes us a tool, but also to discover and love our fellow human beings wherever they are.[12]

Bibliography

Books and Articles

Anderson, A. A. (1989), *2 Samuel*, Word Biblical Commentary 11, Dallas: Word Books.
Arendt, Hannah (1998), *The Human Condition,* Chicago: University of Chicago Press.
Auld, A. Graeme (2011), *I and II Samuel: A Commentary,* Louisville, KY: Westminster John Knox.
Barron, Robert (2015), *2 Samuel,* Grand Rapids, MI: Brazos.
Berlin, Adele (1982), 'Characterization in Biblical Narrative: David's Wives', *JSOT* 23: 69–85.
Fanon, Franz (2008), *Black Skin, White Masks.* Translated by Charles Lam Markmann, London and Chicago: Pluto.
Green, Barbara (2003), *How Are the Mighty Fallen?: A Dialogical Study of King Saul in 1 Samuel,* The Library of Hebrew Bible/Old Testament Studies (Book 365), London: Bloomsbury T&T Clark.

---

10. 'The connotation of courage, which we now feel to be an indispensable quality of the hero in fact already present in a willingness to act and speak at all, to insert one's self into the world and begin a story of one's own' (Arendt 1998: 186).

11. For further explanation see Yamada 2006: 164–77 and Rietz 2006: 192–203.

12. When commencing an analysis of the exploited and oppressed, Franz Fanon's proclamation rings so true: 'I, the man of color, want only this: That the tool never possesses the man. That the enslavement of man by man ceases forever. That it be possible for me to discover and to love man, wherever he may be' (Fanon 2008: 180).

Hackett, Jo Ann (1998), '1 and 2 Samuel', 91–101 in Carol A. Newsom and Sharon H. Ringe (eds), *Women's Bible Commentary*, Louisville, KY: Westminster John Knox.

Halpern, Baruch (2003), *David's Secret Demons: Messiah, Murderer, Traitor, King,* Grand Rapids, MI: Eerdmans Publishing.

Hertzberg, Hans Wilhelm (1960), *1 & 2 Samuel: A Commentary,* Philadelphia: Westminster Press.

Hill, Andrew E. (2006), 'On David's "Taking" and "Leaving" Concubines (2 Samuel 5:13; 15:16)', *JBL* 125 (1): 129–39.

Hye-Jin., ed. (2000), *Unblossomed Flower: A collection of Paintings by Former Military Comfort Women,* Kyonggi-do Province, Republic of Korea: Historical Museum of Sexual Slavery by the Japanese Military.

Kim, Uriah Y. (2008), *Identity and Loyalty in the David Story: A Postcolonial Reading,* Hebrew Bible Monographs 22, Sheffield: Sheffield Phoenix.

Levenson, Jon D. and Baruch Halpern (1980), 'The Political Import of David's Marriages', *JBL* 99: 507–18.

Marguerat, Daniel and Yvan Bourquin (1999), *How to Read Bible Stories*, London: SCM Press.

McCarter, P. Kyle, Jr. (1984), *II Samuel*, The Anchor Bible 9, Garden City, NY: Doubleday.

Morrison, Craig E. OCarm. (2013), *2 Samuel*, Berit Olam Studies in Hebrew Narrative & Poetry, Collegeville, MN: Liturgical Press.

Polzin, Robert (1993), *David and the Deuteronomist: A Literary Study of the Deuteronomic History III: 2 Samuel,* Bloomington: Indiana University Press.

Rietz, Henry W. Morisada (2006), 'Living Past: A Hapa Identifying with the Exodus, the Exile, and the Internment', 192–203 in Mary F. Foskett and Jeffrey Kah-Jin Kuan (eds), *Ways of Being, Ways of Reading: Asian American Biblical Interpretation*, St. Louis, MO: Chalice.

Said, Edward W. (1994a), *Culture and Imperialism*, New York: Vintage Books.

Said, Edward W. (1994b), 'Orientalism', 132–49 in Patrick Williams and Laura Chrisman (eds), *Colonial Discourse and Post-colonial Theory: A Reader*, New York: Columbia University Press.

Yamada, Frank M. (2006), 'Constructing Hybridity and Heterogeneity', 164–77 in Mary F. Foskett and Jeffrey Kah-Jin Kuan (eds), *Ways of Being, Ways of Reading: Asian American Biblical Interpretation*, St. Louis, MO: Chalice.

Newspaper Articles

'Korea and Japan agreed to resolve the issue of the Comfort Women'. *Hankyoreh*, 29 December 2015, http://www.hani.co.kr/arti/politics/diplomacy/723743.html accessed 15 June 2016.

'Japan and South Korea agree WW2 "comfort women" deal'. *BBC*, 28 December 2015, http://www.bbc.com/news/world-asia-35188135, accessed 15 June 2016.

Website

YouTube. 'Herstory'. Last modified 15 January 2014, https://www.youtube.com/watch?v=0CmWdrlv3fI.

THE POLITICS OF ANCIENT AND MODERN BURIAL: REVISITING THE CASE OF RIZPAH

Talia Sutskover

1. Introduction: Burial in Present-Day Israel

The subject of burial seems to act as a battleground between political positions and religious convictions, and not only in biblical times – as shall be shown in the narrative of Rizpah daughter of Aiah (2 Sam. 21.1-14) – but in contemporary times as well.

In Israel of today, Jewish citizens are usually brought to burial by courtesy of the *Chevra Kadisha* (Aramaic 'Holy Society', the official name of the Society), an authorized Jewish-religious organization appointed by the state, whereas non-Jewish citizens (whether Christian, Muslim or others) have their own burial organizations, make their own arrangements and, very often, have their own cemeteries. Public cemeteries in Israel are accessible, spread across the country, and conduct religious burial ceremonies. Only since 1996, after a long public debate, was a secular burial option authorized, and for this purpose several private cemeteries were opened.[1] As for the burial of soldiers, military cemeteries were established in Israel in 1949, one year after the Israeli Declaration of Independence. Today Israel has numerous religious-public cemeteries, some 42 military cemeteries, and around nine private cemeteries that are authorized to carry out secular civic burial.[2]

---

1. It should be stated that even before secular burial was legalized in Israel, the Kibbutzim often conducted this type of burial. On burial in Israel see: http://bfree.org.il/%D7%A7%D7%91%D7%95%D7%A8%D7%94-%D7%91%D7%99%D7%A9%D7%A8%D7%90%D7%9C?gclid=EAIaIQobChMIiuy0sObE1gIVzArTCh0dwAWyEAAYASAAEgJ8t_D_BwE

For a collection of recent newspaper articles regarding burial in Israel published in the newspaper *Globes* go to: http://www.globes.co.il/news/%D7%A7%D7%91%D7%95%D7%A8%D7%94.tag

2. In 2009 the Israeli Knesset approved a legislation prohibiting leaving corpses in the open field. See legislation 6167/09, online: http://elyon1.court.gov.il/files/09/670/061/t06/09061670.t06.htm

Though there is no explicit law in Israel requiring burial to be in the ground, most Israeli citizens request a ground burial, and a minority choose to be cremated.

Burial issues in Israel continue to be a power struggle between religious and non-religious citizens and politicians. Recently, a political-religious crisis regarding the burial of soldiers in Israel was finally resolved. After a two-year public protest (2015–16), authorization was given for non-Jewish soldiers to be buried alongside their peers within the boundaries of military cemeteries.³

Public debate in Jewish Israel about civic burial seems to have been resolved for now, but until civic graveyards were opened the debate was quite fierce and in places continues to be so, even though in many civic burials Jewish rites for the dead continue to be performed by choice (unlike in religious burials, where the rites are mandatory). People want to have a say in the burial of their dear ones. And this leads me back to reconsider the story of a biblical woman who cared deeply about the bodies of her dead and their correct burial and acted upon her feelings. Thus, a contemporary debate may trigger new and unexpected results.

2. Introduction: Rizpah

The biblical narrative of Rizpah, daughter of Aiah (2 Sam. 21.1-14), includes a religio-political crisis around the issue of burial. The story of Rizpah opens with a description of a severe famine cast upon the land of Canaan during the reign of David. The harshness of the famine is described thus, 'And there was a famine in the days of David for three years, year after year' (v. 1).⁴ Given that Yhwh was known to be responsible for bringing rain or withholding it, David seeks him out in an attempt to understand the reason for the long famine.⁵ God answers David that Saul is to be blamed, for 'he put the Gibeonites to death' (v. 1).⁶ The narrator

---

3. http://www.ynet.co.il/articles/0,7340,L-4750050,00.html

4. Scripture quotations throughout, unless otherwise indicated, are my own. I have consulted the RSV, JPS, and NIB. This opening verse connects the episode of 2 Sam. 21.1-14 to 'the days of David', yet its original place is accepted by scholars to be elsewhere in the books of Samuel. According to Smith, the story originally belonged in the earlier days of David, when the battle between the houses of David and Saul was in full force. The narrative seems to fit better right before 2 Samuel 9, which presupposes the killing of the seven sons of Saul (v. 3). Later on, it was placed in its current position, which describes the last days of Saul (Smith 1929: 374; Ben-Yashar 1991: 56; also see Hertzberg 1960: 381; Chavel 2003: 23–52).

5. For references to God as responsible for the rain, see passages such as 1 Kgs 17.14; Jer. 5.24; Joel 2.23; Zech. 10.1 (and also see Ben-Yashar 1991: 58).

6. The connection between bloodshed and the land is well known from other biblical passages, e.g. Num. 35.33-34: 'Do not pollute the land (ולא תחניפו את הארץ) where you are. Bloodshed pollutes the land, and atonement cannot be made for the land on which blood has been shed, except by the blood of the one who shed it. Do not defile the land (ולא תטמא את הארץ) where you live and where I dwell, for I *Yhwh* dwell among the Israelites.' In Gen. 4.10 the blood of Abel cries out from the land, after he has been murdered by his brother.

mentions Saul's persecution of the Gibeonites, despite an existing alliance between the sides: 'Now the Gibeonites were not a part of Israel but were survivors of the Amorites; the Israelites had sworn to spare them' (v. 2). The oath mentioned possibly hints at the pact made between Israel and the Gibeonites at the time of Joshua (Josh. 9.3-27).[7] David appeals to the Gibeonites, asking how he may make amends with them, and the Gibeonites in return demand that seven of Saul's living descendants be killed (2 Sam. 21.3-6). Without any delay, David hands seven of Saul's remaining descendants over to the hands of the Gibeonites. Armoni and Mephibosheth, both sons of Rizpah, Saul's concubine, are executed and so are the five sons of Michal, daughter of Saul.[8] Michal's sons remain unnamed. Only Mephibosheth, son of Jonathan, is mentioned by name and his life is reported to have been spared (verses 7–9). The Gibeonites kill the seven men handed over to them, leaving the dead bodies in the field without burial (verses 9–10). Then Rizpah, daughter of Aiah, silently steps up, stretches her sackcloth over the bodies, and protects them day and night from being eaten by birds and wild animals. She stands there from the beginning of harvest until water poured on them (v. 10). As a result of Rizpah's determined vigil, David is provoked into bringing the seven bodies – together with the bodies of Saul and Jonathan collected from Jabesh Gilead – to a proper burial (verses 11–14). God then puts an end to the famine (v. 14b).

Walters (2008: 453) describes this story as 'the OT at its worst: unpronounceable personal names and gratuitous violence seemingly authorized by God'. In the following discussion I wish to suggest further explanations for the actions of and dynamics between God and Rizpah with regard to the unburied bodies. The data considered here is intended to support the possibility of a rising tension and a rivalry between God and Aiah, to the point that Yhwh is almost forced to lift the famine. But first let us begin with the Gibeonite slaughter, which leads to Rizpah's actions.

---

7. Though the incident in which Saul broke the pact between Israel and the Gibeonites is not described here or anywhere else in the Hebrew Bible, the mentioned pact possibly refers to the one described in Josh. 9.3-27 (McCarter 1984: 443; cf. Smith 1929: 374). In this incident Joshua was deceived by the Gibeonites into making a covenant with them, one that allowed the Gibeonites to live alongside the Israelites in the land of Canaan. According to the law of Deut. 20.16-17, when settling in Canaan the Israelites were commanded to kill foreign nations living nearby, whereas nations living far enough away were spared and given the option of surrendering. Although living nearby, the Gibeonites tricked Joshua into believing they lived far away, thus should be spared.

8. The MT mentions handing over the five sons of Michal (v. 8), but Lagarde's Septuagint and the Peshitta mention Merab, Saul's older daughter (1 Sam. 14.49), instead of Michal. The mention of Merab is in accordance with 1 Sam. 18.19, which tells of her marriage to Adriel the Meholathite who is also mentioned in our pericope (2 Sam. 21.8). In addition, Michal is said to be childless until the day she died (2 Sam. 6.23) (Driver 1913: 352; Smith 1929: 376; Chavel 2003: 28 n. 13; McCarter 1984: 439). Hence, the reader will decide for him- or herself which one of Saul's daughters was originally mentioned in this text.

3. The Meaning of the Gibeonite Execution

The drought described in 2 Sam. 21.1-14 is explained as the result of a broken treaty between Israel and the Gibeonites, for which Saul is blamed (verses 1–2). Although the Gibeonite request to kill the seven Saulide descendants can be regarded as a straightforward act of revenge, it has been suggested that the event carried cultic-symbolic significance since it took place after an extended drought and on a mountain top before Yhwh (2 Sam. 21.9). Perhaps a long drought called for an outstanding sacrifice (Frolov and Orel 1995: 147). Moreover, based on the hypothesis that Gibeon functioned as a cultic centre of the Mesopotamian sun god Šamaš – a hypothesis whose arguments are displayed in the following passages – the Gibeonite slaughter was also seen as an attempt to soothe the wrath of this deity (Dus 1960: 353–74; Heller 1966: 73-9; also see Frolov and Orel 1995: 147).

According to Dus, the three topographic names which include the noun 'sun' – בית שמש (Josh. 15.10, 19.38), עיר שמש (Josh. 19.41), and עין שמש (Josh. 15.7) – also resonate the name of the God Šamaš and hint at his importance in Ancient Israel (Dus 1960: 353). Meaningful connections between Gibeon and the sun are found in the Rizpah narrative and in other biblical pericopes as well. For instance, in the battle description of Joshua 10 the sun in Gibeon is involved in a cosmogonic miracle, as Joshua commands it to stop moving and remain silently in place (Josh. 10.12-13). Dus (1960: 361–64) finds further support for the special connections between Gibeon and the sun in the addition found in the LXX version for 1 Kgs 8.53, 'Then Solomon spoke concerning the house, when he had finished building it, "A sun the Lord made manifest in heaven; he said that he should dwell in deep darkness. Build my house, a remarkable house for yourself, to dwell in anew"' (NETS).[9] Though the exact wording of these lines of Solomon's prayer, expressed at the end of the process of the temple building, is obscure, the theme they carry is that of the manifest phenomenon of the shining sun in contrast to the invisibility of God who prefers the deep darkness, and for whom Solomon prepared a dark dwelling place (Montgomery 1951: 190–1).[10] The connection to Gibeon is established as Solomon's prayer ends and the narrator states that God revealed himself to Solomon in Gibeon for the second time (1 Kgs 9.1-3; the first revelation to Solomon in Gibeon occurs in 1 Kgs 3.4-5). This statement hints at Gibeon's importance as a sacred place of divine revelations (Brooks 2005: 44; Brenner 2009: 207), and it connects the prayer to Gibeon. As regards the lines mentioning the sun in the Greek version of 1 Kgs 8.53, I quote Montgomery (1951: 190): 'Was it cautious censorship which deleted from the Hebrew the first hemistich, preserved however in the Greek?'

---

9. Compare to Burney's translation of the Greek into Hebrew and English: שמש הכין בשמים ה', אמר לשכן בערפל ('The sun hath Yahwe set in heavens, But hath promised to dwell in thick darkness') (Burney 1903: 111).

10. Montgomery finds this same theme in Ps 18:12. Also see his discussion concerning Psalm 19, where God is described as the artist-creator contrasted to his salient creations (Montgomery 1951: 190–1).

Another connection between the sun and Gibeon was suggested to be manifested in our pericope, in 2 Sam. 21.6, 9, with regard to the method of killing that was proposed and performed by the Gibeonites. The verb used to describe the killing of the Saulides is derived from the root *y-k-ʻ* Hif.; and though its exact meaning is debated, the context supports the possibility that the execution bears some connection with the sun (Anderson 1989: 249). The Gibeonites express their request to kill the Saulide boys in the following manner: 'Let seven of his sons be given to us, so that we may hang them up before *Yhwh* (והוקענום לה׳)' (RSV; 2 Sam. 21.6). The RSV translated *y-k-ʻ* as 'hang', whereas Polzin (1969: 236) understands *y-k-ʻ* as 'dismember'. Walters mentions impalement (Walters 2008: 453). The LXX version for 2 Sam. 21.6, 9 translates והוקענום ἐξηλιάζειν, suggesting an execution in the sun, and implying crucifixion (Poulssen 1982: 186–7; Anderson 1989: 249). Dus also argues for a connection between the method of killing and the sun, basing his argument on another biblical occurrence of the same verb, found in Num. 25.4:

> *Yhwh* said to Moses, "Take all the leaders of these people, kill them (והוקע אותם) and expose them before *Yhwh* against the sun, so that *Yhwh*'s fierce anger may turn away from Israel".
>
> ויאמר ה׳ אל משה קח את כל ראשי העם והוקע אותם לה׳ נגד השמש וישב חרון אף ה׳ מישראל

In this passage God commands Moses to kill the leaders of Israel since they submitted to Baal-Peor. The killing in Num. 25.4 is performed 'before *Yhwh* against the sun'. The mention of the sun suggests impalement or leaving the men to die in the sun (Dus 1960: 369–70; Walters 2008: 453).

Poulssen asserts a sympathetic connection between the method of killing and its purpose. Perhaps through the medium of the sun, he says, Yhwh's burning wrath can satiate itself on the bodies, and the people of Israel will be forgiven. The juxtaposition of Yhwh and the sun in Num. 25.4 represents a reunion, he says, 'a mutual permeation, a mysterious oscillation' (Poulssen 1982: 187). But if in our pericope the slaughter of the Saulides is related to the sun, which relates to Šamaš the Mesopotamian sun god, why is the slaughter done on a mountain before Yhwh? Poulssen thus suggests that the sun god is incorporated in Yhwh's force, and not instigated against Yhwh. In any case, the place of slaughter – on a mountain before Yhwh – has been found to support the possibility that the Gibeonites were performing a cultic act intended to end the drought. Other suggestions are that the slaughter was part of a rainmaking ceremony performed by the Gibeonites (Hertzberg 1960: 385; Poulssen 1982: 188), or a fertility ritual carried out by them in the name of the king and in honor of Yhwh (Cazelles 1955: 168–70).[11] The question remains how to understand Rizpah's actions in regard to this possible

---

11. According to Cazelles, the killing of the Saulides was a Gibeonite fertility rite leading to the reintegration of the Gibeonites into Israel (Cazelles 1955: 168–70; Frolov and Orel 1995: 147).

religious ceremonial slaughter, and whether there are further elements in the narrative supporting this cultic interpretation path.

4. Understanding Rizpah's Response

2 Samuel 21.10 describes in detail Rizpah's vigil over the corpses of the seven slaughtered Saulides. Apart from being recognized as a caring and courageous mother, her actions were also seen by commentators as intended to soothe divine rage, or as Hertzberg (1960: 384) remarks: 'Indeed the passage seems to imply that the loving act of the mother helped to ease the restraint of the heavens.' According to Frolov and Orel, Rizpah acted as a political representative of the house of Saul and her success in bringing water served as proof that the alleged sin of Saul had not been the cause of the drought (Frolov and Orel 1995: 147–50).

Further explorations of Rizpah's name and a close reading of the wording used in 2 Sam. 21.10 may shed new light on Rizpah's response. First, the name of Rizpah's mother, Aiah, has often been explained as 'hawk' or 'falcon' (BDB: 17; Noth 1928: 230; Chavel 2003: 29). This was based on contexts such as Lev. 11.14, Deut. 14.13, and Job 28.7. Nevertheless, the similarity of names carried by this biblical character and the Mesopotamian goddess of light and dawn, known as Aya, should not be overlooked. Indeed, connections to Aya, the Mesopotamian goddess, were found in regard to another biblical character, Aiah son of Zibeon the Horite (Aloni 1950: 241), and it would be reasonable to suggest that these connections may also apply to Rizpah, daughter of Aiah.[12]

According to Powell, the Mesopotamian goddess Aya (also known by her Sumerian name Šerda/Šereda) is the personification of the dawn, early morning light, and she is independent of particular heavenly bodies. Aya occurs as the spouse of Šamaš, the Mesopotamian sun god, and is designated in different places as a *kallatum* (bride). This designation is intended to evoke the special status of Aya within a family of astral deities. That is, as *kallatum* she is posited as the wife of Šamaš, daughter-in-law of the Moon and sister-in-law of Ištar (Powell 1989: 447). In the Iahdunlim foundation inscription, dated to the nineteenth century BCE, which includes an account of the building of the temple for the god Šamaš by Iahdunlim king of Mari, Aya is invoked in the curse section, toward the end of the text, lines 149–52. In these lines she is asked to put in a bad word before the

---

12. Commentators have been treating Aiah as Rizpah's father rather than mother (BDB: 17; HALOT: 404; Aloni 1950: 241; Garsiel 1991: 51), perhaps due to the existence of Aiah son of Zibeon (Gen. 36.24; 1 Chron. 1.40), a Biblical male character carrying the same personal name. Yet, because of the feminine grammatical ending and the symbolic allusion to the Mesopotamian goddess Aya, as suggested here, I prefer to see Aiah in this context as referring to a woman, Rizpah's mother.

sun god about anyone who tries to destroy his temple.[13] Significantly, this goddess is turned to when an appeal to Šamaš is called for, and her major role was that of an intercessor with Šamaš (Powell 1989: 450, 454).

Keeping in mind the possibility that the goddess Aya might be invoked in regard to Rizpah the daughter of Aiah, I shall now closely examine the description of her actions described in 2 Sam. 21.10:

> Rizpah daughter of Aiah took sackcloth and spread it out for herself on a rock. From the beginning of the harvest till the rain poured down from the heavens on the bodies, she did not let the birds of the air touch them by day or the wild animals by night.
>
> ותקח רצפה בת איה את השק ותטהו לה אל הצור מתחלת קציר עד נתך מים
> עליהם מן השמים ולא נתנה עוף השמים לנוח עליהם יומם ואת חית השדה
> לילה

Rizpah the daughter of Aiah protects the bodies of the dead boys by spreading her sackcloth over them for what seems to be a long period of time.[14] The mention of the words 'day' יומם and 'night' לילה in proximity with Rizpah, daughter of Aiah, not only expresses her steadfast determination, but also matches and foregrounds the cosmogonic elements related to Aya as the goddess of dawn and the spouse of the sun god.

The mention of 'day' and 'night' together with the phrases 'the birds of the sky' (עוף השמים) and 'animals of the field' (חית השדה) significantly echoes the creation narratives of Genesis 1–2. The first creation narrative describes the making of the beasts and the birds, which follows the creation of the luminaries. In this account the birds are referred to as 'birds of the sky' (Gen. 1.26, 28, 30), but the beasts are called 'beasts of the land' (חית הארץ, Gen. 1.24, 25, 30) rather than 'beasts of the field' (חית השדה), as in the Rizpah narrative. The second creation account includes the exact phrases as in the Rizpah narrative, regarding the birds and the beasts, Gen. 2.19-20:

---

13. The lines in Akkadian: (149) ᵈa-a ka-la-tum (150) be-el-tum ra-bi-tum (151) lu mu-le-mi-na-at a-wa-ti-šu (152) i-na ma-ḫa-ar ᵈUTU a-na da-ri-a-tim. Frayne translates: may the goddess bride Aia, the great lady, put in a bad word about him before the god Šamaš forever (Frayne 1990: 604–8; and see Dossin 1955: 1–28). Aya is also mentioned in the Prologue to the Hammurabi codex of laws (col. I, lines 22–31): Hammurabi states that he is 'the discerning king, obedient to the god Shamash, the mighty one, who establishes the foundations of the city of Sippar, who drapes the sacred building of the goddess Aja with greenery, who made famous the temple of Ebabbar, which is akin to the abode of heaven' (Roth 1997: 77). For more occurrences of Aya in Mesopotamian texts see Powell 1989: 447–55.

14. Interpreters debate how long Rizpah's vigil lasted. According to 2 Sam. 21.10 Rizpah protects the corpses 'from the beginning of the harvest till the rain poured down'. According to v. 9, the execution took place during the first days of the barely harvest, which is April (*Iyyar*). Her vigil lasted until the coming of the November winter rains (Edelman 1992: 776), or perhaps she succeeded in bringing a kind of rare late spring rain in June (Hertzberg 1960, 384; McCarter 1984, 442).

So out of the ground *Yhwh* God formed every beast of the field (כל חית השדה) and every bird of the sky (ואת כל עוף השמים), and brought them to the man to see what he would call them; and whatever the man called every living creature, that was its name. The man gave names to all cattle, and to the birds of the sky (ולעוף השמים), and to every beast of the field (ולכל חית השדה); but for the man there was not found a helper fit for him.

Both 2 Sam. 21.10 and the second account of the creation mention a period of aridity until God moistens the land (Gen. 2.5). The birds of the sky (עוף השמים) and animals of the field (חית השדה) occur together elsewhere, also in contexts of creation and its counterparts, destruction and chaos, e.g. Ezek. 29.5, 31.6, 13, 38.20; Hos. 2.20, 4.3.[15] Hence, the semantic domain of the creation activated in 2 Sam. 21.10 may support the notion that Aiah symbolizes Aya, the goddess of light and dawn, who belongs to the same primordial domain as that of the creation.[16]

The rain coming down in 2 Sam. 21.10 as a result of Rizpah's vigil is described as water pouring down from the sky (עד נתך מים עליהם מן השמים). When rain comes down, it naturally comes from the sky, hence the explicit mention of the sky in this verse is superfluous, and thus underlined. The sky is mentioned once more in the verse, with relation to the birds as discussed above (עוף השמים). Thus, we may argue that the redundant mention of the sky stresses Yhwh's lofty dwelling place in contrast to the land (ארץ), the space where human activity is carried out. In addition, attention is drawn to the contrast between Yhwh, as the sky dweller and the god responsible for the rain; and Aya who, as the goddess of dawn, is perhaps associated with the opposite direction, below rather than above (but see Powell 1989: 449 n. 21). In addition, the meaning of the name Rizpah is known to be a 'glowing coal' (HALOT: 8973), but the homonym rizpha (without the dagesh in the /p/) also brings to mind the meaning 'floor', 'stone pavement' (HALOT 8973). And see Isa. 6.6; Ezek. 40.18; Est. 1.6; 2 Chron. 7.3. Noth (1928: 232) and Chavel (2003: 29 n.15) combine the two akin word forms. The meaning of *Rizpah* as 'rock' or 'floor' supports the contrast already formed between her and God, as he is seated above,

---

15. Ezek. 32.4 includes a variation on this formula; cf. Poulssen 1982: 191.

16. Allusion to the flood narrative can also be found in 2 Sam. 21.10: (a) the falling of the rain for a long period may be a reminder of the flood itself; (b) the phrasing ולא נתנה עוף השמים לנוח עליהם (2 Sam. 21.10) is similar to Gen. 8.9: 'But the dove could find no place to set its feet because there was water over all the surface of the earth' (ותשב אליו אל התבה כי מים על פני כל הארץ ולא מצאה היונה מנוח לכף רגלה); (c) the Flood narrative in Genesis ends with God's promise that he will not bring another flood on the earth ever again. The harvest is mentioned in this statement, as well as day and night in juxtaposition, just as in the description of Rizpah's vigil: 'As long as the earth endures, seedtime and harvest (זרע וקציר), cold and heat, summer and winter, day and night (ויום ולילה) will never cease' (Gen. 8.22). All in all, 2 Sam. 21.10 bears allusions to descriptions of destruction and creation in primeval times.

in the sky, while she is associated not only with the goddess of dawn, but also with the stones in the opposite direction, below.[17] Yet, the mention of the rock in this verse (Rizpah stretches the sackcloth over to the rock, צור) relates to Rizpah's name and highlights its reference to 'rock', and at the same time puts her on the same level as Yhwh, since *ṣur* (צור) is a common designation of Yhwh (e.g. Deut. 32.4; 2 Sam. 22.3, 32; Ps. 95.1).

The verb incorporated to express the stretching of the cloth (נטה) is taken from the sphere of creation, especially of God as creator of the sky. In these contexts God is described as stretching (נטה) the sky as a tent:

Isa. 40.22, It is he who sits above the circle of the earth, and its inhabitants are like grasshoppers; who stretches out the heavens like a curtain (הנוטה כדק שמים), and spreads them like a tent to dwell in (וימתחם כאהל לשבת);

Isa. 51.13, '*Yhwh* your maker who stretched out the heavens (נוטה שמים) and laid the foundations of the earth'.

Ps. 104.2, 'He wraps himself in light as with a garment; he stretches out the heavens like a tent' (עטה אור כשלמה נוטה שמים כיריעה).

The use of sky-creation terminology in 2 Sam. 21.10 implies that Rizpah imitates God's actions, and perhaps symbolically creates an alternative sky over the bodies. It is hard to say whether Rizpah wishes to alarm God, that is, to send him the message that he is not the only existing deity, and that other gods can create the sky as well; or, perhaps, is trying to encourage him to remember his role as creator of the sky and bringer of rain. Maybe her actions carry both messages. In any case, God replies by pouring rain.

The rain does not fall gently but forcibly, as indicated by the use of the verb נתך 'until rain fell upon them from the sky', עד נתך מים עליהם מן השמים (v. 10). The narrator prefers the verb נתך instead of the more expected נתן ('give [rain]') or הוריד ('bring down [rain]'). Ben-Yashar notes that the verb נתך carries the meaning of pouring down forcibly, and occurs in contexts of calamity and destruction, such as in:

Jer. 44.6, 'Therefore, my fierce anger was poured out' (ותתך חמתי, also see 2 Chron. 34.25);

Nah. 1.8, '…Who can endure his fierce anger? His wrath is poured out like fire (חמתו נתכה כאש); the rocks are shattered before him (והצרים נתצו ממנו)';

---

17. Fokkelman acknowledges sets of contrasting pairs deployed throughout the plot of 2 Sam. 21.1-14: rock versus water, heaven versus the field. The rock, he suggests, stands for hardness, the water for softness, life, harvest and growth (Fokkelman 1990: 287). To these sets of contrasting pairs we may add the above offered contrast between Rizpah the daughter of Aiah (down) and Yhwh (up).

and also Dan. 9.11; Jer. 7.20 and 42.18 (Ben-Yashar 1991: 61).[18] Apparently the rain pouring over Rizpah and the bodies is not a rain of blessing, but rather expresses God's anger, thus providing further support for an existing tension between God and Rizpah.

Yhwh neither prevents the execution of the Saulides (cf. Gen. 22.12, Jon. 3.10), nor softens it in any way (cf. 1 Kgs 21.29). As God's possible counterpart, Rizpah is also stubbornly determined as she silently protects the bodies against God's initial demand to punish Saul and his house. Though Rizpah is not given the opportunity to express her feelings and motivations, the ethical dative (*dativus ethicus*) לה following the verb ותטהו in 2 Sam. 21.10, subtly describes the solitude and perhaps loneliness in which Rizpah carries out her actions. The ethical dative in this context can be translated 'for herself', thus marking her isolation. Muraoka explains that the ethical dative expressed in the preposition /l/, followed by a matching pronominal suffix, seems to have the effect of creating a self-contained cosmos around the subject, detached from the surrounding world. According to Muraoka this dative serves to convey the impression that the subject establishes his or her own identity by dissociating himself or herself from their familiar surroundings. Notions of isolation, loneliness, separation, seclusion, or withdrawal often accompany the ethical dative (Muraoka 1978: 497); and can suitably express Rizpah's situation as she alone and unaided confronts God, changes his mind, and wins the support of the king.

5. A Need to Reinforce Divine Powers in the Following Passages

Rizpah daughter of Aiah goes against God's will to punish Saul and his descendants. Rizpah, echoing Aya the Mesopotamian goddess and spouse of Šamaš, spreads a sackcloth over the dead. The use of sky-creation terminology to describe Rizpah's actions signifies the possibility of creating an alternative sky by an alternative deity. These actions clearly irritate Yhwh, who brings down forceful rain. In her actions, Rizpah challenges God and silently fights back. It is not surprising that the songs following the Rizpah narrative reiterate the notions that God is the creator of the sky and bringer of rain. These notions are mentioned in two passages. In 2 Sam. 22.8-14,

... [10] He bowed the heavens (ויט שמים), and came down; thick darkness (וערפל) was under his feet.[11] He rode on a cherub, and flew; he was seen upon the wings of the wind.[12] He made darkness around him his canopy (וישת חשך סביבתיו סכות),

---

18. Ben-Yashar (1991: 60) has a different explanation for Rizpah's vigil, arguing that it was not that the Gibeonites refused to bury the dead, but rather that Rizpah withheld their burial by protecting them from wild animals and thus purposely postponing their natural decay. According to Ben-Yashar she did this because she wanted the blood of the innocent boys to cry out before Yhwh and call for revenge (Job 16.18, Ezek. 24.8-7).

thick clouds, a gathering of water (חשרת מים עבי שחקים).¹³ Out of the brightness before him (מנגה נגדו) coals of fire flamed forth.¹⁴ Yhwh thundered from heaven (מן שמים), and the Most High uttered his voice.

In the second passage, 2 Sam. 23.1-7, God is referred to as 'The ṣur ("rock") of Israel' (v. 3), thus strengthening the cohesion between the two pericopes and forming a direct connection to the rock mentioned in the Rizpah narrative (2 Sam. 21.10). Light, sun, dawn and rain are mentioned together as well in this passage (v. 4), just as in the Rizpah narrative:

> ¹ Now these are the last words of David: The oracle of David, the son of Jesse... ³ The God of Israel has spoken, the rock of Israel (צור ישראל) has said to me: ..., ⁴ he is like the light of morning at sunrise (וכאור בקר יזרח שמש), on a cloudless morning (בקר לא עבות), like the brightness after rain that brings the grass from the earth (מנגה ממטר דשא מארץ).

These two prayers, which follow the Rizpah narrative, seem to aim at the reinforcement of Yhwh's ultimate powers over the sun, light and rain, forces that are both challenged and invoked by the presence and acts of Rizpah daughter of Aiah.

6. Conclusions

The issue of burial indeed has been and is a battle field involving politics and religion. Using this understanding in revisiting Rizpah's story provides the beginning for a new reading.

The Gibeonite execution of the seven descendants of the Saulide house has been considered by commentators not only as revenge against Saul's violent acts toward the Gibeonites, but also as a ritual execution intended to end the three-year famine brought upon Canaan by Yhwh. Seeing the killing as a ritual has drawn attention to Gibeon as a sacred place, uniquely connected with the sun and its personification as Šamaš the Mesopotamian sun god. The discussion offered here has argued that pagan associations are also found to be evoked by Rizpah daughter of Aiah, whose name resembles that of Aya, the Mesopotamian goddess of dawn and light, spouse of Šamaš. An association between the biblical Rizpah daughter of Aiah and the Mesopotamian Aya sheds new light on the understanding of Rizpah's character, who is acting as an equal to Yhwh rather than his inferior. By the act of stretching a sackcloth over the bodies, Rizpah establishes an alternative sky over them. She comes not only as a mother protecting the bodies of her dead children, but as a representative of another deity, challenging Yhwh's judgement. To Rizpah's resilient vigil, God responds with a forceful rain, by which the drought is (temporarily?) stopped. David then collects the bones of the seven victims; and along with the bones of Saul and Jonathan taken from Jabesh Gilead, has them buried in their ancestral grave located in Benjamin at Zela. Only then does Yhwh lift the famine (2 Sam. 21.14).

Brenner (2009: 208) remarks that the story seems to imply criticism of David, who needs a woman identified with Saul's house to remind him of his duty, which is to give honourable burial to the dead of the preceding royal house. To this conclusion I wish to add that not only David needs a reminder but, perhaps, Yhwh needs one too. With her wise gestures and her implied Mesopotamian connections, Rizpah pushes God, not only David, into changing his mind.

Bibliography

Aloni, N. (1950), 'Aiah', *Encyclopedia Biblica* (Hebrew). Bialik Institute, Jerusalem. vol. 1: 241.
Anderson, A. A. (1989), *2 Samuel*. WBC 11; Dallas, TX: Word Books.
Ben-Yashar, Menahem (1991), 'A Study of the Pericope of Rizpah Daughter of Aiah' (Hebrew), *Bet Mikra* 36: 56-64.
Brenner, Athalya (2009), 'Rizpah [Re]membered: 2 Samuel 21:1-14 and Beyond', 207-27 in Athalya Brenner and Frank H. Polak (eds), *Performing Memory in Biblical Narrative and Beyond*. Sheffield: Sheffield Phoenix Press.
Brooks, Simcha Shalom (2005), 'From Gibeon to Gibeah: High Place of the Kingdom', 40-59 in John Day (ed.), *Temple and Worship in Biblical Israel*. London: T & T Clark.
Burney, C. F. (1903), *Notes on the Hebrew Text of the Books of Kings*. Oxford: Clarendon Press.
Cazelles, H. (1955), 'David's Monarchy and the Gibeonite Claim', *Palestine Exploration Quarterly* 87: 165-75.
Chavel, Simeon (2003), 'Compositry and Creativity in 2 Samuel 21:1-14', *JBL* 122: 23-52.
Dossin, George (1955), 'L'inscription de fondation de Iahdun-Lim, roi de Mari', *Syria* 32: 1-28.
Driver, S. R. (1913), *Notes on the Hebrew Text and the Topography of the Books of Samuel*. Oxford: Clarendon Press.
Dus, J. (1960), 'Gibeon – eine Kultstaette des ŠMŠ und die Stadt des Benjaminitischen Schicksals', *VT* 10: 353-74.
Edelman, Diana V. (1992), 'Rizpah', *ABD*: 5: 776.
Exum, J. Cheryl (1997), 'Rizpah', *Word & World*, 17.3: 260-8.
Fokkelman, Jan (1990), *Narrative Art and Poetry in the Books of Samuel*, vol. 3, *Throne and City*. Assen/Maastricht: Van Gorcum.
Frayne, Douglas (1990), *The Royal Inscriptions of Mesopotamia* (=RIM), vol. 4, *Old Babylonian Period (2003-1595 B.C.)*. Toronto: University of Toronto Press.
Frolov, Serge and Vladimir Orel (1995), 'Rizpah on the Rock: Notes on 2 Sam 21:1-14', *Bibbia e Oriente* 37: 145-54.
Garsiel, Moshe (1991), *Biblical Names: A Literary Study of Midrashic Derivations and Puns*. Ramat Gan: Bar Ilan University Press.
Heller, J. (1966), 'Die schweigende Sonne', *Communio Viatorum* 9: 73-9.
Hertzberg, Hans Wilhelm (1960), *1 & 2 Samuel: A Commentary*. OTL; London: SCM Press.
McCarter, P. Kyle Jr. (1984), *II Samuel: A New Translation with Introduction, Notes, and Commentary*. Anchor Bible; Garden City, NY: Doubleday.
Montgomery, James, A. (1951), *A Critical and Exegetical Commentary on The Books of Kings*. New York: Charles Scribner's Sons.

Muraoka, T. (1978), 'On the So-Called Dativus Ethicus in Hebrew', *The Journal of Theological Studies* 29: 495–8.
Noth, Martin (1928), *Die israelitischen Personennamen im Rahmen der gemeinsemitischen Namengebung*. Stuttgart: W. Kohlhammer.
Polzin, R. (1969), '*HWQY*ᶜ and Covenantal Institutions in Early Israel', *Harvard Theological Review* 62: 222–40.
Poulssen, N. (1982), 'An Hour with Rispah: Some Reflections on II Sam 21,10', 185–211 in W.C. Delsman et al. (eds), *Von Kanaan bis Kerala: Festschrift für Prof. Mag. Dr. Dr. J.P.M. van der Ploeg O.P. zur Vollendung des siebzigsten Lebensjahres am 4. Juli 1979: überreicht von Kollegen, Freunden und Schülern*. AOAT 211; Neukirchen-Vluyn: Neukirchener Verlag.
Powell, Marvin A. (1989), 'Aia≈Eos', 447–55 in Hermann Behrens, Darlene Loding and Martha T. Roth (eds), *DUMU-E$_2$-DUB-BA-A: Studies in Honor of Åke W. Sjöberg*. Philadelphia: University Museum.
Roth, Martha T. (1997), *Law Collections from Mesopotamia and Asia Minor*. Atlanta, GA: Scholars Press.
Smith, Henry P. (1929), *A Critical and Exegetical Commentary on the Books of Samuel*. New York: Charles Scribner's Sons.
Sternberg, Meir (1987), *The Poetic of Biblical Narrative: Ideological Literature and the Drama of Reading*. Bloomington: Indiana University Press.
Walters, Stanley D. (2008), '"To the Rock" (2 Samuel 21:10)', *CBQ* 70: 453–64.

Internet Sources

http://elyon1.court.gov.il/files/09/670/061/t06/09061670.t06.htm
http://bfree.org.il/%D7%A7%D7%91%D7%95%D7%A8%D7%94-%D7%91%D7%99%D7%A9%D7%A8%D7%90%D7%9C?gclid=EAIaIQobChMIiuy0sObE1gIVzArTCh0dwAWyEAAYASAAEgJ8t_D_BwE
http://www.globes.co.il/news/%D7%A7%D7%91%D7%95%D7%A8%D7%94.tag
http://www.ynet.co.il/articles/0,7340,L-4750050,00.html
NETS, Paul D. McLean and Bernard A. Taylor (trans.), *New English Translation to the Septuagint: 3 Reigns*; http://ccat.sas.upenn.edu/nets/edition/11-3reigns-nets.pdf

RIZPAH [RE]MEMBERED[1]

Athalya Brenner-Idan

Introduction: On Secondary Burial and Rizpah Now

Talia Sutskover, in her study of the Rizpah narrative in this volume (pp. 43–55), explains how Judaism has a fetish about proper burial with all ceremony of human remains. Proper burial is 'dust to dust' (Gen. 3.19): no coffin is allowed unless in special circumstances, and cremation is religiously out of the question. This is the age-old practice which is mandatory for Jewish remains. This is valid in the case of primary (immediately after a person's death) or secondary (incarceration of remains after a time) burial. Throughout the ages, Jews asked to be buried in the Holy Land – as a primary or secondary resting place.

Secondary burial is considered as important a duty as primary burial. This attitude extends to bones, body parts, ashes and so on. The biblical expressions that translate into '[the dead] was gathered to his kin/people/fathers' (as in Gen. 25.8, 49.29 and 33; Judg. 2.10 and many more), and the textual contexts of such expressions, attest to their inclusion of secondary burial.[2]

---

1. The first version of this study was originally published as 'Rizpah [Re]Membered: 2 Samuel 1-14 and Beyond', 207–27 in *Performing Memory in Biblical Narrative and Beyond*, edited by A. Brenner and F. H. Polak, Sheffield: Sheffield Phoenix, 2009. It is now expanded, revised and framed by a new introduction and a new conclusion.

2. A good example for this is Jacob's death (Gen. 49.29-33). He dies in Egypt but asks for permanent (secondary) burial in Canaan, echoing the same expression: 'Then he instructed them [his sons], saying to them, "I am about to be gathered to my kin. Bury me with my fathers in the cave which is in the field of Ephron the Hittite, the cave which is in the field of Machpelah, facing Mamre, in the land of Canaan, the field that Abraham bought from Ephron the Hittite for a burial site – there Abraham and his wife Sarah were buried; there Isaac and his wife Rebekah were buried; and there I buried Leah – the field and the cave in it, bought from the Hittites". When Jacob finished his instructions to his sons, he drew his feet into the bed and, breathing his last, he was gathered to his people' (JPS 1985).

The Israeli state is famous for its efforts to bring fallen soldiers home for burial, which is a bargain point often with its foes. It also brings 'home' the remains of Zionist founders and other national heroes who long ago died in the Diaspora, to house their remains in the holy land.[3] This is a matter of state policy. However, ultra-orthodox practices can carry this duty to extremes.

Nowadays in Israel, when human bones are discovered in an excavation – in archaeological digs, road building, or laying foundations for new housing – the ultra-orthodox go into violent protests, including clashes with the police, to the point of hindering the work until it is determined whether the bones discovered are Jewish or not, because if they are Jewish – and this can be approximately determined by investigations of Jewish sources about such locations, historical circumstances and conjectures too – they should be reburied with all the required religious ceremonies before the work proceeds. Ironically, archaeological excavations designed to acquire knowledge about Jews and Judaism have been stopped for a prolonged period because of this reason, not to mention other building activities. This care for administering secondary burial, even after thousands of years, is as hot a protest topic for the ultra-orthodox (non-Zionist) communities in Israel[4] as the Shabbat and refusal to serve in the IDF (Israel's army).

In January 2020 the seventy-fifth anniversary of the liberation of the Auschwitz-Birkenau extermination camps was marked in Israel. Fifty-something foreign dignitaries and heads of state came to participate in the occasion, under the banner 'Remembering the Shoah, Fighting Antisemitism'. Probably not incidentally, local newspapers were full of stories that in Auschwitz-Birkenau, because of the heavy rains in 2019, large surface areas of land have been exposed at the camp locations. Vast quantities of human remains and ashes, previously scattered round the crematoriums or superficially buried, were exposed. Those remains are for the most part Jewish. An international committee is now beginning to deal with the problem, taking into account Jewish *halakhah* as well, and they are already saying that it is a complicated issue. An Israeli religious official, on 23 January 2020,

> implored participants in last week's World Holocaust Forum to assist in retrieving the bone fragments, writing: 'This is a complex engineering and logistical project that requires the guidance and advice of engineers and hydrologists. We call upon the heads of states participating in the World Holocaust Forum that before occupying yourself with memorializing the memory of the victims, it is more important to occupy yourself with their

---

3. One example. Theodor Herzl, the visionary of Zionism, died in Vienna and was interred there in 1904. His remains were brought to Israel in 1949 and interred in the National Civil Cemetery on the mountain called after him, Har Herzl. A proper [state] burial ceremony was conducted in 1950. His children's remains were brought over much later, in 2006.

4. Ultra-orthodox communities in Israel largely define themselves as non-Zionist and even anti-Zionist and have done so since the inception of the state. To be sure, there are many religious groups, less radical, that are declared Zionists.

dignity. We appeal to you with a humanitarian request – to help carry the burden of this complex project so that after 75 years, the bones of the Jewish victims of the Holocaust who were murdered while sanctifying G-d's name will be brought to Jewish burial and everlasting rest.[5]

What has this to do with the biblical Rizpah? A lot, I think. It may be argued that what Rizpah wants is a primary burial for her dear ones, since they were refused that and were hanged to dry instead. However, by the time they are buried the corpses are, to all intents and purposes, at a secondary stage: they are bones; and yet, Rizpah persists. And in that, for current readerly sensibility, she refracts current emotions and current preoccupations.

Hadar Goldin and Oron Shaul were captured as soldiers by Hamas at the Gaza Strip in August 2014. It is believed that both are dead, and that Hamas (a Palestinian group that controls the Gaza Strip) is holding their remains.

> Talks for their [Goldin and Shaul] remains, and living Israelis being held by the terror group, have failed to reach any breakthroughs in over five years, despite high levels of public sympathy for their cause.[6]

And yet the two mothers, Leah Goldin and Zehava Shaul, persist in their efforts, nationally and internationally, to get help for bringing their sons 'home': that is, for proper Jewish burial, undoubtedly of a secondary nature.

When this study was originally published, the focus was on general, English-speaking cultural-contextual afterlives of the biblical Rizpah and 'her' story. It is reproduced here, with changes and additions, as placed also against the context of current Israeli practices and beliefs. Reading it after Sutskover's contribution to this volume, whose contemporaneous contextual position is the same, demonstrates how context may stimulate dissimilar research results about biblical texts, even when started backwards from a similar research and contextual position.

Prior to Rizpah: Several Textual and Other Issues

A three-year famine is somehow attributed, by Yhwh himself, to Saul's killing of the Gibeonites. A remedy is sought by blood revenge: seven live members of the nearly extinct Saulide house, two sons by Rizpah and five by Michal, are killed and their bodies publicly displayed. Rizpah keeps vigil over the bodies. After a while King David is told. He collects the 'bones' of the dead, and Saul's and Jonathan's

---

5. https://www.theyeshivaworld.com/news/featured/1826213/horrifying-thousands-of-human-bone-fragments-visible-in-auschwitz-photos.html, with photographs there. [Accessed January 2020]

6. https://www.timesofisrael.com/mother-of-slain-soldier-held-in-gaza-charges-pm-doing-more-for-pardoned-convict/ [Accessed January 2020]

bodies, and has them buried. Yhwh then lifts the famine, presumably by ending the drought that caused it. A strange and horrifying story, a 'text of terror' to borrow from Phyllis Trible's coinage.

Even before getting to Rizpah and her actions[7] (properly speaking only v. 10; consequences in verses 11-14), the text is perplexing and difficult to understand. let us repeat briefly the main questions of readers, including scholars. To begin with, there is a textual/historical problem in the wider sense. There is no other mention in the biblical text concerning a conflict between Saul and the Gibeonites, even though the toponym 'Gibeon' is well-linked to David and his heir Solomon.[8] Historically, as possibly evidenced by the chapter's textual placing, it is difficult to contextualize within David's chronological story, although the claim is for its occurring at the beginning of his reign. In view of David's and later Solomon's special links to Gibeon, at least as reflected in the biblical text, it is easy to jump to the conclusion that this is an etiological-tendentious story, establishing those links with a sacred place (where Solomon has an initiation dream, in 1 Kings 3 as well as in a second revelation, 1 Kings 9), with yet another attempt to 'explain' divine regret about Saul and his House's demise.

Another set of issues concerns the Gibeonites' demand and action, and David's agreement to accede to them. Neither the oracular procedure nor God's assent here is easy to follow. Worth noting is that, when all is seemingly done and the Saulides are executed, the famine is still not lifted. Here comes the final set of issues, that concerning Rizpah, her action and its consequences. For, if David as well as his readers wish for closure, this comes not after acceding to the Gibeonites' demand, but only after Saul, Jonathan and the impaled sons of Saul's house are brought to burial in their ancestral area (verses 13-14).[9] It would therefore seem that the story, cryptic and problematically without a precise event-flow context, undermines its own main message: on the one hand, it seems to be an anti-Saulide, pro-David polemics; on the other hand, it seems to imply criticism of David, who needs a woman identified with Saul's house to remind him of his duty – to give honorable burial to the dead of the preceding royal house. In that framework, then, Rizpah is but a tool for educating David.[10]

---

7. The text of 2 Sam. 21.1-14 I used, Hebrew and English, is from the Unbound Bible site (homepage: http://unbound.biola.edu/, then search for your passage or idiom).

8. The toponym Gibeon appears in the HB thirty-eight times; the generic singular 'Gibeonite' once in Neh. 3.7, and the generic plural 'Gibeonites' six times, only in our chapter. The main clusters of occurrences are about Joshua and his negotiations, then protection of Gibeon (Josh. 9–10), the struggle between Abner and David's supporters (2 Sam. 2–3), and information linked with David and Solomon in 1 Kings, 1 Chronicles (several) and 2 Chronicles 1 (twice).

9. For a rewriting of this passage while deleting Rizpah completely, see Flavius Josephus, *Antiquities*, 7.12.1 and p. 76 below. Other ancient sources too grapple with the questions set briefly above, but these texts are not the subject of this study.

10. That Mephibosheth son of Saul has the same name as Jonathan's son, who appears later in David's court and is allegedly spared because of David's oath to Jonathan (21.7; cf. 2 Sam. 9, 16.4, 19.25-31), presents another difficulty of detail.

Rizpah: Preliminary Considerations

Indeed, apart from the single verse disclosing her action, and the narration of consequences, Rizpah is a 'silent witness' albeit not a passive one. All in all she is named in the HB four times: once as Saul's secondary wife, never heard of before, whom Abner 'comes to', to the chagrin of Ish-Bosheth son of Saul (2 Sam. 3.7), and as a trigger for Abner's planned secession from Saul's house; and three times in the present chapter (verses 8, 10, 11). All we know about her is her male-relational status – to Saul after he has died, a passive relationship [not marriage, not in so many words!] with Abner, motherhood to two sons, and her conduct toward the family corpses. No more. On that slim basis, we can read summaries such as the following:

> **RIZPAH** (PERSON) [Heb. רצפה]. The daughter of Aiah and concubine of Saul ben Kish, first king of Israel. She bore Saul two sons, Armoni and Mephibaal (Mephibosheth). Nothing is known of her life during Saul's reign. During Eshbaal's brief reign, she became the focus of Abner's unsuccessful attempt to depose his inexperienced nephew and rule Israel in his stead (2 Sam. 3.7). By having sexual relations with the former king's concubine, Abner tried to lay claim to the throne by virtue of his possession of the royal harem. During the early years of David's joint reign over Israel and Judah, Rizpah's two sons were ritually executed along with the five sons of Merab, Saul's eldest daughter, in an effort to end a three-year famine that had been plaguing the land (2 Sam. 21.1-14) ... Rizpah is reported to have kept a vigil over the seven dead bodies, keeping away birds and animals of prey until rain fell and ended the drought – from mid-April until October or November. David then is said to have had the bones of the seven victims gathered up, and to have had them buried along with the exhumed bones of Saul and Jonathan, who had been buried in Jabesh-gilead, in the family ancestral tomb located in Benjamin at Zela. (Edelman 1997[11])

This summary is far from unusual, and undoubtedly constrained by considerations of space and importance. I do not cite it here in order to insult Diana Edelman, whose work I usually appreciate highly. I do so in order to point out that so-called 'minor' female figures in the HB are often exploited not only by/in the text itself – to make a point extraneous to 'themselves' – but also by readers/interpreters, who largely repeat the text's main points, adding on various considerations and assumptions such as (in this case) Abner's attempt to realize a personal ambition through her (or: perhaps he simply loved her for her own sake? Can this option be entertained as well?), or attributing Rizpah's motivation for her act to pious observance of burial customs, or motherly feelings, by way of filling the biblical gaps.

My own intention is to remember female figures such as Rizpah and also re-member them. By re-membering I mean the process of tracing the refragmentation

---

11. See also Edelman 2000: 145–6.

and regrouping of narratives in which they feature, and their being enlisted for fresh contextual uses by contextual readers. My first attempt into this territory was to try and reconstruct a first-person, partly fictive, informed midrashic portraits that take into account the *Nachleben* of such figures. Such *Nachleben* perennially updates in favor of the reteller, or the reteller's fancy or needs: and as such, is worth tracing more for understanding the producer of the biblical figure's *Nachleben* than of the biblical figure's biblical 'life', although the latter may be illustrated afresh as well.

Thus in *I Am: Biblical Women Tell their Own Story* in the chapter on Rizpah (Brenner 2005: 120–32, 225–6), I used several sources for looking at Rizpah rather than at the relational male figures the story illustrates: from her assumed female genealogy [Rizpah daughter of Aiah] and a wordplay on her name to the midrash and Flavius Josephus – the latter deletes her completely from the 'events' of 2 Samuel 21, since her action seems to reflect badly on David – to two twentieth-century Hebrew plays in which she features. Other sources such as Internet sites were mentioned only briefly in that book. Here I am leaving behind the first-person mode but would like to commence from where I left off in that book. My central question remains that of retelling and memory/memorizing, as applied to this minor figure. In this I looked for Rizpah traditions not only in Hebrew sources but also outside those sources.

Rizpah Traced on the Internet: Classification of Materials

I have limited myself to internet materials, as a conscious exercise in cultural analysis. Of course, I cannot and do not wish to ignore the fact that internet sources themselves are or may be processed from other textual, non-verbal and media objects. However, because of the internet's dissemination and accessibility, it is highly suitable for research into the process of contextualizing, hence creating life/culture through and alongside the recreation of the Bible.

Looking for internet traces, for traces they are, of Rizpah in current Western cultures, yielded first four types of materials and then an additional fifth. Those are:

1. Translations and retellings of 2 Samuel 21, moving Rizpah more to the story's foreground.
2. Rizpah as a personal name in the early to post-modern periods.
3. Nineteenth-century poetry, with Rizpah at its centre.[12]
4. Contemporary women's charismatic churches and other organizations; and finally,
5. Rizpah connections to some Freemasons' temples, or 'shrines'.

---

12. I have not been able to find twentieth-century poems relating to Rizpah on the internet, hence the choice of nineteenth-century poems.

1. Rizpah Translations, Paraphrases and Retellings

Translations, paraphrases, retellings and straightforward sermons extolling Rizpah in general terms for her deeds, also attributing to her maternal and theological motives that are 'silent' in or 'missing' from the HB text, are many. Such texts would customarily allow the exemplum Rizpah much more space and significance than she receives in the biblical text, considerably and dramatically expanding on the single biblical verse (v. 10) describing her actions. These texts, interesting as they may be, with their central message, common to feminist and non-feminist contemporary readers alike, share a message: through her non-verbal persistence a pious woman [yes!] may teach a man (King David) a lesson by her behaviour, even when she is unimportant and he is an elevated king and God's chosen. Such interpretive texts are not surprising in that they differ from the source text in amplification and processing. They do spell out an extra moral lesson for men and women, but not in a revolutionary or novel fashion.

I do not wish to discuss such renderings at length beyond pointing out the relatively common romancing of two features, namely the praise Rizpah receives for her textual silence; and the value of proper burial. Two examples will suffice here.

In September 2003, forty female representatives participated in an Asian Ecumenical Consultation, 'Overcoming Violence against Women and Children', held in Manila. The group was sponsored by the Christian Conference of Asia and hosted by the National Council of Churches in the Philippines.

> Early Biblical and theological insights of women's wisdom and liberation were provided by Dr Muriel Orevillo-Montenegro from Silliman University in the Philippines. Using texts such as those in 2 Samuel – the story of strength through silence...some possibilities of working differently were explored.[13]

In a blog dated 15 October 2004, Marilynn Griffith – female and African-American, from Florida, describing herself as 'disciple/writer' and 'strange but wonderful' – cites the biblical text of 2 Samuel 21 together with a paraphrase of a sermon, ultimately applied to her Christian situation. The burial issue is taken up as central and made into a *proper* burial issue, that is, ultimate homing into the bosom of Christ.[14]

I use the word 'romancing' deliberately, since it seems to me that the consumers' context dictates their understanding, then gap filling, of the biblical text. Working backwards from the silence commonly and culturally enforced on South Asian women, it is relatively easy to attribute silence to the literary Rizpah as a matter of technique or situation whereas, in the HB, the reason for her literary silence may

---

13. *In Unity* Spring/Summer 2004, read online, http://www.ncca.org.au/__data/page/2217/04_SS_06.pdf. [Accessed 2019]

14. http://rhythmsofgrace.blogspot.com/2004/10/rain-from-heaven.html. [Accessed 2019]

be different. Frank Polak, working from the perspective of discourse analysis, thinks that the whole passage hangs on Rizpah's silence (Polak 2009, esp. 48–50).[15] But my tendency is to fill the gap differently: in my opinion the passage hangs on her persistence in action. Now, who is right here? Moreover, why does Rizpah do as she does? It is customary to attribute her action to her wish to bring the bodies, her sons' and other kin's bodies, to burial since burial is a sacred value in the HB. This is indeed possible by citing the many examples of narrated burials, together with ceremonies and places linked to them, in the HB. However, those sources talk more about *proper* burial than about burial *per se*. And there is one more possibility: that Rizpah objects to the [foreign?] custom of displaying a dead adversary's body as trophy, to the shame caused by the performative element certainly sought by the Gibeonites, more than to anything else. Or perhaps was her concern not necessarily for the *proper burial*, that is, ceremonial and in one's own family grave, as David gratuitously does at the end, but simply for the end of the shameful, public spectacle and the return of family honour in *any* form of burial?

It is interesting, in these and in more examples, that the Rizpah figure is adopted as emblematic by non-Western women, so that a marginal woman figure is magnified into an exemplum for and by marginalized women. This, however, is not always the case,[16] and certainly does not hold for the next category.

2. *The Name Rizpah and its Contexts in Family Trees/Genealogical Lists*

www.genealogy.com is a mine of information. For instance, there is a discussion thread about Rizpah Laforge (1793–1882, Somerset County, NJ);[17] and a digital book at the University of Pennsylvania has a Rizpah in its eighteenth- to nineteenth-century genealogies linked to 'The early Village'.[18] Truman Ames, a lawyer born in 1851 and residing in Lake County, Illinois, was originally from a Vermont/Pennsylvania family. There were eight siblings: 'Walter W., Lydia W., Edmund, *Rizpah*, Truman, Watie M., Lillie P. and Luella'.[19] In official registries as well as genealogy forums, there are Rizpahs in Vermont and other New England areas, and across the Canadian border. Even in 2008, a woman from North Carolina named *Rizpah* Stone, whose father's mother was called Ruby Hockaday, was

---

15. Also in a discussion of this contribution's first draft, in an Amsterdam-Tel Aviv workshop at Tel Aviv University, February 2005.

16. A quick search using Google blogsearch beta (http://search.blogger.com/?q=rizpah&hl=en&ie=UTF-8&x=20&y=6&filter=0&ui=b lg&sa-&start=0) will show 128 early twentieth century postings, mainly by women, using Rizpah as an emblem. As far as I can ascertain, there are no clear race delimiters here, although most postings are gendered female. See also http://www.womensministries.cc/prayer_january06.htm. [Accessed 2019]

17. http://genforum.genealogy.com/laforge/messages/198.html etc. [Accessed 2019]

18. http://www.libraries.psu.edu/do/digitalbookshelf/27995405/27995405_part_02.pdf. [Accessed 2019]

19. http://www.usgennet.org/usa/sd/state/tluc/page101.html. [Accessed 2019]

looking for an ancestor. She was then a young woman: the father she never met was born in the 1940s.[20]

The locations as well as family histories point mainly to white, Protestant environments where the name Rizpah was, if not exactly popular, then at least used fairly widely. (That the name is now less common seems to be clear.) Why was it, for a while, a noticeable given biblical name? This is difficult to determine. Perhaps an identification of Rizpah with Mary Magdalene (and other women called Mary),[21] made by some, because part of their wish to prepare Jesus' body for a proper (secondary!) burial on the third day after his death. And this appears also in at least one strand of Rizpah-inspired poetry/literature.

3. Nineteenth-Century Rizpah Poetry

My search for poetry was not infinite: to be sure, given more time and effort, more examples of Rizpah poems in the English language could have been found,[22] and probably prose too.[23] However, the laws of Internet search and distribution would perhaps indicate that the examples below (and reproduced in *Appendix 1*) are the most famous for, or most often read by, contemporary readers.

The most popular and often cited poems are from the second half of the nineteenth century. They are written by male poets: Buchanan, Tennyson, Kendall and Bryant. This gender factor is interesting; first, in view of the greater attachment of twentieth-century female readers to the Rizpah figure, as already shown and as will be shown also below, under 'Charismatic Churches'; and second because, unlike the female-gendered Rizpah usages cited, only Buchanan focuses on Rizpah's alleged theological dimensions, while the other three poets use her figure as a stepping stone for social, political and religious critique at large.

Robert Williams Buchanan (1841–1901), in *The Earthquake* [1885], ll. 110–23, calls Rizpah 'mother of nations' (l. 110) and explicitly equates her with Jesus' mother Mary and the taking of Jesus' body from the Cross ('Madonna', ll. 115, 123). This link may explain further and implicitly the attachment of Christian female readers to the Rizpah figure. I have not checked the Church Fathers and early modern interpreters for such an interpretation: this would be another project. At any rate, an interpretation such as this, without assuming actual knowledge of the

---

20. http://www.jenforum.com/hockaday/messages/328.html. [Accessed 2019]

21. Mark 16.1; Matt, 28.1; Lk. 24.10; John 20.1

22. One line in Christopher Smart (1722–1771) *Jubilate Agno*: Fragment B, Part 1 ('let Rizpah rejoice with the Eyed Moth who is beautiful in corruption'); Edward Hayes Plumptre (1821–1891), *Rizpah Daughter of Aiah*; Frances E.W. Harper (1824–1911), *Rizpah, the Daughter of Aiah*; Felicia Dorothea Hemans, née Browne (1793–1835), *The Vigil of Rizpah*, in *A Century of Sonnets* (ed. Paula Feldman), 409. Several of those and possibly others are to be found in the Electronic Poetry Project of Emory University, under several headings.

23. For instance, C. E. Israel (1961), in his novel about Rizpah, which I have not been able to read.

poem, may also bolster the adoption of Rizpah as an emblem figure for charismatic women churches (below).

Alfred Lord Tennyson's (1809–92) ballad 'Rizpah', written in 1880, is perhaps the most famous Rizpah poem. But is it about the biblical Rizpah? Not really. The ballad is a soliloquy of a dying woman, obviously delivered just before her death to another [silent but strongly implied as audience] woman. As the ballad unfolds, we understand that the dying woman is poor and disreputable, her listener bourgeois and conventionally pious. The speaker – 'Rizpah' – is explaining to her listener how her son was convicted of robbery and executed, part of the sentence being to leave his body to rot in a metal cage without possibility of burial. She has spent years collecting the son's bones and finally managed to bury them all, which is certainly a secondary burial. In her talk she attacks the conventional piety of her listener, which is implied by the unfolding story, and justifies her own morbid action by mother's love and the higher demands of decency (burial).

Tennyson put '17–' at the beginning of the poem, indicating that the monologue/conversation takes place in the eighteenth century. Indeed, the poem is based on a true story that happened in Shoreham, Sussex, in 1792. A highway robbery on the mail at the Goldstone Bottom, committed by a Shoreham man named Rook as an accomplice to a man called Howell, resulted in the perpetrators' execution by hanging.[24] The recovery of the bones from the gibbet by Rook's mother was used by Tennyson about 100 years later, together with the biblical story, for social critique of class and religion, which he did quite often in his poetry, recycling older myths and events (such as Dante's *Divine Comedy* in *In Memoriam*) for critique of Victorian conventions he perceived as unjust. However, apart from the imperfect similarity in the two figures' preoccupation with their sons' dead bodies, Tennyson's *Rizpah* bears little similarity to the biblical Rizpah.

In his poem 'Rizpah' Henry Kendall (1839–82), an Australian poet, embeds an elaboration of 2 Sam. 21.10 within a passer-by's message to David: he actually uses the few words of v. 11 – 'and David was told what Rizpah daughter of Aiah, Saul's *pilegesh*, had done' – as a narrated frame in which the events that occur in one biblical verse are expanded, with other figures (such as a watchman) added. And he stops there: for Kendall in this poem, David does not act upon being told.

---

24. 'In the 18th century the mail was delivered on horseback. On 30 October 1792, a crook by the name of Edward Howell undertook the robbery of the mail coach at the Goldstone Bottom, with his accomplice a young man named James Rook. James Rook gave away his involvement at the Red Lion, Shoreham, and the two highwaymen were arrested for the robbery from John Stephenson (the boy delivering the mail) of half a sovereign. They were tried and found guilty at the Spring Assizes at Horsham and sentenced to death. The hangings took place on 26 April 1793 before a large crowd at the Goldstone. After the two guilty men were hanged, the bodies were saturated in tar and enclosed in a gibbet, an iron frame with the chains fastened to the bodies' (http://www.glaucus.org.uk/GoldMail.htm).

But David, son of Jesse, spake no word,
But turned himself, and wept against the wall.

The point here is not whether David did bury the sons: this is outside the poem and goes beyond his apparent pain upon hearing the story (an addition to the biblical text and undoubtedly in David's favor); is of no consequence to what happens here. From this point onwards the poem becomes an unambiguous critique of the American civil war, foregrounding Rizpah as a symbol par excellence of the situation of women/ mothers, citing also Rachel and her quest for her sons (Jer. 31.14). Rizpah (singular) becomes American Rizpahs (plural). Once again, perhaps a different slant to the biblical story.

William Cullen Bryant (1794–1878), an American poet and journalist, begins his 'Rizpah' poem by quoting 2 Sam. 21.9-10. He then lets Rizpah tell her story of v. 10, at great length, in a monologue: that is, Bryant gives her a voice, which she lacks in the biblical text. In addition to describing her vigil in great detail, and dwelling upon her maternal sufferings, Rizpah has an ethical critique. Her sons have not sinned: the alleged sin was their father's; and yet, they were sentenced to death, and an ignoble death at that. The issue of collective/cross-generational punishment is raised and defined as unjust.

The poems are of course very different from each other. But the [male] poets' tendency to use the Rizpah figure for social critique (apart from in Buchanan's case) is clear. Another feature worth noting is the voice granted to Rizpah by Tennyson (although his Rizpah is certainly not the biblical Rizpah!) and by Bryant. Apparently, these two poets do not recognize strength in Rizpah's silence but in her action – and in the speech they award her.

4. Contemporary Charismatic Churches and Other Women's Organizations

The *Daughters of Rizpah*[25] is a charismatic African American church run by Pastor Jacqueline E. McCullough, CEO and President, who founded the church in 1986.

> Daughters of Rizpah is an international urban evangelistic ministry with a traditional missionary grassroots focus. Technologically on the cutting edge, Daughters of Rizpah functions as a publishing and distribution company that provides services to the community, both nationally and internationally by promoting family enhancement, educational development and spiritual renewal.[26]

Pastor McCullough, a former nurse, also runs an organization known as *Beth Rapha*: while the web site claims this is Hebrew for 'House of Healing',[27] this seems more like Aramaic to me – at any rate, the house is dedicated to healing through

---

25. http://www.rizpah.org/. [Accessed 2019]
26. http://www.rizpah.org/aboutdaughters.htm. [Accessed 2019]
27. http://www.bethrapha.org/index2.html. [Accessed 2019]

prayer. Both organizations seem like big and healthy businesses, based in Brooklyn, New York but with many urban branches across the US.

There is also another Rizpah association of women dedicated to nursing, and an organization called 'Daughters of Rizpah': 'Women coming together praying for families, churches, leaders, schools and the nations;[28] and a company called Rizpah. com offers religious links, and more.[29] One text will perhaps suffice here to illustrate this latter-day Rizpah attachment and what it means in terms of the biblical story's latter-day articulation.

> This [Rizpah's actions, ABI] is a metaphor for how relentless our intercessory prayers should be. We should determine to cover those in sin and those in need with our prayers so that Satan can't devour them, be it daytime or nighttime. Rizpah was not deterred by hunger, by exhaustion, by the stench of the bodies, by her grief, by the hopelessness of her situation, or by the reactions of those passing by. She was single-minded in her goal to see that the sons and the grandsons of a king were properly buried. Her persistence paid off. When David was told what Rizpah was doing, not only were her own sons buried, but so were the bones of Saul and Jonathan and the bodies of Saul's grandsons as well.
>
> If an earthly king such as David would yield to the demands of a persistent concubine named Rizpah, how much more will a loving heavenly Father hear and answer the persistent prayers of mothers in Zion who long for the salvation of souls and not just physical bodies? We must be persistent in prayer. God wants to answer our prayers for restoration.
>
> Abraham persisted in prayer for Lot, and Lot was saved. Jacob persisted in prayer, and the Lord blessed him. Moses persisted in prayer for the sins of the Israelites, and they were not destroyed ...
>
> God will hear the persistent prayer of the church today![30]

Elements such as (proper) burial, persistence, action, motivation, and somehow also prayer are all combined in an updated figure. Rizpah's intercessory powers are compared to Abraham's and Moses', her praying powers (!) to Jacob's. Ultimately, she becomes not only an emblem of the church but the Church itself.

Last but not least, there is a seemingly unrelated 'Daughters of Rizpah Janitorial Service' in Jacksonville, FL.[31] I have no idea who the Janitorial service owner/s is/are, from the viewpoint of colour. It is clear, though, that the energetic Daughters of Rizpah church has chosen her emblematic matron not only because of her biblical character as imagined and re-imaged but also and mainly for her colour:

28. http://womenofrizpah.cabanova.com/. [Accessed 2019]
29. http://www.rizpah.com/. [Accessed 2019]
30. http://www.womensministries.cc/prayer_january06.htm. [Accessed 2019]
31. http://directory.jacksonvilledirect.info/daughters-rizpah-janitorial-jacksonville-435-clark-road/. [Accessed 2019] An older link, http://www.drjclean.com/index.html, was much more informative but does not work anymore. However, it seems now that the firm has branches and franchises also in other US cities

for in biblical Hebrew Rizpah means 'burning coal' (so also in Isa. 6.6), hence 'black'. Perhaps this understanding can be applied to the name choice of the Florida Service company as well.

5. A Rizpah Shrine

There exists a Freemasonry-related 'Mystical Order of the Shrine'. The story is a little strange, to say the least, and perhaps well-worth quoting verbatim from the website. (The full quote is to be found in *Appendix 2*).

Gleaned from various Shriners' sites as well as from the *Wikipedia* site,[32] it would seem that the Shriners, or *Ancient Arabic Order of the Nobles of the Mystic Shrine* [*AAONMS*, almost an anagram of 'Masons'], are an order attached to the Freemasons. Until 2000, an aspirant member had to complete either the Scottish Rite or York Rite degrees of Masonry to be eligible for Shrine membership, but now any Master Mason can join. Established in New York City in the 1870s, the Shriners are best known for organizing fun events. Members of the Shrine are immediately recognizable by the fezzes they wear and are often seen in parades and as clowns in the Shrine Circus. However, the Shrine is also noted for its charitable works, most notably the Shriners' hospitals for children, which provide medical treatment to children free of charge.

The Shriners' lodges or, as they call them, 'temples' or 'mystical temples', were usually given Arab names, such as Abdallah, Abu Bekr and Rameses, with few exceptions.[33] There are three shrines in Kentucky: one of them, the Rizpah Shrine, is in Madisonville. However, how it came to its name could not be found, since the URLs given do not seem relevant at this time. One of them does not work; and the second loops through commercial information without delivering 'secretive' Shriners' and Freemasons' 'secrets'.[34]

Why Rizpah, then? This remains unclear. What is nevertheless striking is the choice of a biblical name; of a biblical female figure at that, for a male-centred institution; and the connection to healing, be it accidental or otherwise, as also apparent in the discussion of the charismatic women's churches and organizations.

Concluding Remarks

The journey undergone in this study took me through different contexts: from reflections of burial, primary and especially secondary, in modern Jewish /Israeli culture; through a biblical text with a silent although highly active figure at its centre,

---

32. http://en.wikipedia.org/wiki/Shriners. [Accessed 2019]

33. http://www.iremshrine.org/Shrines.htm lists all shrines by name, location and contact details. Other sites give the meanings of the names and their derivation, when known. [Accessed 2019]

34. Variously as http://www.rizpahtempel.org/ or http://rizpahtemple.com. [Accessed 2019]

Rizpah, a 'burning coal' that is not consumed by its own fire; through internet alleyways of Rizpah *Nachleben* in – principally – English-speaking Christian culture, early modern to modern to post-modern.

Apart from translations and scholarly interpretations, available non-Jewish/Israeli sources were classified into groups: translations, interpretations, retellings and take-offs from the biblical texts; Rizpah as a personal name in the early to post-modern period; nineteenth- and twentieth-century poetry, with a 'Rizpah' at its centres; contemporary women's charismatic churches and other organizations; and Rizpah 'shrines'. I was hoping to answer some questions, namely: What are the common ideological parameters, if any, that can be deduced from each cluster/group/classified category? Does the genre or form (genealogies, poetry, religious info/propaganda) reflect or shape the re/membering? Can time/place characteristics be defined as decisive or significant for Rizpah usage? What is she used for?

At the end of this search I find myself unable to answer these questions in a way that will satisfactorily make sense of the disparate materials I discovered, to bundle my findings – interesting as they may be – into a meaningful whole. Perhaps such an endeavor is, ultimately, a reductionist exercise neither possible nor advisable. I can see no direct line of historical or cultural development in what was here presented. What I can see are certain modes of *use* and adaptation to changing conditions of time, gender, class, personal status – in certain locations. I can understand why South Asian women and also White women from the American Bible Belt would interpret Rizpah's silence not only as a virtue but also as a tool for effecting change; I can also see why some male interpreters would see it as such as well, within the framework of upholding traditional female virtues. The same applies to various other attempts to find in the biblical story's gaps additional elements that could update it to specific readers' concerns. A tenuous link produced (and evident in Buchanan's poem) between Rizpah and Mary may support the relative popularity of Rizpah as a first name, but nevertheless does not explain its race provenance (apparently White) in the early modern and modern period, and its status as less fashionable today; and I know nothing about its colour provenance now. The choice of attributing emblematic 'black' significance to Rizpah is understandable from the name's meaning in Hebrew ('burning coal'), but the timing of this choice remains inexplicable. The political use of Rizpah by the poets cited (Tennyson, Kendall, Bryant; not Buchanan, whose use is religious more than political) does not require justification, since the biblical story itself is highly political and can be taken further. What amazes me is that only one poet – Kendall – uses it directly to criticize David and other persons of authority, whereas this is done repeatedly by woman readers; a gender differential is apparent here. Finally, the Rizpah shrine remains enigmatic.

This inconclusive picture, strands that form a loose mosaic, may be the result of non-sufficient information, defective search, lack of patience, Internet (my chosen medium) slant for US sources, especially when the language search is English; but it may also point to the possibility that the *Nachleben* of biblical figures, like other cultural myths, may be unpredictable and at times impossible to tame into tidy categories. Recording the ways in which the memories of biblical figures or images are [re]constructed or manufactured may be more fruitful than stating too easily that this or the other interpretation, or usage, is 'right' or 'wrong'. This is equally true outside scholarship as well as in it.

Rizpah as a name has not been used in Jewish communities; it is not used as such in modern Israel. This does not necessarily reflect a negative attitude to the biblical name bearer. Rather, a homonym *rişpāh* appears in Hebrew vocabulary, already a few times in the HB as *rişphāh*,[35] that is, with a minimal shift of the medial consonant /p/ to /ph/. The word designates 'floor', '[tiled] ground', from the Hebrew root *r-ş*-ph ('lay in order'). Over time the word shifted back to the pronunciation *rişpāh*, with 'floor', 'bottom' and the like the common meaning from talmudic times on and including nowadays.[36] This common usage would therefore seem to preclude naming a newborn female Rizpah, *pace* the biblical figure's valorization in tradition and interpretation.

Finally. In contemporary Israel, where women (and men) invest so much effort in bringing their dead, usually soldiers, to secondary burial 'at home' if the original burial place is unknown, such as in case of war, and where traditional culture requires such burial as a religious and humane duty, the biblical Rizpah figure – resistant to political power as she is, religiously correct as she is – is *not* used as a symbolic masthead in relevant cases. I find this amazing, and strange: biblical figures have been enlisted as cultural heroes in Jewish/Israeli ethos for less spectacular actions. However, this is not the case here. This may be connected with the downgrading of the HB (*TaNaKh*) at least in secularist Israeli society in recent decades: the HB is now less of an inspirational model than in previous decades.[37]

Appendix 1: The Poems

Robert Williams Buchanan (1841–1901)
From *The Earthquake* [1885],[38] ll. 110–23

O Rizpah, Mother of Nations, the days of whose glory are done, Moaning
    alone in the darkness, thou countest – the bones of thy Son!
The Cross is vacant above thee, and He is no longer thereon –
A wind came out of the night, and He fell like a leaf, and was gone.
But wearily through the ages, searching the sands of the years,
Thou didst gather His bones together, and wash them, Madonna, with tears.

---

35. Ezek. 42.3; 2 Chron. 7.3.

36. See the site of the Academy of the Hebrew Language, the Historic Dictionary, https://maagarim.hebrew-academy.org.il/Pages/PMain.aspx?koderekh=31488&page=1

37. As is made amply clear by Lammfromm in her study in this volumes, pp. 119–37. Lammfromm's case study is Elijah the Prophet, but her conclusions are valid beyond this topic.

38. http://mysite.wanadoo-members.co.uk/robertbuchanan/html/quake2.html#rizpah.

They have taken thy crown, O Rizpah, and driven thee forth with the swine, But the bones of thy Son they have left thee; yea, kiss them and clasp – they are thine!
Thou canst not piece them together, or hang them up yonder afresh, The skull hath no eye within it, the feet and the hands are not flesh.
Thou moanest an old incantation, thou troublest the world with thy cries – Ah God, if the bones should hear thee, and join once again, and arise!
In the night of the seven-hill'd City, discrown'd and disrobed and undone, Thou waitest a sign, O Madonna, and countest the bones of thy Son!

Alfred Lord Tennyson (1809–1892), British[39]
Rizpah

17–
I.
Wailing, wailing, wailing, the wind over land and sea–
And Willy's voice in the wind, 'O mother, come out to me'.
Why should he call me to-night, when he knows that I cannot go?
For the downs are as bright as day, and the full moon stares at the snow.
II.
We should be seen, my dear; they would spy us out of the town.
The loud black nights for us, and the storm rushing over the down,
When I cannot see my own hand, but am led by the creak of the chain, And grovel and grope for my son till I find myself drenched with the rain.
III.
Anything fallen again? nay–what was there left to fall?
I have taken them home, I have number'd the bones, I have hidden them all.
What am I saying? and what are *you*? do you come as a spy?
Falls? what falls? who knows? As the tree falls so must it lie.
IV.
Who let her in? how long has she been? you–what have you heard? Why did you sit so quiet? you never have spoken a word.
O–to pray with me–yes–a lady–none of their spies–
But the night has crept into my heart, and begun to darken my eyes.
V.
Ah–you, that have lived so soft, what should *you* know of the night, The blast and the burning shame and the bitter frost and the fright?
I have done it, while you were asleep–you were only made for the day. I have gather'd my baby together–and now you may go your way.

---

39. http://home.att.net/~TennysonPoetry/rizpah.htm as well as many other sites.

VI.
Nay–for it's kind of you, Madam, to sit by an old dying wife.
But say nothing hard of my boy, I have only an hour of life.
I kiss'd my boy in the prison, before he went out to die.
'They dared me to do it', he said, and he never has told me a lie.
I whipt him for robbing an orchard once when he was but a child–
'The farmer dared me to do it', he said; he was always so wild–
And idle–and couldn't be idle–my Willy–he never could rest.
The King should have made him a soldier, he would have been one of his best.
VII.
But he lived with a lot of wild mates, and they never would let him be good;
They swore that he dare not rob the mail, and he swore that he would; And he took no life, but he took one purse, and when all was done
He flung it among his fellows–I'll none of it, said my son.
VIII.
I came into court to the Judge and the lawyers. I told them my tale,
God's own truth–but they kill'd him, they kill'd him for robbing the mail.
They hang'd him in chains for a show–we had always borne a good name–
To be hang'd for a thief–and then put away–isn't that enough shame?
Dust to dust–low down–let us hide! but they set him so high
That all the ships of the world could stare at him, passing by.
God 'ill pardon the hell-black raven and horrible fowls of the air,
But not the black heart of the lawyer who kill'd him and hang'd him there.
IX.
And the jailer forced me away. I had bid him my last goodbye; They had fasten'd the door of his cell. 'O mother!' I heard him cry. I couldn't get back tho' I tried, he had something further to say, And now I never shall know it. The jailer forced me away.
X.
Then since I couldn't but hear that cry of my boy that was dead,
They seized me and shut me up: they fasten'd me down on my bed. 'Mother, O mother!'–he call'd in the dark to me year after year–
They beat me for that, they beat me–you know that I couldn't but hear; And then at the last they found I had grown so stupid and still
They let me abroad again–but the creatures had worked their will.
XI.
Flesh of my flesh was gone, but bone of my bone was left–
I stole them all from the lawyers–and you, will you call it a theft?–
My baby, the bones that had suck'd me, the bones that had laughed and had cried–
Theirs? O no! they are mine–not theirs–they had moved in my side.
XII.

Do you think I was scared by the bones? I kiss'd 'em, I buried 'em all– I can't
    dig deep, I am old–in the night by the churchyard wall.
My Willy 'ill rise up whole when the trumpet of judgment 'ill sound, But I
    charge you never to say that I laid him in holy ground.
XIII.
They would scratch him up–they would hang him again on the cursed tree.
    Sin? O yes–we are sinners, I know–let all that be,
And read me a Bible verse of the Lord's good will toward men–
'Full of compassion and mercy, the Lord'–let me hear it again;
'Full of compassion and mercy–long-suffering'. Yes, O yes!
For the lawyer is born but to murder–the Saviour lives but to bless.
He'll never put on the black cap except for the worst of the worst,
And the first may be last–I have heard it in church–and the last may be
    first. Suffering–O long-suffering–yes, as the Lord must know,
Year after year in the mist and the wind and the shower and the snow.
XIV.
Heard, have you? what? they have told you he never repented his sin. How
    do they know it? are *they* his mother? are *you* of his kin?
Heard! have you ever heard, when the storm on the downs began,
The wind that 'ill wail like a child and the sea that 'ill moan like a man?
XV.
Election, Election and Reprobation–it's all very well.
But I go to-night to my boy, and I shall not find him in Hell.
For I cared so much for my boy that the Lord has look'd into my care, And
    He means me I'm sure to be happy with Willy, I know not where.
XVI.
And if *he* be lost–but to save *my* soul, that is all your desire:
Do you think that I care for *my* soul if my boy be gone to the fire? I have
    been with God in the dark–go, go, you may leave me alone– You never
    have borne a child–you are just as hard as a stone.
XVII.
Madam, I beg your pardon! I think that you mean to be kind,
But I cannot hear what you say for my Willy's voice in the wind–
The snow and the sky so bright–he used but to call in the dark,
And he calls to me now from the church and not from the gibbet–for hark!
    Nay–you can hear it yourself–it is coming–shaking the walls–
Willy–the moon's in a cloud–Good-night. I am going. He calls.

Henry Kendall (1839–82), Australian poet[40]

Rizpah
SAID one who led the spears of swarthy Gad,
To Jesse's mighty son: 'My Lord, O King,
I, halting hard by Gibeon's bleak-blown hill
Three nightfalls past, saw dark-eyed Rizpah, clad
In dripping sackcloth, pace with naked feet
The flinty rock where lie unburied yet
The sons of her and Saul; and he whose post
Of watch is in those places desolate,
Got up, and spake unto thy servant here
Concerning her – yea, even unto me: –
"Behold", he said, "the woman seeks not rest,
Nor fire, nor food, nor roof, nor any haunt
Where sojourns man; but rather on yon rock
Abideth, like a wild thing, with the slain,
And watcheth them, lest evil wing or paw
Should light upon the comely faces dead,
To spoil them of their beauty. Three long moons
Hath Rizpah, daughter of Aiah, dwelt
With drouth and cold and rain and wind by turns,
And many birds there are that know her face,
And many beasts that flee not at her step,
And many cunning eyes do look at her
From serpent-holes and burrows of the rat.
Moreover," spake the scout, "her skin is brown
And sere by reason of exceeding heat;
And all her darkness of abundant hair
Is shot with gray, because of many nights
When grief hath crouched in fellowship with frost
Upon that desert rock. Yea, thus and thus
Fares Rizpah", said the spy, O King, to me'.
But David, son of Jesse, spake no word,
But turned himself, and wept against the wall.
We have our Rizpahs in these modern days
Who've lost their households through no sin of theirs,
On bloody fields and in the pits of war;
And though their dead were sheltered in the sod
By friendly hands, these have not suffered less
Than she of Judah did, nor is their love

---

40. http://whitewolf.newcastle.edu.au/words/authors/K/KendallHenry/verse/PoemsOfKendall/rizpah.html and others.

Surpassed by hers. The Bard who, in great days
Afar off yet, shall set to epic song
The grand pathetic story of the strife
That shook America for five long years,
And struck its homes with desolation – he
Shall in his lofty verse relate to men
How, through the heat and havoc of that time,
Columbia's Rachael in her Rama wept
Her children, and would not be comforted
With that high patience that no man attains,
For tidings, from the bitter field, of spouse,
Or son, or brother, or some other love
Set face to face with Death. Moreover, he
Shall say how, through her sleepless hours at night,
When rain or leaves were dropping, every noise
Seemed like an omen; every coming step
Fell on her ears like a presentiment
And every hand that rested on the door
She fancied was a herald bearing grief;
While every letter brought a faintness on
That made her gasp before she opened it,
To read the story written for her eyes,
And cry, or brighten, over its contents.

William Cullen Bryant (1794–1878), American poet and journalist[41]

Rizpah

And he delivered them into the hands of the Gibeonites, and they hanged them in the hill before the Lord; and they fell all seven together, and were put to death in the days of the harvest, in the first days, in the beginning of barley-harvest.
And Rizpah, the daughter of Aiah, took sackcloth, and spread it for her upon the rock, from the beginning of harvest until the water dropped upon them out of heaven, and suffered neither the birds of the air to rest upon them by day, nor the beasts of the field by night.
2 Samuel, xxi. 10
Hear what the desolate Rizpah said,
As on Gibeah's rocks she watched the dead.
The sons of Michal before her lay,
And her own fair children, dearer than they:
By a death of shame they all had died,
And were stretched on the bare rock, side by side.
And Rizpah, once the loveliest of all

41. http://www.4literature.net/William_Cullen_Bryant/Rizpah/.

That bloomed and smiled in the court of Saul
All wasted with watching and famine now,
And scorched by the sun her haggard brow,
Sat mournfully guarding their corpses there,
And murmured a strange and solemn air;
The low, heart-broken, and wailing strain
Of a mother that mourns her children slain: –
"I have made the crags my home, and spread
On their desert backs my sackcloth bed;
I have eaten the bitter herb of the rocks,
And drunk the midnight dew in my locks;
I have wept till I could not weep, and the pain
Of the burning eyeballs went to my brain.
Seven blackened corpses before me lie,
In the blaze of the sun and the winds of the sky.
I have watched them through the burning day,
And driven the vulture and raven away;
And the cormorant wheeled in circles round,
Yet feared to alight on the guarded ground.
And when the shadows of twilight came,
I have seen the hyena's eyes of flame,
And heard at my side his stealthy tread,
But aye at my shout the savage fled:
And I threw the lighted brand to fright
The jackal and wolf that yelled in the night. –
"Ye were foully murdered, my hapless sons,
By the hands of wicked and cruel ones;
Ye fell, in your fresh and blooming prime,
All innocent, for your father's crime.
He sinned – but he paid the price of his guilt
When his blood by a nameless hand was spilt;
When he strove with the heathen host in vain,
And fell with the flower of his people slain,
And the sceptre his children's hands should sway
From his injured lineage passed away. –
"But I hoped that the cottage-roof would be
A safe retreat for my sons and me;
And that while they ripened to manhood fast,
They should wean my thoughts from the woes of the past;
And my bosom swelled with a mother's pride,
As they stood in their beauty and strength by my side,
Tall like their sire, with the princely grace
Of his stately form, and the bloom of his face. –
"Oh, what an hour for a mother's heart,
When the pitiless ruffians tore us apart!

When I clasped their knees and wept and prayed,
And struggled and shrieked to Heaven for aid,
And clung to my sons with desperate strength,
Till the murderers loosed my hold at length,
And bore me breathless and faint aside,
In their iron arms, while my children died.
They died – and the mother that gave them birth
Is forbid to cover their bones with earth. –
'The barley-harvest was nodding white,
When my children died on the rocky height,
And the reapers were singing on hill and plain,
When I came to my task of sorrow and pain.
But now the season of rain is nigh,
The sun is dim in the thickening sky,
And the clouds in sullen darkness rest
Where he hides his light at the doors of the west.
I hear the howl of the wind that brings
The long drear storm on its heavy wings;
But the howling wind and the driving rain
Will beat on my houseless head in vain:
I shall stay, from my murdered sons to scare
The beasts of the desert, and fowls of air'. –

Appendix 2: The Shriners, in Their Own Words

In August, 1870, William J. Florence, a prominent American actor traveling in Europe, was enthralled by a magnificent pageant presented by the Council from Egypt in Marseilles, France. Mr Florence related this experience to his personal friends, Dr Walter M. Fleming, in New York. Dr Fleming was a noted Masonic scholar, and he utilized this ability plus his knowledge of Arabian and Egyptian literature to contrive a ritual. This brilliant physician spaced mystery and enchantment through the manuscript and submitting it to actor Florence and eleven other distinguished men, explained it was his desire to form a order that would act to relax and appeal to the humoresque portion of human nature after being subjected to the continuous serious presentation of the Knight Templar Orders and Scottish Rite Degrees.

These thirteen founders of what was to be known as 'The Ancient Arabic Order of the Nobles of the Mystic Shrine' decided the prerequisite to membership would be members of the Masonic Order who has attained the status of Knight Templar and/or Thirty-Second degree Scottish Rite Masons. The first 'Temple' was founded in New York on September 26, 1872, and named 'Mecca'. The Shrine enjoyed rapid growth. The National Order was founded June 6, 1876.

On June 25, 1888 Rameses Temple in Toronto, Ontario, Canada, was chartered and the Order became the 'Shrine of North America', the name 'Imperial' was adopted to signify the International Order.

In Kentucky, Temples were chartered as follows: Kosair in Louisville in 1886; El Hasa in Ashland in 1906; Oleika in Lexington in 1908; Rizpah in Madisonville in 1909. The Shrine held annual conventions, and for the first fifth years fun and fellowship were the only net results.

With the passing of World War 1, the men who composed the membership of the Shrine geared their activities toward deeds of more exalted usefulness. At the Imperial Council Session held in Portland, Oregon, in June 1920, the Shrine 'found its soul'. The representatives authorized the formation of the 'Shriners' Hospitals for Crippled Children' to be supported by an annual assessment of each Noble. The first Hospitals for the treatment of orthopedically handicapped children was opened by the Shrine at Shreveport, Louisiana, on September 16, 1922. The Lexington, Kentucky, unit was opened November 1, 1926. The Shrine now operates 19 Orthopedic Hospitals and three Burn Institutes, the first of which was opened in Galveston, Texas, on March 20, 1966. Just as the Shrine has made America conscious of the crippled child, it is now performing the same humanitarian act in the fields of treatment and research of burned children.

The tremendous financial load of the Shriners Orthopedic and Burns programs of today must necessarily be supplemented by income in addition to the assessment of each Shriner. Football games, circuses, paper sales and other projects are conducted annually for this great charitable undertaking. Wills, bequests and the 'Living Trust' are earnestly solicited from all friends of mankind.

The Shriners Hospitals for Children have zealously earned and cautiously protect the proud title of 'THE WORLD'S GREATEST PHILANTHROPY'.[42]

Bibliography

Brenner, Athalya (2005), *I Am: Biblical Women Tell their Own Story*, Minneapolis: Fortress Press, 120-32, 225-6.

Brenner, Athalya (2009), 'Rizpah [Re]Membered: 2 Samuel 1-14 and Beyond', 207-27 in *Performing Memory in Biblical Narrative and Beyond*, edited by A. Brenner and F. H. Polak, Sheffield: Sheffield Phoenix.

Edelman, Diana V. (1997), 'Rizpah', *ABD CD-ROM* (= 1992).

Edelman, Diana V. (2000), 'Rizpah', 145-6 in *Women in Scripture*, edited by C. Meyers, T. Craven and R. Kraemer, Grand Rapids: Eerdmans.

Israel, Charles E. (1961), *King Saul's Concubine; RIZPAH*, New York: Simon & Schuster.

Polak, Frank A. (2009), 'Negotiations, Social Drama and Voices of Memory in Some Samuel Texts', 46-71 in *Performing Memory in Biblical Narrative and Beyond*, edited by A. Brenner and F. H. Polak, Sheffield: Sheffield Phoenix.

---

42. http://www.grandlodgeofkentucky.org/shrine.html. See also http://www.shri-nershq.org/ for the children's hospitals supported.

Internet Sources

https://maagarim.hebrew-academy.org.il/Pages/PMain.aspx?koderekh=31488&page=1 [Accessed 2019]
http://www.4literature.net/William_Cullen_Bryant/Rizpah/ [Accessed 2019]
http://www.bethrapha.org/index2.html [Accessed 2019]
http://genforum.genealogy.com/laforge/messages/198.html [Accessed 2019]
http://www.grandlodgeofkentucky.org/shrine.html [Accessed 2019]
http://home.att.net/~TennysonPoetry/rizpah.htm http://www.dryclean.com/index.html [Accessed 2019]
http://www.iremshrine.org/Shrines.htm [Accessed 2019]
http://www.jenforum.com/hoc [Accessed 2019]
http://www.glaucus.org.uk/GoldMail.htmkaday/ [Accessed 2019]
http://www.libraries.psu.edu/do/digitalbookshelf/27995405/27995405_part_02.pdfhttp://directory.jacksonvilledirect.info/daughters-rizpah-janitorial-jacksonville-435-clark-road/ [Accessed 2019]
http://mysite.wanadoomembers.co.uk/robertbuchanan/html/quake2.html#rizpah [Accessed 2019]
http://www.ncca.org.au/__data/page/2217/04_SS_06.pdf [Accessed 2019]
http://www.rizpah.com/ [Accessed 2019]
http://www.rizpah.org/ http://www.rizpah.org/aboutdaughters.htm [Accessed 2019]
http://rizpahtemple.com http://www.rizpahtempel.org/ [Accessed 2019] http://rhythmsofgrace.blogspot.com/2004/10/rain-from-heaven.html [Accessed 2019] http://search.blogger.com/?q=rizpah&hl=en&ie=UTF8&x=20&y=6&filter=0&ui=blg&sa–&start=0 [Accessed 2019]
http://www.shrinershq.org/ [Accessed 2019]
http://www.usgennet.org/usa/sd/state/tluc/page101.html.messages/328.html [Accessed 2019] http://whitewolf.newcastle.edu.au/words/authors/K/KendallHenry/verse/PomsOfKendall [Accessed 2019]
http://en.wikipedia.org/wiki/Shriners [Accessed 2019]
http://www.womensministries.cc/prayer_january06.htm [Accessed 2019]
http://www.womenofrizpah.cabanova.com//rizpah.html [Accessed 2019]
http://unbound.biola.edu/ [Accessed 2019]

Intermezzo

On (Heroic) Death beyond
the Hebrew Bible

COMMEMORATING FIRST WORLD WAR SOLDIERS AS MARTYRS

Jan Willem van Henten

This contribution is a slightly revised version of a chapter originally published in a volume about cross-cultural martyrdom, focusing on the canonization, contestation and afterlives of martyrs.[1]

The theme of martyrdom is contested not only because martyrs themselves are contested – a person can be a martyr for the in-group and an enemy or even terrorist for others – but also because many ethnic and religious groups have their own 'canon' (authoritative list) of martyrs, and these canons compete with each other. Both the origin of the concept of martyrdom (classical Greece, Hellenistic Judaism, Early Christianity, Islam) and the definition of martyrdom are heavily debated (van Henten 2020; van Henten and Saloul 2020) and this contribution, therefore, follows a discursive approach focusing on the commemoration of soldiers as martyrs. Whatever the motivations and convictions of these soldiers may have been, they were made into martyrs by who commemorate them. The rhetoric and pictorial programme of these commemorations imply at least that they are supposed to have been vindicated by God after their death.

Heroic death on the battlefield is a marginal theme in the Hebrew Bible, but Hebrew Bible passages can play an important role in the 'scripturalized' commemoration of 'martyrs' from later times, as we will see further on in this essay.

Why have martyrs interested me for almost forty years? Documents and artefacts about martyrs can be seen as windows into the identity constructions of the communities who commemorate them: they reflect a power struggle which is remarkably won by the martyrs; and, whatever people say, religion and politics are often closely and tightly interconnected in commemorations of martyrs, from antiquity up to the present day (van Henten 1997; 2009).

In the following case study from the modern European context – which, largely, is my own context (I am Dutch) – we can see how martyrdom may be constructed

---

1. A first version of this article was published in Ihab Saloul and Jan Willem van Henten (eds), *Martyrdom: Canonisation, Contestation and Afterlives*. Amsterdam: Amsterdam University Press, 2020, 153–79. It is here revised and reproduced with thanks to AUP.

in the case of military death, from the Hebrew Bible on, relying on materialities as well as texts, and motivated by politics as well as religion.

1. Introduction: Commemorating the Fallen of First World War as Martyrs

Martyrdom traditions have become a fascinating framework of reference for commemorating soldiers and other victims of mostly military violence during the First World War.[2] Hence, individual persons who were believed to have made an exceptional sacrifice during the First World War are sometimes being commemorated as martyrs. One example of such a person is the nurse Edith Cavell, who is, among other things, commemorated as a 'nurse, patriot, and martyr' on her memorial outside Norwich Cathedral.[3] The Germans executed Cavell on 12 October 1915 because of the help she had given to Allied soldiers trapped in occupied Belgium. Edith Cavell was a devout Anglican and widely perceived as a Christian martyr, as several monuments imply. Her statue in London at St Martin's Place near Trafalgar Square is mainly secular in tone but surmounted by a Cross and Virgin with Child. Such a commemoration is common in Turkey as the successor of the Ottoman Empire, but much rarer in countries of northwest Europe (Hettling and Echternkamp 2013: 31, 36–9). This makes the exceptions all the more interesting.[4] One of these cases concerns Arthur Winnington Ingram, the bishop of London who also served as the chaplain of the London Rifle Brigade and the London Royal Naval Volunteers. Winnington-Ingram is very explicit in a 1914 speech for the bereaved families of British soldiers killed by identifying the dead soldiers as martyrs:[5]

> You have lost your boys, but what are they? Martyrs – martyrs as really as St Stephen was a martyr – martyrs dying for their faith as really as St Stephen, the first martyr, died for his. They looked up when they died in the trenches, or in the little cottage where they were carried, they looked up and they saw JESUS standing on the right hand of GOD. And he is keeping them safe for you there when the time comes. Covered with imperishable glory they pass to deathless life.[6]

---

2. I warmly thank Tamara Breugelmans (Amsterdam), Jan de Vries (Nijmegen), Gregor Langfeld (Amsterdam), and Peter Pässler (VDK, Kassel), for very helpful comments and references.

3. This memorial sculpture was erected by Henry Pegram in 1918 and moved to its present location in 1993. It was restored in 2014. Description: https://historicengland.org.uk/listing/the-list/list-entry/1210795 [consulted 10 April 2017].

4. For surveys concerning the commemoration of British and German soldiers including those of the First World War, see Goebel 2013: 199–224 and Hettling and Echternkamp 2013: 123–58. See also Winter 1998; Capdevilla and Voldman 2006: 149–79.

5. Snape 2008: 191. Further references in Carpenter 1949; Bell 2013.

6. Winnington-Ingram 1914: 75; Wolffe 2015: 23.

The bishop obviously connects the fate of the fallen with St Stephen facing death: 'I see heaven open and the Son of Man standing at the right hand of God' (Acts 7.56[7]). Wolffe connects the bishop's speech with a 1914 painting by James Clark, entitled the 'Great Sacrifice', which was widely reproduced in the early months of the war and in the Christmas 1914 issue of *The Graphic*.[8] The painting draws an analogy between a fallen soldier and Jesus' crucifixion, with Jesus looking down compassionately on the soldier, suggesting that the soldier died for Jesus Christ and that Jesus shared in his suffering.[9] Wolffe (2015: 24) comments:

> If the confidence of such equations between Christian martyrdom, the sacrifice of the war dead, and even the sacrifice of Christ himself seem disconcerting to later generations, they need to be seen in their context as a logical consequence of the demonising of the Germans, as a pastoral response to the need to offer consolation to the bereaved, and also as an effort by Christians to shape the national response in a manner that affirmed rather than marginalised Christianity. Winnington-Ingram, it should be recalled, was speaking into a cultural context in which others readily found a more secular nationalistic framework to make sense of the war casualties.

The tension between a secular and nationalistic framework of interpretation on the one hand, and a religious perspective on the other, is the main focus of John Wolffe's discussion of the commemoration of British soldiers as martyrs.[10] My focus in this contribution is different: I will concentrate on the articulations of martyrdom itself in the commemorations of fallen soldiers as martyrs, including the use of biblical passages in support of such interpretations.

The first thing that comes to mind is that a definition of the martyr figure remains implicit in Bishop Winnington-Ingram's 1914 speech. However, in a sermon preached on 28 November 1915, he is more explicit about what being a martyr means for him. He states that he considers every soldier who fell during the war a martyr: he looks upon 'everyone who fights in this war as a hero, and upon everyone who dies in it as a martyr' (Evans 2007: 66–7; Bell 2013: 127; Wolffe 2015: 24). Winnington-Ingram, therefore, considerably broadens the concept of martyrdom in comparison to the 'classical martyrs' in Judaism and Christianity, who usually die in a forensic context (van Henten 2012a). His martyrs remind one of the battlefield martyrs in the older Muslim traditions about martyrdom

---

7. Quotations from the NT are from the NRSV unless otherwise stated.

8. A British weekly illustrated newspaper, published in London 1869-1932, with wide influence on contemporaneous art.

9. King 1993: 246. Cf. a stained glass window with a crucifixion and a soldier in uniform at the foot of the cross in the English Martyrs (Roman Catholic) church at The Sands, Whalley, Ribble Valley, Lancashire, http://www.iwm.org.uk/memorials/item/memorial/42656 [consulted 10 April 2017].

10. Cf. Capdevilla and Voldman 2006: 164–9.

(Kohlberg 1997). The second point that strikes the reader is that Winnington-Ingram remains vague about the cause of martyrdom. This may have been obvious for him, something like 'for God and King', but once again it is quite different from older martyrdom accounts, which often highlight the martyr's motivation. Instead, the bishop makes a bold statement by drawing an analogy between the fallen soldiers and St. Stephen. This implies that he focuses on those who stayed behind: the reinterpretation of the death of the fallen as martyrs provides meaning and significance to their death, as well as consolation for their relatives and friends. The analogy with Stephen also implies the prospect of a resurrection, which is explicitly mentioned in the quotation: the fallen would be safe in the presence of Jesus Christ until the end of times: 'And he is keeping them safe for you there when the time comes. Covered with imperishable glory they pass to deathless life' (1914: 75, above). This implies that the soldiers are privileged because their resurrection had already taken place, similar to the resurrection of the martyrs in the early Christian tradition.

We can consider Winnington-Ingram's speeches about the fallen to be an eye opener for the implicit and sometimes explicit configuration of the deceased soldiers as martyrs on war memorials and in military cemeteries. In the remaining part of my contribution I will focus on several cases of the commemoration of soldiers killed in the First World War which are thematically related, because biblical motifs and older martyrdom traditions play an important role in their commemoration in artwork with religious motifs. I will look particularly at mosaics in two of the four German military cemeteries in West Flanders, Belgium; a statue of Saint Edmund connected with killed soldiers of the First World War in the Anglican St Edmund King and Martyr Church in Dudley, West Midlands, England; and, finally, a stained glass window with a memorial inscription in All Saints' Church at Huntingdon, Cambridgeshire, also in the United Kingdom.

2. The German Military Cemeteries at Hooglede and Menen, Belgium

There are currently four German military cemeteries in West Flanders (Belgium), which go back to the years of the war itself and preserve the bodily remains of more than 100,000 German soldiers who are commemorated as national heroes.[11] The four cemeteries, where also soldiers from other cemeteries that no longer exist were reburied, are Vladslo-Praetbosch,[12] which includes two statues by Käthe Kollwitz; the so-called student cemetery of Langemark-Poelkapelle, which

---

11. Freytag and Van Driessche 2011: 163-238, see https://oar.onroerenderfgoed.be/publicaties/RELT/7/RELT007-008.pdf [consulted 2 March 2016]. And in general: Mosse 1979; Hettling and Echternkamp 2013.

12. https://inventaris.onroerenderfgoed.be/erfgoedobjecten/94250 [consulted 5 April 2017].

is well-known and turned into a more general memorial site that is visited frequently;[13] and the cemeteries that will be discussed in detail (Hooglede and Menen). They are taken up together in a UNESCO application for the list of heritage locations in danger.[14] There is a myth about the cemetery at Langemark, suggesting that the German soldiers buried there were young students who sacrificed their life happily and with glowing patriotism 'on the altar of the fatherland'.[15] George Mosse considers this patriotic glorification of a sacrificial death on the battlefield a deliberate association with Jesus Christ's Passion and a strategy for interpreting the fallen's death from the perspective of the sacred.[16] The solidarity unto death of the soldiers implies that they are models for the living, which echoes a motif in classical martyr texts.[17] The motif of a patriotic self-sacrifice, which is beneficial for the nation, is expressed in the maxim 'Germany must live, even when we have to die' ('*Deutschland muss leben, und wenn wir sterben müssen*'), by Heinrich Lersch (1914), which is currently located at the back of the inner entrance building at Langemark. The two lines of text were originally put on a wall in front of the so-called grave of the comrades at Langemark between 1932 and 1934.[18] Scholars have also associated the many oaks planted in these cemeteries with martyrdom, because the oak is the German tree from immemorial times and a symbol of posthumous afterlife in nature (Freytag and Van Driessche 2011: 169).

For my discussion, the most interesting features of these cemeteries are the mosaics at Hooglede and Menen, which are directly connected with the fate and commemoration of the fallen soldiers and clearly built on biblical and Christian motifs. One concerns a mosaic on the inside wall of a gallery with arches at the cemetery at Hooglede. It shows a majestic Jesus Christ with two human figures on his right and two on his left, and an inscription pointing to its commemorative function. The other concerns the cemetery at Menen, which includes a small octagonal chapel with beautiful mosaics on the inside, with symbols deriving from the book of Revelation. This chapel has rightly been interpreted as a representation of Revelation's heavenly Jerusalem (Freytag and Van Driessche 2011: 171, 173). Both cemeteries must have been redesigned under the supervision of Robert Tischler (1885–1959), the chief architect of the Association for the Care of the German Military Cemeteries (*Volksbund Deutsche Kriegsgräberfürsorge*, VDK),

---

13. Description: https://inventaris.onroerenderfgoed.be/erfgoedobjecten/83766 [consulted 20 April 2018].

14. http://whc.unesco.org/en/tentativelists/5886/ [consulted 11 April 2017].

15. Ketelsen 1985; Mosse 1979: 6–7; Mosse, 1990: 70–4; Freytag and Van Driessche 2011: 166, 171, 181–3; 194.

16. Mosse 1979: 4; Mosse 1990: 7–8, 35; Freytag and Van Driessche 2011: 166.

17. Mosse 1979: 7; Freytag and Van Driessche 2011: 166; 171; van Henten 2011: 300–27.

18. Freytag and Van Driessche 2011: 171. During the Nazi period Lersch's maxim was used for other memorial sites as well: Hettling and Jörg Echternkamp 2013: 136–40.

from 1926 to 1959.[19] Tischler was a warm supporter of Hitler and he used secular and fascist-nationalistic motifs in his design of the military cemeteries in the Nazi period. After the Second World War he clearly built on Christian motifs for the decoration of the cemeteries, and even included chapels in some of them as sacred spaces of remembrance.[20]

Hooglede

The cemetery of Hooglede dates from 1917, when there was a great need for burial space because of the third Battle at Ieper, which started in July 1917.[21] Before the Second World War the cemetery was mainly a meadow, with endless rows of crosses with a triangle top.[22] From 1937 onward a hall of honour was built with open arches on the front side – a Neo-Roman propylaeum (30 metres wide and 6 metres long), in technical terminology.[23] This hall was included in the new sacralised set-up of the cemetery, which was constructed between 1954 and 1959 and is roughly similar to the present state. Standing in front of the entrance in the low south wall of natural stone, with a plaque with the text '*Deutscher Soldatenfriedhof Hooglede* 1914–1918' (German Military Cemetery Hooglede 1914–1918), one looks up to a rectangular piece of land of ca. 1.8 hectare that slightly ascends and that has rows of lying granite gravestones, each containing two names of deceased soldiers, the date of their death, the number of their grave and sometimes also their military rank (Freytag and Van Driessche 2011: 168, 202). In between the stones there is grass, extensive stretches of heather and forty-three groups of five standing crosses from basalt lava rock. The heather reflects the wish of the VDK, the association that was for a long time responsible for maintaining the cemetery, to have a 'flourishing grave field' (*blühender Gräberfeld*) at Hooglede (Freytag and Van Driessche 2011: 202). At the west and east sides there are oak and maple trees and there are a few poplars behind the hall of honour, which is built of sandstone from Ibbenbüren.[24]

19. About the VDK, see Gudenberg 1969; Soltau 1981; http://www.volksbund.de/home.html [consulted 14 April 2017]; Kuberek 1990; Fuhrmeister 2007.

20. Lurz 1983; Kirchmeier, *Eine Festung, die eine Friedhof ist: in Stein gefassten Ideologie – 75 Jahre Totenburg Quero.* VDK leaflet (2014), http://docplayer.org/30529801-Eine-festung-die-ein-friedhof-ist.html [consulted 26 April 2018].

21. https://inventaris.onroerenderfgoed.be/erfgoedobjecten/95266 [consulted 12 April 2017]. Freytag and Van Driessche 2011: 174–75.

22. The numbers of the soldiers buried at Hooglede differ slightly: Freytag and Van Driessche (2011: 179, 191–2; 199) consistently mention 8247 persons, but https://inventaris.onroerenderfgoed.be/erfgoedobjecten/95266 [consulted 12 April 2017] and http://www.volksbund.de/kriegsgraeberstaette/hooglede.html [consulted 14 April 2017] refer to 8241 German soldiers and 16 Russian soldiers.

23. https://inventaris.onroerenderfgoed.be/erfgoedobjecten/95266 [consulted 12 April 2017].

24. Freytag and Van Driessche 2011: 168, 179; https://inventaris.onroerenderfgoed.be/erfgoedobjecten/95266 [consulted 12 April 2017].

During the adaptations at Hooglede in the fifties of the previous century, four of the open spaces below the arches in the hall were covered, two rooms were created and a mosaic was included in the inner wall at the back of the hall. Two of these renovations include explicit and elaborate religious imagery, which implies that all the buried soldiers were from that time on remembered and honoured from a religious perspective. The room at the west side is closed off on the inside by a wrought-iron screen through which a square memorial in bronze in the middle can be seen, designed and sculpted by Fritz Schmoll genannt Eisenwerth in 1956-1957.[25] The memorial looks like an altar and on top of it is a small square metal cupboard with a cross on top. The sides of the cupboard are open; on the east side lies a book with the names of all the soldiers buried here. The east side of the memorial has an inscription above a wreath: '*HIER RUHEN DEUTSCHE SOLDATEN 1914-1918*'. Its west side contains a relief of an angel; and the other two sides have the head of an animal in the middle, possibly a lion. The most explicit religious imagery concerns the Christ mosaic at the centre of the hall (Figure 5.1), designed in 1956 by Franz Grau (1910-1992),[26] a German artist from Munich who also designed the mosaic inside the famous war memorial for the fallen German soldiers at El Alamein (1955), and several other war monuments with very obvious Christian motifs.[27]

The large central figure in this mosaic, several metres high, is a seated Jesus Christ in a long robe with a halo, against a mainly brick-red background. The Christ figure as well as the other human figures are presented in combinations of pastel colours: light green, yellow, blue, red, green etc. Slight variations of colour articulate their forms. Although Christ's throne is invisible, the folding lines of his robe and his bended knees presuppose that he is seated (Welscher 1999: 124). He wears a long robe and his feet rest on a semicircle which has several layers in slightly different colours. His right arm is lifted towards the onlookers, his fingers form a gesture of speaking. In his left hand he carries a scroll, the bottom of which rests on his left upper leg. Two characters are inscribed on the scroll: an Alpha and an Omega. Two smaller figures stand to his left, both holding their hands together

---

25. Küppers 2003/2004: 352; Freytag and Van Driessche 2011: 202. https://inventaris.onroerenderfgoed.be/erfgoedobjecten/95266 [consulted 12 April 2017]. The VDK's chief architect, Robert Tischler, used to contract artists from the Munich region for the artwork of the cemeteries: in addition to Fritz Schmoll genannt Eisenwerth and Franz Grau also Willy Guglhör and others; see Vancoillie 2017: 13, http://www.riha-journal.org/articles/2017/0150-0176-special-issue-war-graves/0162-vancoillie [consulted 23 April 2018].

26. The mosaic was produced by the firm Gustav van Treeck, Werkstätte für Mosaik und Glasmalerei (Munich).

27. Welscher 1999: 25-26, 124. See also the artwork by Franz Grau at the war cemeteries of Lommel (Belgium, 1959), Berchtesgaden-Schönau (Germany, 1956), Orglande (France, 1961) and Marigny (France, 1961).

Figure 1 Mosaic by Franz Grau. The Military Cemetery at Hooglede, Belgium. Photo: Jan Willem van Henten

in front of their breast. One of them is clearly a woman with long hair, wearing a long robe and sandals. Her feet and lower legs are clearly visible. The other person, sometimes also identified as a woman,[28] is closer to Christ and wears a long robe that meets the ground, so that her or his feet are invisible. S/he also has long dark hair, and the bottom side of the face may depict a beard. The dress of Christ and the two figures to his left looks timeless, and clearly builds on Byzantine iconographic traditions. The two human figures to Christ's right, also smaller than he is, are by the look of their faces clearly males. They wear military clothes: their boots as well as the round buckle of their belts are clearly visible. The identification of the two men, although bareheaded, as soldiers seems certain because of the helmet held in the left hand by one of them. One of these men holds his arms and hands in front of him, close to his breast. The other one holds his right arm and hand in a similar position. The upper part left and right of the Christ figure shows the inscription '1914–1918 in memoriam', which clearly connects the mosaic with the funerary context of the war cemetery.

The central figure probably represents Christ as ruler and/or judge of humankind, in line with the well-known iconographical tradition of *Christus*

---

28. Freytag and Van Driessche 2011: 171, https://inventaris.onroerenderfgoed.be/erfgoedobjecten/95266 [consulted 12 April 2017].

Pantokrator (majestic, almighty, in glory; and see below). The abstract half-circle, with several concentric layers, may symbolize the earth or the rainbow. The identification of the two figures at the left is difficult, also because the gender of one of them is ambiguous. The two figures at the right can easily be identified as two of the soldiers who were buried at Hooglede. This is implied by their military dress, which matches the contemporary context and is supported by the inscription '1914–1918 in memoriam', which explicitly links the buried fallen soldiers in the graveyard to the mosaic. What is the meaning of the entire scene? Freytag and Van Driessche (2011: 171, 202) briefly discuss the meaning of this mosaic and suggest that the scene indicates that the soldiers, after their heroic death, are taken up in heaven as just persons (*'Dieses Bildnis verweist auf die Soldaten als "Gerechte", die in den Himmel aufgenommen werden'*). This implies that the soldiers were vindicated directly after death, as were martyrs in early Jewish and Christian traditions (e.g. 2 Macc. 7.9, 11, 14, 23, 28–29; *Acts of the Scillitan Martyrs* 15). The anonymous author of the description on the Belgian heritage list at Hooglede suggests that the scene represents Jesus Christ as judge of the world, making the V-sign with his right hand (but this is not correct, see below), and flanked by four mourning and praying persons, two soldiers and two women.[29] Both interpretations seem plausible, but in both cases a convincing argument is missing.

Since the Christ figure in the centre obviously builds on Christian iconographic traditions, the clue to the meaning of the entire mosaic scene may be found in a particular iconographical tradition about a collective, with Christ as the central figure. Three of those iconographical traditions come to mind. The first tradition concerns the so-called *Dominus legem dat* or *Traditio legis* iconography, which is attested in antiquity from the fourth century CE onward and implies that Jesus Christ revealed the law in analogy to Moses.[30] The second iconographical tradition, attested from the Middle Ages onward, is Christ in Glory (*Majestas domini*).[31] The third relevant tradition is that of the *Deesis*, an early-Christian and Byzantine representation that is analogous to Christ in Glory in the West, but with different details.[32] Additional arguments for the interpretation of the pictorial programme of the Hooglede mosaic can be found in other mosaics created by Franz Grau, including those in the chapel at Menen (below).

The *Dominus legem dat* pictorial tradition builds on the transfer of the Torah scrolls by the Romans in 71 CE as told by Flavius Josephus, and highlights Rome as the supreme Christian city. This iconographical programme may have been triggered by the Emperor Julian's failed attempt to rebuild the Jerusalem Temple (Noga-Banai 2015). The Jesus figure of Franz Grau closely matches the depiction

---

29. https://inventaris.onroerenderfgoed.be/erfgoedobjecten/95266 [consulted 12 April 2017].

30. Spera 2000; Arbeiter 2007; Noga-Banai 2015.

31. Berger 1926; Meer 1938; Schiller 1971: 233–49; Poilpret 2005.

32. Walter 1968; Schiller 1971: 195; Onasch 1993: 83–4; Cutler 1987; Gilsdorf 2012; Neff 2007: 372–3.

of the haloed Christ of the *Dominus legem dat* tradition, who stands or sits in the centre of the scene, has an open scroll in his left hand, and raises his right arm with an open hand. The Apostle Paul stands at the right of Jesus, turned towards him; and the Apostle Peter, who can be recognized by the crosier in his left hand, stands at Jesus' left side, supporting or receiving the scroll with his right hand.[33]

The scene at Hooglede matches the *Dominus legem dat* tradition but also deviates from it in several ways: the figures at Jesus Christ's right and left side, four altogether, can hardly be identified with the apostles Peter and Paul (below). The document held in Christ's left hand probably does not refer to the Law. It has a flat surface and can be an open scroll, but also a tablet or a codex. Most importantly, the characters Alpha and Omega are depicted on it, and this detail links the document to the book of Revelation, where Jesus is introduced by the words 'I am the Alpha and the Omega' (Rev. 21.6). The characters Alpha and Omega, symbolizing supreme power in Revelation, are elsewhere in that book associated with God (1.8; 22.13), but in Rev. 21.6 they refer to Jesus Christ. This may imply that the scene at Hooglede points in particular to the well-known passage in Revelation 21 about a new heaven and a new earth. If so, the message for those remembered and honoured at Hooglede, and for the visitors, would be quite appropriate. Read in its immediate context the passage highlights the words of a figure seated on a throne, indicating a renewal of everything as well as the vindication of the 'conquerors', who can easily be associated with the deceased soldiers. The gesture of the raised right arm and the (slightly malformed) open hand of which thumb, index finger and middle finger are stretched and little finger and ring finger flexed against the palm of the hand, supports the interpretation that Jesus conveys a message about the soldiers, because it points to the act of speaking (Roberts 1998: 54). Rev. 21.5-7 reads:

> (5) And the one who was seated on the throne said, 'See, I am making all things new.' Also he said, 'Write this, for these words are trustworthy and true.' (6) Then he said to me, 'It is done! I am the Alpha and the Omega, the beginning and the end. To the thirsty I will give water as a gift from the spring of the water of life. (7) Those who conquer will inherit these things, and I will be their God and they will be my children.'

The seated one on the throne, associated with Jesus Christ in Revelation 21, can be identified with the Christ figure of the mosaic scene. The words that have to be written down, according to Rev. 21.5, strengthen the connection, because they can be identified with the book or the scroll in Jesus' left hand. The self-identification 'I am the Alpha and the Omega' also confirms the message of the words, which is about the renewal of everything, the gift of living water to the thirsty[34] and salvation

---

33. Noga-Banai 2015: 158–61. The scene can include additional figures, like sheep or lambs; and Christ's feet sometimes rest on clouds, heaven or a terrestrial globe.

34. Cf. Rev. 22 about the river of the water of life flowing from the throne of God and of the Lamb through the middle of the street of the heavenly Jerusalem (22.1-2).

to the 'conquerors', i.e. those who live by the message of the book of Revelation (van Henten 2012b). From the perspective of the *Dominus legem dat* tradition and the interconnections with Revelation 21, the mosaic points to the vindication of the buried soldiers and a renewal of their life in the heavenly Jerusalem. We will see that a similar message is evoked by part of the imagery of the Menen mosaics.

The Christ in Glory pictorial tradition is thematically related to the iconography of *Dominus legem dat*. Once again Jesus Christ is portrayed seated on a throne with either a globe or a book in one of his hands. He is often depicted together with four figures, which matches the Hooglede mosaic. These figures are the four evangelists, sometimes depicted together with their symbols.[35] A coloured drawing at the beginning of Matthew's Gospel in a codex with the Gospels from Tournai (ca. 900) depicts Jesus Christ in a way similar to Franz Grau's mosaic – although in a very different style. Jesus sits on the throne within a large halo, has lifted his right arm and hand slightly, and holds a book in his left hand. This book must be the collection of the four Gospels. In the four corners the symbols of the four evangelists are depicted, each with a book, i.e. their Gospels.[36] The *Majestas Domini* tradition can help to explain the number of four human figures accompanying Jesus Christ in the Hooglede mosaic scene, although the identification of these figures may be different. The tradition also helps to interpret one detail that so far has not been discussed: Jesus Christ is sitting upon a rainbow. The rainbow is a regular element of the *Majestas Domini* tradition, which depicts Jesus Christ as being seated above a rainbow or a sphere.[37] The biblical context presupposed by the Christ in Glory iconography is the heavenly courtroom in Revelation 4–5, which includes a transfer of power to the Lamb that was slaughtered as well as its glorification (Rev. 5.12-13).[38] The half circle of the rainbow supports this interconnection, because a rainbow of emerald surrounds the divine throne according to Rev. 4.3 (Neff 2007: 372). The *Majestas Domini* tradition may also suggest a specific interpretation of the depiction of Jesus' raised right hand with the gesture of the fingers (above). The image of Jesus' right hand in the *Majestas Domini* tradition is usually interpreted as a gesture of blessing.[39]

---

35. E.g. The Hague, Koninklijke Bibliotheek, MS 78 D 40 folio 63r Miniature of MD with 4 evangelists and their symbols. Also without evangelists, e.g.: Lund University Library Medeltidhandskrift 5 folio 77v: http://www6.ub.lu.se/fsi/server?source=Laurentius/Mh_5/Mh_5-f_77_v.tif&profile=mats_stor&type=image [consulted 13 April 2017].

36. The Hague, Museum Meermanno-Westreenianum, MS 10 B 7 Folio 11v. Details: http://www.arkyves.org.proxy.uba.uva.nl:2048/view/byvmss_1328/ [consulted 13 April 2017].

37. Schiller 1971: 233; 236; Markus 2013: 135. Cf. the Iconclass description 11D321: '"Majestas Domini": Christ in mandorla seated in a rainbow or sphere and accompanied by the Tetramorph', Waal 1985: 27.

38. Schiller 1971: 200. Sometimes Christ in Majesty is associated with the Last Judgement.

39. E.g. on the baptismal font of the Tryde Church, Scania, Markus 2013: 137. O'Neill 1996: 182; Supercic 2009: 206.

The half circle symbolizing the rainbow brings us to a third relevant iconographic tradition, because it builds on the early-Christian and Byzantine representation of Christ that is called the *Deesis*. This tradition is analogous to the *Majestas Domini* in the West.[40] The *Deesis* depicts a seated Jesus Christ as *Pantokrator* with a book on his left knee, raising his right hand in benediction. Near him are figures who address their prayers of intercession to Christ.[41] This iconographical tradition gives us, perhaps, a hint about the identification and meaning of the two figures at the left of Jesus in Hooglede. In the *Deesis* Christ is often flanked by the Virgin Mary and John the Baptist in the role of intercessors. The gesture of their hands in front of them symbolizes both adoration and entreaty. Sometimes Mary and John kneel before Christ.[42]

In what ways are these related older Christian iconographical traditions useful for the interpretation of the mosaic at Hooglede? In line with the *Dominus legem dat* tradition, which may have influenced the *Majestas Domini* tradition, the book or scroll held in Jesus Christ's left hand becomes a focal point. This identification of the book with the Law is not supported by other details of the scene. The book could be the four Gospels, in line with the *Majestas Domini* iconography; but the most plausible interpretation is that it is associated with the Apocalypse because of the letters Alpha and Omega inscribed on it. The entire book of Revelation or, more plausibly, the message for the 'conquerors' highlighted in Revelation 21 (above) may be represented by the book image, because that association matches the funeral setting of the scene very well. The book points in that case to the 'victory' of the soldiers as well as their reward in heaven. The book may at the same time be associated with the 'book of life' referred to in Rev. 20.15: 'and anyone whose name was not found written in the book of life was thrown into the lake of fire'. This passage is part of the judgement of the dead described in Rev. 20.11-15. If the 'book of life' is alluded to by the mosaic, it would highlight the vindication of the fallen soldiers. In that case another association in line with the *Majestas Domini* and *Deesis* traditions becomes obvious: the heavenly courtroom of Revelation may be evoked by the imagery of the scene. From this perspective, the scene would anticipate the vindication of the deceased soldiers by their incorporation in the 'book of life' after the intercession of Mary and John the Baptist. However, the identification of the two figures at Jesus' left side is not certain. If we interpret the two figures in line with Franz Grau's El Alamein mosaic (1955), which commemorates fallen German soldiers from the Second World War and depicts a symmetry of twice three figures – three soldiers and three women, plausibly wives or mothers of soldiers – the two figures at Hooglede could also represent female relatives of the soldiers: wives, mothers and/or sisters (Welscher 1999: 25–6).

40. Neff 2007: 372–3; Woodfin 2011: 76. Also Connor 2016: 27–8.
41. Walter 1968; Walter 1970. The iconographical tradition of the Deesis has also been interpreted as a representation of the celestial hierarchy pointing to the divine Logos, see for references n. 32.
42. Walter 1968: 312–16; Cutler 1987: 145–7, 151; Gilsdorf 2012: 133–6; Woodfin 2011: 64–76.

Menen

The cemetery at Menen also dates from 1917 (above) and was also extensively adapted in the fifties (Vancoillie 2013). It is a meadow with trees (mainly oaks and acorns) and bushes, with lying granite gravestones (52 x 52 cm), with up to twenty names per stone. This is a design that is characteristic for the VDK's chief architect Robert Tischler, who focused on the military collective of the deceased and was not interested in the fate of the individual (Lurz 1983: 69). A huge number of soldiers is buried at Menen, 47,864 soldiers, because bodies from other cemeteries have been moved over to this location.[43] The cemetery covers about three hectares and has a polygonal structure – roughly a pentagon – with an octagonal chapel roughly in the middle. This chapel, built of large blocks of pink iron sandstone ('Wesersandstein'), is highlighted right at the entrance, because the gate of the entrance building gives access to a stone path leading up to the chapel. This setup invites the visitor to 'march up' to the chapel. The cross on top of the chapel's pointed roof – a large cross built in the wall – and especially the extensive religious imagery inside imply that the deceased are commemorated at Menen from a sacral perspective, providing consolation to and triggering praise from visitors in terms of Christian religion. The relief above the architrave of the entrance door displays a lying angel blowing a trumpet, which reminds one immediately of the seven angels with trumpets in Revelation (Rev. 8.7, 8, 10, 12; 9.1, 13; 11.15). It may represent the seventh angel who announces the rule of God and his Messiah in the context of the heavenly courtroom (Rev. 11.15-19). If so, this implies that the visitor is invited, so to say, to enter the virtual world depicted in the book of Revelation.[44] The setting, with a sacred building in the middle, is very similar to the Second World War military cemetery at Donsbrüggen (Germany), which was also designed by Robert Tischler (Figure 5.2). The building at Donsbrüggen is rectangular, but it also has a long stone path leading up to the entrance and a lying angel blowing a trumpet above it.[45]

The interconnections with the book of Revelation are strongly supported by the mosaics with twenty-eight (4 x 7) symbolic figures on the walls inside the chapel, designed by Franz Grau (1959).[46] Some of them clearly point to imagery deriving from Revelation, including a wounded lamb with a small halo and the characters

---

43. http://www.volksbund.de/kriegsgraeberstaette/menen.html [consulted 14 April 2017]; https://inventaris.onroerenderfgoed.be/erfgoedobjecten/95675 [consulted 14 April 2017]; Freytag and Van Driessche (2011: 191) mention a slightly higher number of 48,049 deceased.

44. The anonymous author of http://www.volksbund.de/kriegsgraeberstaette/menen.html [consulted 14 April 2017] mentions that the imagery of the walls derives from a picture Bible.

45. I owe this observation to Dr Jan de Vries, Nijmegen (The Netherlands).

46. They were produced by the Firma Vereinigte Süddeutsche Werkstätten für Mosaik und Glasmalerei GmbH, München-Solln.

Figure 2 Memorial building by Robert Tischler. The German Military Cemetery at Donsbrüggen, Germany. Photo: Jan de Vries

Alpha and Omega.[47] Five of the eight octagonal interior walls are covered with dark grey or green mosaics on which figures in gold are illuminated in varying ways, depending on where one stands and whether the light comes from the entrance or from one of the windows in the two other walls.[48] One of these golden figures displays an abstract city with many slimline towers, which has been interpreted as the heavenly Jerusalem (Rev. 21; Freytag and Van Driessche 2011: 171). I cannot discuss the entire pictorial programme of this chapel's interior here and would like to highlight only two points. The lower symbol on three of the walls concerns various types of tree, sometimes just above an extension of the wall as a simple altar on which a book of names can be displayed. In this funerary context, highlighting symbols from Revelation, these trees plausibly symbolize the 'tree of life' mentioned in Rev. 22.14: 'Blessed are those who wash their robes [NRSV; cf. 7.14; KJV: who 'do his commandments'], so that they have the right to the tree of life and may enter the city by the gates.' This imagery would imply that the fallen soldiers are vindicated and have access already to the heavenly Jerusalem, analogous to the fate of the ancient martyrs.[49]

47. For a description of the interior of the chapel, see Freytag and Van Driessche 2011: 216–17; https://inventaris.onroerenderfgoed.be/erfgoedobjecten/95675 [consulted 14 April 2017].

48. The mosaics were created by Franz Grau and dated to 1959 by Welscher (1999: 124). See also Freytag and Van Driessche 2011: 216–17. The twenty-eight symbols include the Christ monogram IHS, the cross, a winged lion and a winged ram, angels with books, various birds, a chalice with bunches of grapes, ears of wheat, lambs and trees.

49. Freytag and Van Driessche (2011: 171, 216–17) argue that the imagery of the chapel symbolizes the sacrifical cult and the soldiers' resurrection, and also suggest that their death was compared to Jesus' death.

Figure 3 Mosaic of the Tree of Life, by Franz Grau. Chapel of the German Military Cemetery at Menen, Belgium. Photo: Jan Willem van Henten

The second point concerns the polished octagonal pillar at the centre of the chapel, which is guarded by four animal figures who stand with their back attached to the pillar in the form of a cross. These animals are small lions reminding one of the reliefs of lions on the square memorial in bronze at Hooglede, which is no surprise because the pillar was created by the same artist as the memorial, Fritz Schmoll genannt Eisenwerth (above).[50] The number 'four' reminds one of the four creatures around the divine throne in Revelation 4–5, the first of which is identified as a lion (4.7). Strikingly, the elongated capital that connects the pillar at its top to the red-brick ceiling is of humanlike figures, four adult women with children of various ages, who seem to be mourning. Obviously, visitors are inclined to interpret these mourning figures from the perspective of the funerary context. Plausible

---

50. Küppers 2003/4: 351; Freytag and Van Driessche 2011: 216. Fritz Schmoll genannt Eisenwerth himself refers to the animals as lions in a handwritten invoice to the VDK dated March 14, 1959, preserved in the VDK archives.

associations are the identification of the women and children with the spouses and children of the deceased soldiers, or of the young soldiers themselves with their mothers. This very unusual detail of a capital existing partly of human figures may well be another evocation of Revelation imagery. In Jesus' decree for his followers in Philadelphia (Rev. 3.7-13) he makes a promise to those who have kept his word of patient endurance to keep them from the hour of trial, the last judgement (3.10), and also to reward those who 'conquer' by giving them access to the heavenly Jerusalem and making them a pillar in God's temple: 'If you conquer, I will make you a pillar in the temple of my God; you will never go out of it. I will write on you the name of my God, and the name of the city of my God, the new Jerusalem that comes down from my God out of heaven, and my own new name' (Rev. 3.12). This symbolism of the pillar in God's temple points to the vindication of the soldiers as well as their relatives, similar to the message of Rev. 22.2, 14 discussed above. For the visitor of the chapel, this imagery has the same double function as bishop Winnington-Ingram's words: it points to the vindication and heavenly reward of the fallen and, therefore, also implies consolation for those staying behind.[51]

3. The Commemoration of Soldiers in the St Edmund King and Martyr Church in Dudley and All Saints' Church at Huntingdon

In the United Kingdom, reinterpretations of fallen soldiers' death in the context of post-war memorials interconnect more explicitly with martyrdom traditions than the two German cemeteries at Flanders. I will conclude this contribution with a brief discussion of two cases in which fallen soldiers are commemorated by associating them with earlier famous heroes who are remembered as martyrs.[52]

---

51. Cf. Freytag and Van Driessche 2011: 171: 'Wieder ist die Intention, die auferstandenen Soldaten symbolisch in die sakrale Sphäre zu heben und den Besuchern Trost zu spenden, indem das Leben nach dem Tod gepriesen wird'.

52. E.g. the small English Martyrs Memorial Chapel at Preston (north-west of Manchester), which is part of the Roman-Catholic Church of St Thomas of Canterbury and the English Martyrs, i.e. Roman Catholics who were executed under treason legislation (1534–1680). The chapel was converted from the church baptistery. Its name suggests that it is devoted to the English Martyrs of previous centuries, but in fact it commemorates 142 soldiers who belonged to the parish and had fallen during the First World War. The names of the dead are inscribed on the oak panels at either side of the altar of the chapel, with a crucifixion scene in the centre. On the wall opposite the altar there is a stained glass window with the words, 'Pray for the soldiers of this parish who died in the Great War, 1914 to 1918 to whose memory this chapel is dedicated'. See https://www.warmemorialsonline.org.uk/memorial/190935/ [consulted 25 April 2018]. A direct qualification of fallen soldiers as martyrs is found on a simple monument, with a cross on top, in a hamlet west of Itchen Abbas and north-east of Winchester. The stone base of the cross has an inscription that has 'Martyr Worthy' as heading, twelve names of fallen soldiers below it in smaller characters, and a comment in large characters below the names: 'Faithful unto Death'. See https://www.warmemorialsonline.org.uk/memorial/197224/ [consulted 25 April 2018].

Inside the Anglican church of St Edmund King and Martyr in Dudley (West Midlands, UK) is a wooden pedestal surmounted by a painted plaster figure of St Edmund.[53] St Edmund was King of East Anglia from 855 CE to 870 CE. Abbo of Fleury tells how he was defeated during one of the Viking invasions and refused to denounce his Christian identity and venerate pagan deities. As a consequence, he was bound to a tree and executed with arrows, and finally beheaded.[54] There is a dedicatory inscription on a plaque at the base of the statue that associates the saint with the fallen soldiers of the First World War:

> THIS STATUE OF
> ST EDMUND KING AND MARTYR
> IS IN MEMORY OF
> THE MEN
> WHO GAVE THEIR LIVES
> IN THE WAR
> 1914–1918[55]

A much more complex case that interconnects fallen soldiers with martyrs and builds on several religious motifs and biblical passages concerns All Saints' Church at Huntingdon, Cambridgeshire. The Church has beautiful stained-glass windows, many of which depict saints who are important in the Anglican tradition (Pevsner 1968: 269). The east window depicts the 'tree of life', with numerous saints and images on its branches.[56] On top is the monogram of Jesus. Below the monogram there are four registers, the two highest of which depict two series of four saints, most of whom have been venerated as martyrs.[57] The highest ones, with the largest figures, show St Martin, St George, St Oswald and St Edmund with their banners – four saints who are important in the English tradition.[58] The second register from above shows older Christian saints: St John the Baptist, St Felicitas, St Dorothea and St Pancratius. St Felicitas may be the companion of Perpetua with

---

53. http://www.iwm.org.uk/memorials/item/memorial/48056 [consulted 25 April 2018].
54. Young 2015. http://dx.doi.org/10.1080/0015587X.2015.1030909 [consulted 26 April 2018].
55. http://www.iwm.org.uk/memorials/item/memorial/48056 [consulted 25 April 2018].
56. East window, stained glass by the Kempe Company, 1920.
57. Exception: St Martin.
58. For St Edmund see above. St George, executed at the order of Emperor Diocletian, became the patron saint of England in the Tudor period and is celebrated on St George's Day (23 April) – Meier 2010: 161–2. St Oswald was King of Northumbria from 634 until his death. He is venerated as a saint because he was killed during the Battle of Maserfield and, as Bede tells us, prayed for the soul of his soldiers when he was about to die – Bede, *Hist. eccl.* 3; Butler 1756–1759 s.v. St Oswald King and Martyr; Stancliffe and Cambridge 1995; Smith 2008: 598. St Martin was appointed bishop of Tours in 371 CE, and became a popular saint within several Christian denominations – Meier 2010: 131–2.

the same name, who died with Perpetua in Carthage in 203 CE; or Felicitas of Rome, who had seven sons and was tortured to death with them during the rule of Antoninus Pius (138–61 CE).[59] Another but less likely interpretation in the context of the other saints in this register reads this name as a corruption of Felec, a local saint from Cornwall from the fifth or sixth century.[60] St Dorothea died, according to tradition, in 311 as a virgin martyr at Caesarea Mazaca (Spain; Meier 2010: 49–50). Saint Pancras allegedly died as a martyr, being 14 years old, in Rome in 304 CE. The one but lowest register, with smaller images, concerns Jesus' birth, crucifixion (two scenes in the centre), and burial. The lowest register shows four angels carrying unfolded scrolls inscribed with quotations from Revelation.[61] These words include an adapted quotation of Rev. 22.14 (according to part of the manuscript tradition): 'Blessed are they that do his commandments, that they may have right to the tree of life, which is in the midst of the paradise of God'. The first part of the quotation matches the KJV of this verse: 'Blessed are they that do his commandments, that they may have right to the tree of life and may enter in through the gates into the city'. The last part of the inscription is an explanation of the meaning of the 'tree of life', which is a symbol of paradise, here identified with the heavenly Jerusalem.

Interestingly, the 'tree of life' of the east window, with saints and martyrs, is explicitly connected with the commemoration of those who fell during the First World War. A dedicatory stone tablet, set within a carved wooden frame, is placed on the north wall of the nave. It states that the window glass was dedicated by survivors of the war. It commemorates the 55 (?)[62] soldiers fallen during the war as follows:[63]

† TO THE GLORY OF GOD†
THE EAST WINDOW OF THIS CHURCH AND
THIS TABLET HAVE BEEN OFFERED BY MANY
WHOSE

59. Both saints with the name Felicitas are included in the Martyrologium Romanum, and their 'anniversaries' are 7 March and 23 November respectively.

60. https://en.wikipedia.org/wiki/Felec_of_Cornwall [consulted 25 April 2018].

61. http://www.iwm.org.uk/memorials/item/memorial/288 [consulted 25 April 2018].

62. There is conflicting information about the number of names: the Imperial War Museums mention 63 names of the deceased on the memorial, but list 66 names: https://www.iwm.org.uk/memorials/item/memorial/288 [consulted 25 April 2018]. The Roll of Honour of the Ministry of Defence and the Royal British Legion mentions only 55 names: http://www.roll-of-honour.com/Huntingdonshire/HuntingdonAllSaints.html [consulted 25 April 2018].

63. See also the plaque in the churchyard with the inscription: *TO THE MEN OF / 1914–1918 WHO / WROUGHT FOR / MANKIND A GREAT / DELIVERANCE / ALSO TO THOSE WHO / IN 1939-1945 / SERVED AND DIED / TO PRESERVE OUR / GLORIOUS HERITAGE.* – http://www.iwm.org.uk/memorials/item/memorial/66203 [consulted 25 April 2018].

> HOMES, LIBERTIES AND LIVES WERE
> PRESERVED THROUGH THE SACRIFICE OF THOSE WHO DIED
> AND THE DEVOTION OF
> THEIR COMRADES, IN REMEMBRANCE OF
> ... [names of fallen]
> WHO GAVE THEIR LIVES IN THE GREAT WAR 1914-1919
> **"THEY WERE A WALL UNTO US BOTH NIGHT AND DAY"**
> I SAM XXV 16.[64]

The inscription expresses thanks by those who survived for the sacrifice of the fallen (note the words 'sacrifice of' and 'gave their lives'), whose death is interpreted as a beneficial death. The soldiers saved their fellow-citizens (and their possessions) and enabled them to live on in freedom. It also commemorates the devotion of the deceased's fellow-soldiers who remained alive. The quotation of 1 Sam. 25.16 ('They were a wall unto us both night and day') interprets the patriotic self-sacrifice from a religious perspective, highlighting the protection offered by the soldiers 'day and night'.[65] This quotation also invites the visitor to read the inscription in combination with the message that the window expresses, which would associate the fallen soldiers with the 'tree of life' saints. The inscription clearly states that the window and the tablet belong together. The analogy between the fallen and the saints of the tree suggests that the soldiers too fulfilled God's commandments in extreme circumstances at the expense of their life; and, as a consequence, that they deserve a similar reward, i.e., 'have a right to the tree of life', as the quote from Revelation in the lowest register of the window states. Such a fate is neither depicted by the tree nor stated by the inscription on the tablet but seems to be the logical implication of the interconnection of the fallen soldiers and the mostly martyred saints of the tree, who according to Church tradition have already been resurrected.

4. Conclusion

My search into the commemoration of fallen soldiers of the First World War as martyrs started with a very explicit quote from Bishop Arthur Winnington-Ingram, who called deceased British soldiers 'martyrs' and compared them with St Stephen, the first Christian martyr. My case studies of two German military cemeteries in West Flanders, Belgium, a statue of Saint Edmund connected with

---

64. http://www.iwm.org.uk/memorials/item/memorial/288; http://www.roll-of-honour.com/Huntingdonshire/HuntingdonAllSaints.html [both consulted 25 April 2018]. Emphasis by the present author.

65. This quotation is taken from the story of David and Nabal, when David's men claim to have supplied Nabal (and his possessions) services of unrequited protection all through the season, so that his peaceful agricultural activities can be continued unhindered. As such, the biblical context is quite different from the recontextualized text in the inscription.

First World War soldiers in the Anglican church of St Edmund King and Martyr in Dudley (West Midlands, UK), and a stained glass window with a memorial inscription in All Saints' Church at Huntingdon (Cambridgeshire, UK), show implicit and explicit associations with martyrdom. The artwork by Franz Grau and Fritz Schmoll genannt Eisenwerth builds on Christian pictorial and literary traditions that suggest that the soldiers are vindicated as martyrs, and sojourn in the heavenly Jerusalem with God and Jesus Christ. A cluster of allusions to passages from Revelation helps to articulate this message (Rev. 3.7-13; 4.3, 7; 20.11-15, 21; 21.5-7 and 22.14).

The mosaic at Hooglede may also build on the iconographical traditions of the *Dominus legem dat*, the *Majestas domini* and the Deesis. A more explicit commemoration of the fallen soldiers as martyrs is found in the two churches within the United Kingdom by way of a direct association with previous martyrs, either St Edmund (Dudley), or a combination of early Christian and older English martyrs (Huntingdon). The latter commemoration also builds on traditions about the 'tree of life' and paradise, and quotes Rev. 22.14 and 1 Sam. 25.16, which function here – in the framework of martyrdom – as pointers to the soldiers' beneficial death and their reward in Paradise.

Bibliography

Arbeiter, Achim (2007), 'Die mosaiken', in: Jürgen Rasch and Achim Arbeiter (eds.), *Das Mausoleum der Constantina in Rom*. Mainz: Philipp von Zabern, 124–47.

Bede, Venerabilis (731), *Historia ecclesiastica gentis Anglorum*.

Bell, Stuart (2013), 'Malign or Maligned? – Arthur Winnington-Ingram, Bishop of London, in the First World War', *Journal for the History of Modern Theology* 20: 117–33.

Berger, Robert (1926), *Die Darstellung des thronenden Christus in der romanischen Kunst*. Reutlingen: Gryphius Verlag.

Butler, Alban (1756–1759), *The Lives of the Fathers, Martyrs, and Other Principal Saints: Compiled from Original Monuments, and Other Authentick Records*, 4 vols. London: n.p.

Capdevilla, Luc, and Danièle Voldman (2006), *War Dead: Western Societies and the Casualties of War*. Transl. by Richard Veasey. Edinburgh: Edinburgh University Press.

Carpenter, Spencer Cecil (1949), *Winnington-Ingram: The Biography of Arthur Foley Winnington-Ingram, Bishop of London, 1901–1939*. London: Hodder and Stoughton.

Connor, Carolyn (2016), *Saints and Spectacle: Byzantine Mosaics in their Cultural Setting*. New York: Oxford University Press.

Cutler, Anthony (1987), 'Under the Sign of the Deesis', *Dumbarton Oaks Papers* 41: 145–54.

Evans, Suzanne (2007), *Mothers of Heroes, Mothers of Martyrs: World War I and the Politics of Grief*. Montreal/Kingston: McGill-Queens University Press.

Freytag, Annette and Van Driessche, Thomas (2011), 'Die Deutschen Soldatenfriedhöfe des Ersten Weltkriegs in Flandern', *Relicta* 7: 163–238.

Fuhrmeister, Christian (2007), 'Der Volksbund Deutsche Kriegsgräberfürsorge e.V. im 20. und 21. Jahrhundert. Bemerkungen aus Sicht der politischen Ikonographie', in: Ellen Ueberschär (ed.), *Soldaten und andere Opfer?: Die Täter-Opfer-Problematik in der deutschen Erinnerungskultur und das Gedenken an die Opfer von Krieg und Gewaltherrschaft*. Rehburg-Loccum: Verlag Evangelische Akademie, 45–66.

Gilsdorf, Sean (2012), 'Deēsis Deconstructed: Imagining Intercession in the Medieval West', *Viator* 43: 131–74.
Goebel, Stefan (2013), 'Brüchige Kontinuität: Kriegerdenkmäler und Kriegsgedenken im 20.Jahrhundert', in: Hettling and Echternkamp, *Gefallenengedenken*, 199–224.
Gudenberg, Eberhard von (1969), *Volksbund Deutsche Kriegsgräberfürsorge e.V.: 50 Jahre Dienst am Frieden*. Kassel: Pressehaus.
Henten, Jan Willem van (1997). *The Maccabean Martyrs as Saviours of the Jewish People: A Study of 2 and 4 Maccabees*, JSJSup 57. Leiden: Brill.
Henten, Jan Willem van (2009). 'Martyrdom, Jesus' Passion and Barbarism', *BibInt* 17: 239–64.
Henten, Jan Willem van (2011), 'Martyrium II. Martyriumidee', *Reallexikon für Antike und Christentum* 24: 300–27.
Henten, Jan Willem van (2012a), 'Noble Death and Martyrdom in Antiquity', in: Sebastian Fuhrmann and Regina Grundmann (eds.), *Martyriumsvorstellungen in Antike und Mittelalter: Leben oder Sterben für Gott?* Leiden: Brill, 85–110.
Henten, Jan Willem van (2012b), 'The Concept of Martyrdom in Revelation', in: Jörg Frey, James A. Kellhoffer and Franz Toth (eds), *Die Johannesapokalypse: Kontexte und Konzepte / The Revelation of John: Contexts and Concepts*. Tübingen: Mohr Siebeck, 587–618.
Henten, Jan Willem van (2020). 'Early Jewish and Christian Martyrdom', in: Paul Middleton (ed.), *The Wiley Blackwell Companion to Christian Martyrdom*. Chichester: Wiley-Blackwell, 72–87.
Henten, Jan Willem van, and Ihab Saloul (2020). 'Introduction', in: Ihab Saloul and Jan Willem van Henten (eds), *Martyrdom: Canonisation, Contestation and Afterlives*. Amsterdam: Amsterdam University Press, 11–31.
Hettling, Manfred and Echternkamp, Jörg (2013), *Gefallenengedenken im globalen Vergleich: nationale Tradition, politische Legitimation und Individualisierung der Erinnerung*. München: Oldenbourg.
Hettling, Manfred and Jörg Echternkamp (2013), 'Heroisierung und Opferstilisierung: Grundelemente des Gefallenengedenkens von 1813 bis heute', in: Hettling and Echternkamp, *Gefallenengedenken*, 123–58.
Ketelsen, Uwe-K. (1985), 'Die Jugend von Langemarck. Ein poetisch-politisches Motiv der Zwischenkriegszeit', in: Thomas Koebner, Ralph-Peter Janz and Frank Trommler (eds), *'Mit uns zieht die neue Zeit'. Der Mythos der Jugend*. Frankfurt a. M.: Edition Suhrkampf, 68–97.
King, Alexander MacIan (1993), *The Politics of Meaning in the Commemoration of the First World War in Britain 1914–1939*. Dissertation. University College London.
Kirchmeier, Fritz (2014), *Eine Festung, die eine Friedhof ist: in Stein gefassten Ideologie – 75 Jahre Totenburg Quero*. Leaflet of the VDK, http://docplayer.org/30529801-Eine-festung-die-ein-friedhof-ist.html [consulted April 26, 2018].
Kohlberg, Etan (1997), *Medieval Muslim Views on Martyrdom*. Amsterdam: Koninklijke Nederlandse Akademie van Wetenschappen.
Kuberek, Monika (1990), 'Die Kriegsgräberstätten des Volksbundes Deutsche Kriegsgräberfürsorge', in: Michael Hutt (ed.), *Unglücklich das Land, das Helden nötig hat, Leben und Sterben in den Kriegsdenkmälern des Ersten und Zweiten Weltkrieges*. Marburg: Jonas Verlag, 75–90.
Küppers, Barbara (2003/2004), *Fritz Schmoll genannt Eisenwerth (1883–1963): Kunstgewerbler, Innenarchitekt und Bildhauer in München*. Dissertation Technische Universität München/ Weimar: VDG.

Lurz, Meinhold (1983), '"... ein Stück Heimat in fremder Erde": Die Heldenhaine und Totenburgen des Volksbunds Deutsche Kriegsgräberfürsorge', *Arch+* 71: 66–70.

Markus, Kersti (2013), 'Baptism and the King's Coronation: Visual Rhetoric of the Valdemar Dynasty: Some Scanian and Danish Baptismal Fonts', in: Krista Kodres and Anu Mänd (eds), *Images and Objects in Ritual Practices in Medieval and Early Modern Northern and Central Europe*. Newcastle: Cambridge Scholars Publishing, 122–42.

Meer, Frederik van der (1938), *Maiestas Domini: théophanies de l'Apocalypse dans l'art chrétien: étude sur les orgines d'une iconographie spéciale du Christ*. Rome: Pontificio Istituto di Archeologia Cristiana.

Meier, Esther (2010), *Handbuch der Heiligen*. Darmstadt: Wissenschaftliche Buchgesellschaft.

Mosse, George (1979), 'National Cemeteries and National Revival: The Cult of the Fallen Soldiers in Germany', *Journal of Contemporary History* 14: 1–20.

Mosse, George (1990), *Fallen Soldiers: Reshaping the Memory of the World Wars*. New York: Oxford University Press.

Neff, Amy (2007), 'Byzantine Icons, Franciscan Prayer: Images of Intercession and Ascent in the Upper Church of San Francesco, Assisi', in Timothy Johnson (ed.), *Franciscans at Prayer*. Leiden: Brill, 357–82.

Noga-Banai, Galit (2015), 'Dominus legem dat: von der Tempelbeute zur römischen Bildtinvention', *Römische Quartalschrift* 110: 157–74.

Onasch, Konrad (1993), *Lexikon Liturgie und Kunst der Ostkirche, unter Berücksichtigung der Alten Kirche*. Rev. ed. Berlin: Buchverlag Union.

O'Neill, Philip (1996), *Enamels of Limoges 1100–1350*. New York: Metropolitan Museum of Art.

Pevsner, Nikolaus (1968), *Bedfordshire and the County Huntingdon and Peterborough. Buildings of England*. Harmondsworth: Penguin.

Pickles, Katie (2007), *Transnational Outrage: The Death and Commemoration of Edith Cavell*. Basingstoke: Palgrave Macmillan.

Poilpret, Anne-Orange (2005), *Maiestas Domini: une image de l'Eglise en Occident, Ve-IXe siècle*. Paris: Cerf, 2005.

Roberts, Helene (1998), *Encyclopedia of Comparative Iconography: Themes Depicted in Works of Art*. Vol. 1. Chicago: Fitzroy Dearborn.

Schiller, Gertrud (1971), *Die Ikonographie der Christlichen Kunst*. Vol. 3, die Auferstehung und Erhöhung Christi. Gütersloh: Gütersloher Verlag.

Schiller, Gertrud (1980), *Die Ikonographie der Christlichen Kunst*. Vol. 4.2, Maria. Gütersloh: Mohn.

Smith, Julia (2008), 'Saints and their Cults', in: T. F. X. Noble (ed.), *The Cambridge History of Christianity*. Vol. 3. Cambridge: Cambridge University Press, 581–605.

Snape, Michael (2008), *The Royal Army's Chaplain Department 1796–1953: Clergy under Fire*. Woodbridge: The Boydell Press.

Soltau, Hans (1981), *Volksbund Deutsche Kriegsgräberfürsorge: Sein Werden und Wirken*. Kassel: Volksbund Deutsche Kriegsgräberfürsorge.

Spera, Lucrezia (2000), 'Traditio Legis et Clavium', in: Fabrizio Bisconti (ed.), *Temi di iconografia paleocristiana*. Rome: Pontificio istituto di archeologia cristiana, 288–93.

Stancliffe, Clare, and Eric Cambridge (1995), *Oswald: Northumbrian King to European Saint*. London: Paul Watkins.

Supercic, Ivan (2009), *Croatia in the Late Middle Ages and the Renaissance: A Cultural Survey*. Philip Wilson Publishers, 2009.

Vancoillie, Jan (2013), *De Duitse militaire begraafplaats Menen Wald. Geschiedenis van de Duitse militaire graven in Zuid-West-Vlaanderen*. Wevelgem: Jan Vancoillie.

Vancoillie, Jan (2017), 'From Field Grave to Comrades' Grave. The German First World War Graves on the Flanders Front'. *RIHA Journal* 0162 | 27 June 2017. http://www.riha-journal.org/articles/2017/0150-0176-special-issue-war-graves/0162-vancoillie [consulted 23 April 2018].

Waal, Henry van de a.o. (1985), *An Iconographic Classification System*. Haarlem: North-Holland Pub. Co.

Walter, Christopher (1968), 'Two Notes on the Deesis', *Revue des études byzantines* 26: 311–36.

Walter, Christopher (1970), 'Further Notes on the Deësis', *Revue des études byzantines*: 161–87.

Welscher, Leonore (1999), *Rhythmus in Form und Farbe: Lebenswerk des Künstlers Franz Grau*. Hannover: Benatzky Druck und Medien.

Winnington-Ingram, Arthur (1914), *A Day of God: Being Five Addresses on the Subject of the Present War*. London: Wells, Gardner, Darton.

Winter, Jay (1998), *Sites of Memory. Sites of Mourning: The Great War in European Cultural History*. Cambridge: Cambridge University Press.

Wolffe, John (2015), '"Martyrs as Really as St Stephen was a Martyr"? Commemorating the British Dead', *International Journal for the Study of the Christian Church* 15: 23–38.

Woodfin, Warren T. (2011), *The Embodied Icon: Liturgical Vestments and Sacramental Power in Byzantium*. Oxford: Oxford University Press.

Young, Francis (2015), 'St Edmund, King and Martyr in Popular Memory since the Reformation', *Folklore* 126: 159–176. http://dx.doi.org/10.1080/0015587X.2015.1030909 [consulted April 26, 2018].

Part II

KINGS

THE TWO WOMEN IN SOLOMON'S JUDGEMENT: READING CROSS-TEXTUALLY WITH CHINESE SOURCES*

Wei Huang

Introduction

The story of Solomon's judgement (1 Kgs 3.16-28) has been generally viewed as a story demonstrating Solomon's judicial wisdom. Readers from Chinese contexts are familiar with the story of two women judicially contending for one child too, because different versions of the story were recorded both in Chinese Buddhist scriptures and in Chinese secular writings.

This essay focuses mainly on presenting the differences between the two literatures, biblical and Chinese, on two issues: the judge's judicial wisdom, and the two women's personal social status. The juxtaposition of the Hebrew and Chinese sources will reveal how cultural contexts produce variants. At the same time, it will be seen how the female characters are manoeuvred to support the social norms and customs in both contexts.

It is not surprising that Chinese people in general are not familiar with the Hebrew Bible. But, when they hear about the story of Solomon's judgement, they would soon find it as familiar as if they have heard it somewhere else. This is indeed the case. The story has its Chinese counterparts which have been transmitted and retold in various Chinese literature strands. Owing much to the pioneering research of Hugo Gressmann, there has long been awareness that there are more than twenty-two similar stories in world folklore and literature about the dispute between two women about a single living child (Gressmann 1907). Because of the existence of numerous parallels and analogues in different cultures, tracing the provenance of the theme story

---

* An early version of this paper was presented at the Society of Biblical Literature International Meeting in Berlin, summer 2017, in the seminar session on Contextual Interpretation of the Bible. Special appreciation is due to Athalya Brenner-Idan, who inspired me a great deal in the formation of this essay.

became a natural query for scholars.¹ This essay will focus on the differences between the two women by comparing the biblical story with other Chinese versions. Even if the narratives have a common story of two women contending for one child in a judicial scene, they are differently constructed in regard to the marital status or the situation of the two women. It can be clearly seen that the authors manipulate the two female characters in order to fit them into the cultural context of their own tradition.

Juxtaposing the Different Chinese Versions

There is more than one version of the story in Chinese literatures.² Zhongshu Qian [錢鍾書] (1910–1998), the very famous Chinese classicist, also a critic and a writer, has collected a variety of different versions of this story in Chinese traditional literature, the Chinese Buddhist scripture and the Bible (Qian 2007: vol. iii, 1587). Qian was most likely the very first Chinese scholar who mentioned the story of Solomon's judgement together with those Chinese versions. In his huge four-volume work *Limited Views: Essays on Ideas and Letters* [*Guanzhui bian* 管錐編], first published in 1979,³ the stories were categorized and generalized under the subject 'settling a lawsuit under careful scrutiny' [察情斷案] (vol. iii, 5). In the time period without computer and electronic search tools, it was extraordinary that Qian selected and compiled the materials depending on his own memory of the massive literature. This voluminous work 'is now properly recognized as the culmination of Zhongshu Qian's study of literature, broadly conceived, in both the Chinese and Western traditions' (Egan 1998: 1).

Qian's work, however, was not organized in a modern academic manner. It followed a traditional Chinese form of 'random notes' or 'reading notes', rather than a full-scale classical commentary or a formal paper. He juxtaposed the texts that belong to different traditions and tried to show a connection between them. Of course, the stories were taken out of their original contexts. Qian claimed that this was not simply a comparative method. His aim was to 'strike a connection' [打通] between Chinese literature and foreign literature in order to extract new meaning (as stated by Egan 1998: 15–16).⁴ This 'strike a connection' is truly quite a vague term which Qian did not explain much in his work. Ronald Egan discussed the term's meaning and Qian's methodology in the Introduction to his selective translation of *Limited Views*. He points out that 'the connections' Qian strikes

---

1. For instance, see Brewster 1962. In his essay Brewster mentions that many scholars are in favour of the Hebrew Bible story as the original, while some have defended the originality of the Indian version, known also in China.

2. Gaster (1969: 493) mentioned two in Chinese classic literature.

3. Unfortunately, the chapter discussed in the article was not included in Ronald Egan's selected translation of *Limited Views* (Egan 1998).

4. The phrase *da tong* [打通] is his own explanation. Qian explained his purpose in a letter to his friend.

between Chinese and Western works served two purposes, one of which is to investigate common tendencies in language, aesthetic principle, or thought (Egan 1998: 17–22). When Qian freshly juxtaposed several passages or items drawn from their original settings, 'striking a connection' not only just served to highlight similarities/dissimilarities but also to inform oneself 'about the many permutations of an idea or variations on a theme that human consciousness has created' (Egan 1998: 22). That is to say, the purpose of our research is to bring 'the connections' between the two (Chinese and Western) or among more cultural traditions, allowing mutual understanding in a cross-cultural manner.

For us Chinese, it was/is unlikely to admit biblical texts as one of the religious and cultural resources in our traditions. The method Qian practised, i.e. juxtaposition, became obviously valuable for us to understand a 'new' text from the context of our 'old' texts. As biblical scholar Archie C. C. Lee has pointed out, the fact that several great living religions have their deep roots in Asia should be taken seriously in biblical interpretation (Lee 2000), which he termed 'cross-textual interpretation' (Lee 1993a; 1993b). A fruitful cross-textual interpretation requires a creative dialogue and interaction between the two (or more) texts.[5] The confidence for a possible cross-textual interpretation lies in the belief that we would understand ourselves better when we understand others properly.

In this essay I shall bring the Chinese sources into a cross-textual reading. Two of these sources, the *Fengsu Tongyi* and the *Chalk Circle,* are from non-religious settings; the other two, *Sūtra of the Wise and the Foolish* and *Jātakas,* are from Buddhist traditions.

Cutting or Tugging?

The *Fengsu tongyi* [風俗通義] (*Comprehensive Discussion of Customs*) is a collection of stories and legends about folk customs compiled by the Late Han official-scholar Ying Shao [應劭] (140–206 CE) around 195 CE. Ying Shao claimed that his work 'is comprehensive with regard to the wrongs and errors in prevailing customs' (in Knechtges and Chang 2014: 1945). The story about the two women and one baby boy was a short one, occupying a small portion in one chapter of the book. Instead of cutting the boy in half as Solomon required, the judge asked the two women to compete by grasping the boy from an attendant who was holding the boy at the same distance from each.

Much later in the Yuan dynasty (1271–1368), the story appeared in a longer play script, *The Chalk Circle* [灰闌記], written by Li Qianfu [李潛夫]. The text which we have today is the one anthologized by Zang Maoxun [臧懋循] (1550-1620) in his collection entitled *Yuan qu xuan* [元曲选] (*An Anthology of Yuan*

---

5. Archie Lee used 'Text A' to indicate Asian texts, while 'Text B' refers to the Bible (Lee 2002).

Opera) (Li 2014).⁶ In this play script, the story was obviously expanded. Not only do the two women have names, but also more characters were added in the story. Similar to the version in the *Fengsu tongyi*, the judge orders the two women to compete by pulling the child out of a chalk circle drawn around him on the floor.

The 'tug of war' motif can also be discerned in the two Buddhist versions. Originally the *Jātaka* was written in Pāli, the sacred language of a branch of Buddhism known as Theravāda Buddhism (Appleton 2016). It contains more than 500 stories about the previous lives of the Buddha (or the Bodhisatta, which was his name before his awakening).⁷ The *Jātaka* tradition can be traced further back to the third century BCE (Huang 2013: 16). Early Buddhists used those stories to illustate the biography of the Buddha, and the long path from Bodhisatta to Buddhahood. In their view, the stories were not simply folktales but instructional tales. The *Jātaka* stories are very popular in Theravāda Buddhist countries, i.e. Sri Lanka, Burma, Laos, Cambodia and Thailand. Even if it was never fully translated into Chinese as a canon, some of the *Jātaka* stories were known to the Chinese through the Chinese version of the Tibetan *Tripiṭaka* (Xianlin Ji 1963: 76).

One of the Chinese sources, the *Sūtra of the Wise and the Foolish*, was labelled as foreign in Qian's book: the most obvious reason for this is that the story is not among the Confucian classics, but included in the Buddhist scriptures. In fact, the transmission of Indian Buddhist narratives to China was a long and complicated process.⁸ The monk Seng You [僧祐] compiled the *Chu Sanzang ji ji* [出三藏集記] (*Collected Notes on the Making of the Tripiṭaka*), which included the *Sūtra of the Wise and the Foolish*. Seng You also made some bibliographical comments, suggesting that the *Sūtra of the Wise and the Foolish* was recorded and edited by eight monks as early as the year 445 CE. The *Sūtra* was composed much later than the *Jātaka* and a bit later than the *Fengsu tongyi*. Here is the relevant chronological table of composition for the four sources.

Jātaka	3rd century BCE
Fengsu tongyi	195 CE
Sūtra of the Wise and the Foolish	445 CE
Chalk Circle	13th–14th centuries CE

With regard to the story we are discussing here, in *Jātaka* the sage (as one of the Buddha's previous lives) draws a line on the floor, lays the child in the middle of the line,

---

6. More than 500 years after its composition, the Yuan opera *The Chalk Circle* was rearranged into the Peking opera and many other local operas through its European and American manifestations: Du 1995: 307–25.

7. The Pāli text was collated by Fausbøll 1877–1896. For the English translation of the *Jātaka*, see Cowell and Rouse 1907. Based on these two, Guo and Huang translated more than 100 stories into Chinese (Guo and Huang 1985).

8. The role Central Asia played in the process was an important issue (Mair 1993: 1).

and asks each of the two women to pull one hand of the child. In the *Sūtra of the Wise and the Foolish*, the king (as one of the previous lives of the Buddha) does not draw a line, but asks the two women to engage in a tug of war by pulling the child's hand.

The different means of judging the case of the two biblical women indicate the authors' different attitudes in building the male protagonist's character. In 1 Kgs 3.24-25, Solomon orders that the living child be cut in half. This was obviously not what Solomon would actually want to happen in the biblical story. However, it does sound like a solution lacking empathy or understanding. Hence, Carole R. Fontaine points out that this narrative of the blameless infant's execution reveals habitual abuses of power at court, and grants King Solomon not a great image from a humanistic point of view (Fontaine 1994b). On the other hand, Robert D. Miller understood Solomon in this narrative as a 'trickster' of folklore literature, who 'displays his wisdom by his foolishness, by taking things too literally' (Miller 2011: 504). In contrast, the male protagonists in the Chinese versions do not share with Solomon a similar 'trickster' character.

Interestingly, there is another story about two men disputing a bolt of cloth in the *Fengsu tongyi*. In this story, the cloth was indeed cut in two by the judge's order, and each man got a half. Then, after the trial, the judge sends somebody to secretly listen to the conversation between the two men. The owner is then heard grumbling about the injustice he has received, while the other man praises the judge's kindness. In this way the judge finds out who the true owner is and settles the case in a just happy end.

Moreover, the same story of two persons disputing one piece of cloth appears in the *Sūtra of the Wise and the Foolish* just after the two women's case. Both cases are judged by the same king.[9] It was quite clear that the Chinese author was aware of the 'cutting in half' motif in judging this type of lawsuit. However, in all the Chinese versions, the authors chose not to use the 'cutting the child in half' motif in the two women's case. Instead, a 'tug of war' motif was applied. The male protagonists are never depicted as 'tricksters' but are always positive figures, representing the social values and norms of Chinese society. At the same time the female characters, with their marginal status in society, serve as a foil to the male protagonists and their positive qualities.

Female Goblins and Prostitutes

At the very beginning of the biblical story, the narrator informs the audience about two women coming before the king for justice. The two women are presented as nameless

9. The English translation of the story can be seen in Frye 1981: 213. However, this is an English translation of the *Sūtra of the Wise and the Foolish* from Mongolian, while the actual text is preserved in Tibetan and translated from a Chinese source. I compared the Frye translation with the Chinese version of the stories in discussion. To a large extent, the translation did follow the Chinese text, even though it was translated several times from Chinese to Tibetan to Mongolian to English. Another very informative paper discussing the transmission process of the two women/one son case from India to Tibet through the Chinese Buddhist Texts is Xiaoping Feng 1986.

prostitutes (*zônôt*). Mentioning their profession so early in the story functions, first and foremost, to serve the need of plot development. Their marginalized and socially isolated occupation perfectly explains the reason why they share a communal household, with no male protector and no servants in attendance, thus no witness to solve the dispute (Brenner 1985: 81–2; Bird 1989: 132–3). As Fontaine notes, 'the *zônôt* of 1 Kings 3 are functional "widows"' (Fontaine 1994a: 155). On the other hand, the two women are indistinguishable from each other in terms of name, profession or physical features, hence 'equal' in the story. The key to recognizing the true mother is to elicit the true mother's maternal feelings. In the mindset of the biblical authors, they assume that the true mother would display her maternal compassion, transcending jealous possession in order to save her child's life, just as Moses' mother gives up her child to another woman in order to save his life (Lasine 1989: 70).

The assumption that the false mother would fail to express maternal compassion for her own child works in all the Chinese versions. They are very instructive in the sense of trying to teach the readers that only maternal compassion could help identify the true mother. In the *Sūtra of the Wise and the Foolish*, the story is extremely simplified, with no description of the two women. They are absolutely 'equal': the text simply uses the expression 'two mothers' [二母]. The reason for the simplification can be explained by the fact that the *Sūtra of the Wise and the Foolish* was composed much later then the *Jātaka* and the *Fengsu tongyi* (see above, p. 112). The *Sūtra* combined two cases (the two women's case, and the cloth case) together. It seems that the *Sūtra* assumes that the readers are familiar with the stories. In the *Jātaka*, the false mother is designed to be a female goblin who wishes to have the baby in order to eat it (Cowell and Rouse 1907: 164). By the end of the *Jātaka* version, the sage emphasizes to the female goblin the spiritual principle of cause and effect, saying: 'you committed sin in old time and so were born as a goblin; and now you still go on committing sin, blind fool that you are' (Cowell and Rouse 1907: 164). In the biblical version, the false mother is equated with a true prostitute (Bird 1974: 61). Nevertheless, the socially inferior prostitute is able to display maternal compassion similar to that of other (decent) women (Brenner 1985: 82).

The *Chalk Circle* is the latest among all the versions discussed. It is an elaborate and well-expanded story about the two women's case. In this version, the true mother has a name: Zhang Haitang [張海棠]. She has been a prostitute, but later married Ma Junqing [馬均卿], a wealthy man, as his second wife and bore him a son. The first Mrs Ma, the man's first wife, remains nameless. She conspires with her paramour Zhao, an officer of the local court, to murder her husband. Mrs Ma puts poison in the husband's soup and asks Haitang to present it to him. After Mr Ma's death, the first Mrs Ma, with Zhao's help, accuses Haitang of murdering their husband and claims Haitang's son as her own in order to get the dead husband's inheritance. At the court, Zhao attempts to prove Haitang's crime by reference to her former occupation as a prostitute. In the end, the Capital Court reverses the decision of the lower court, thanks to Haitang's brother Zhang Lin [張林] and the impartial judge Bao Zheng [包拯].[10]

---

10. The play script was first translated into French in 1832, then into German in 1925: see Wenwei Du 1995: 308.

Bao Zheng was a historical figure from the northern Song dynasty (960–1127). The story praises his righteousness in solving an unjust case against an ordinary person, which in Confucian tradition is in accordance with the image of the ideal official. Likewise, the positive characters (those who are favoured in the story, e.g. the true mother Haitang and her brother who saves Haitang from a false accusation) are well-behaved from the perspective of Confucian values.

Prostitution as life occupation is morally inferior but is still tolerated in biblical society (Brenner 1985: 78). Such is also the situation in the Chinese society the *Chalk Circle* describes. It is totally acceptable for the wealthy Mr Ma to marry Haitang even though she has been a prostitute. However, because of her former occupation as a prostitute, she can be second wife only. After she gives birth to his son, Haitang undoubtedly becomes the story's positive female figure: at any rate, she is the true mother. As a true mother in a lawful marriage, her new identity can surpass her former marginalized status as a prostitute. In the meantime, the woman whose word cannot be trusted is characterized as a prostitute (Bird 1989: 132). So, the case as it comes before Solomon seems 'impossible' to solve for a (Chinese) judge if both women are actually prostitutes. This prostitute stereotype is also present in the *Chalk Circle*. At the local court, when the true mother's status is questioned, Haitang's former occupation as a prostitute is one of the reasons for convicting her as a murderer. In contrast, Haitang's brother is the positive male figure in the story. Due to the father's early death and the family's ensuing poverty, the brother has to leave his home town, his mother and sister, seeking a job, as has already been stated at the beginning of the play script. Before he leaves, the brother condemns his mother for letting Haitang become a prostitute. Later, as a clerk at the Capital Court, he works under Judge Bao. Haitang's case can finally be completely cleared due to his help. It would seem that women must wait passively for men to, eventually, come to their rescue.

It is worth mentioning that the Chinese play *The Chalk Circle* was adapted by the famous German playwright Bertolt Brecht (1898–1956) in his work *The Caucasian Chalk Circle*. Brecht reversed the judgement scene, so that in his play (in Scene 5) the 'true' mother is the adoptive mother Grusha, who has been a maid in the house of a Caucasian city governor. Thus for him a woman's maternal love is not necessarily bound up with biological kinship, blood relationship or low class: the educational function of his story lies in the argument that humane, maternal feelings supersede other factors. The birth mother, the governor's wife who abandons her son at the beginning, wants her son back only in order to inherit the governor's property. This shows how a biblical theme (in this case in the story about Solomon's judgement) may receive continued, secondary and tertiary, afterlives in Western literature via Chinese literature.

Conclusion

In each and every version of the five discussed in this essay (the biblical story and the four Chinese examples), it is the judge's wisdom that is praised. Be the judge

King Solomon, or the previous lives of the Buddha, or upright government officials, all the judges are male characters. Biblical scholars remind us that details gleaned from the story may illuminate the life and social circumstances of the two women (Brenner 1985: 81). By juxtaposing these versions, we can clearly observe that the judges' 'wisdom' is obtained at the price of manoeuvring the two woman figures. Social norms require that a true mother show her maternal compassion directly; on the other hand, a false mother can be a female goblin who has committed a sin in her previous life, a morally inferior prostitute, an adulteress, a murderer or a woman who covets others' property.

In addition, the Chinese texts require male characters to act as righteous and impartial persons in order to present a positive image. In the Chinese versions, one would never expect the male heroes to behave outside of the social norms and values. Unlike the biblical narrative, where Solomon might be depicted as a 'trickster', in the Chinese versions the previous life of the Buddha, the upright officials and the brother of the true mother Haitang, are all flawless. Also, it must be remembered, in all these versions it is a boy that the two women are contending for.

Appendix

Since there is no English translation of the *Fengsu tongyi*, here is my translation of the two stories that parallel the biblical narrative about Solomon's judgement.

The first story is about two men disputing one bolt of cloth.

> There was a man from Linhuai County who held a bolt of cloth to sell in the market. He put on the cloth over himself due to the rain on his way to the market. Then came another man begging for sharing the shelter from the rain. Thus the first man yielded an area fitting one head. The rain stopped. They should have said goodbye to each other. But a struggle happened. Each said, 'My cloth'. They went to the court, each telling his own words. The governor of the county and also the prime minister Xue Xuan heard the case. Neither of the two men could be convinced. Xuan said, 'The cloth is only worth about several hundreds. Enough for you arguing with one another to the county court!' Then Xuan called the minor official to cut the cloth in two. Each man got a half. After that Xuan sent someone secretly to listen to their conversation. The second man said, 'How kind our governor is!' The first man said, 'Bah!' The owner of the cloth grumbled about the injustice he received. Xuan said, 'Yes, I originally know that you are the owner.' He condemned the second man. The man confessed his guilt and returned the cloth to the owner.m   (Ying 1980: 422)

The second story is in the same chapter of the first but appears further after two other stories. This one is about two women contending for a son.

> There was a wealthy family at Yingchuan County. The two brothers lived together. Both of their wives got pregnant. After a few months, the elder brother's wife suffered a miscarriage. She thus remained indoors. When the day came, both

went to the delivery house together. The younger brother's wife gave birth to a boy. At night the boy was stolen. They had a lawsuit. For three years, the county court could not settle the case. The prime minister Huang Ba came and sat down in front of the hall. He asked an attendant to hold the boy, standing in the middle between the two women about ten strides away from each. Then he shouted at the women, 'Go and take your boy by yourself!' The elder brother's wife held the boy tight and quick. The boy cried loudly. The younger brother's wife was so afraid of hurting the boy. She loosened her grip and let go with her heart broken badly. The elder brother's wife was quite happy. Ba said, 'This is the son of the younger brother's wife.' He condemned the elder brother's wife. She then confessed her guilt. (Ying 1980: 423)

Bibliography

Appleton, Naomi (2016), *Jātaka Stories in Theravāda Buddhism: Narrating the Bodhisatta Path*, London: Routledge.
Brecht, Bertolt (1965), *The Caucasian Chalk Circle*, trans. Eric Bentley, New York: Grove Press.
Bird, Phyllis A. (1974), 'Images of Women in the Old Testament', 41–88 in R. R. Ruether, ed., *Religion and Sexism: Images of Woman in the Jewish and Christian Traditions*, New York: Simon and Schuster.
Bird, Phyllis A. (1989), 'The Harlot as Heroine: Narrative Art and Social Presupposition in Three Old Testament Texts', *Semeia* 46: 119–39.
Brenner, Athalya (1985), *The Israelite Woman: Social Role and Literary Type in Biblical Narrative*, Sheffield: JSOT Press.
Brewster, Paul G. (1962), 'Solomon's Judgement, Mahosadha, and the Hoei-Kan-Li', *Folklore Studies* 21: 236–40.
Cowell, E. B. and W. H. D. Rouse (trans.) (1907), *The Jātaka, Vol. VI: No. 546: The Mahā-Ummagga-Jātaka*. Retrieved from https://www.sacred-texts.com/bud/j6/j6012.htm (accessed 30 August 2019).
Du, Wenwei (1995), 'The Chalk Circle Comes Full Circle: From Yuan Drama Through the Western Stage to Peking Opera', *Asian Theatre Journal* 12/2: 307–25.
Egan, Ronald (1998), 'Introduction', 1–26 in Egan, *Limited Views: Essays on Ideas and Letters, Selected and Translated by Ronald Egan*, Cambridge, MA: Harvard University Asia Center.
Fausbøll, V., ed. (1877–1896), *The Jātaka Together with its Commentary being Tales of the Anterior Births of Gotama Buddha*, 6 vols., London: Trübner and Co.
Feng, Xiaoping (1986), 'The Spread of an Indian story" of two mothers contending for one son" in Tibet', *Journal of Xizang Minzu University (Philosophy and Social Sciences Edition)* 3: 36–42. [冯小平，《印度 "二母争子" 故事在西藏的流传》，《西藏民族学院学报》社会科学版，1986年第3期，第36 - 42页].
Fontaine, Carole R. (1994a), 'The Bearing of Wisdom', 143–60 in Athalya Brenner (ed.), *A Feminist Companion to Samuel and Kings*, Sheffield: Sheffield Academic Press.
Fontaine, Carole R. (1994b), 'A Response to 'The Bearing of Wisdom', 161–7 in Athalya Brenner, ed., *A Feminist Companion to Samuel and Kings*, Sheffield: Sheffield Academic Press.
Frye, Stanley (1981), *Sūtra of the Wise and the Foolish (mdo mdzangs blun), or Ocean of Narratives (üliger-ün dalai)*, translated from Mongolian, Dharamsala: Library of Tibetan Works and Archives.

Gaster, Theodor H. (1969), *Myth, Legend, and Custom in the Old Testament: A Comparative Study with Chapters from Sir James G. Frazer's Folklore in the Old Testament*, Vol. II, New York: Harper & Row.

Guo, Liangjun, and Baosheng Huang (trans.) (1985), *Selected Stories from the Jātaka*, Beijing: People's Literature Publishing House [郭良鋆、黄宝生译，《佛本生故事选》，北京：人民文学出版社，1985].

Gressmann, Hugo (1907), 'Das salomonische Urteil', *Deutsche Rundschau* 130: 212–28.

Huang, Baosheng (2013), 'On the *Jātakas*', 15–26 in Huang, *Selected Papers on Buddhist Studies*, Beijing: China Social Sciences Press. [黄宝生，《<本生经>浅论》，载于《梵学论集》，北京：中国社会科学出版社，2013，第15–26页].

Ji, Xianlin (1963), 'On the Pali text of the *Jātaka*', *World Literature* 5: 73–6. [季羡林，《关于巴利文<佛本生故事>》，《世界文学》，1963年05期，第73–6页].

Knechtges, David R., and Taiping Chang (eds) (2014), *Ancient and Early Medieval Chinese Literature: A Reference Guide*, Leiden: Brill.

Lasine, Stuart (1989), 'The Riddle of Solomon's Judgement and the Riddle of Human Nature in the Hebrew Bible', *JSOT* 45: 61–86.

Lee, Archie C. C. (1993a), 'Genesis 1 from the Perspective of a Chinese Creation Myth', 186–98 in Graeme Auld, ed., *Understanding Poets and Prophets: Essays in Honour of George W. Anderson*, Sheffield: Sheffield Academic Press.

Lee, Archie C. C. (1993b), 'Biblical Interpretation in Asian Perspective', *Asian Journal of Theology* 7: 35–9.

Lee, Archie C. C. (2000), 'Biblical Interpretation as Dialogical Process in the Context of Religious Pluralism', 201–9 in Daniel Jones Muthunayagon (ed.), *The Bible Speaks Today*, Delhi: ISPCK.

Lee, Archie C. C. (2002), 'Cross-Textual Interpretation and its Implications for Biblical Studies', 247–54 in Fernando F. Segovia and Mary Ann Tolbert (eds), *Teaching the Bible: Discourses and Politics of Biblical Pedagogy*, New York: Orbis Books.

Li, Qianfu [Li Xingdao] (2014), 'Huilanji,' 1–49 in Zang Maoxun, ed. *Yuanqu xuan. Xuxiu Siku Quanshu jibu*, vol. 1760, Shanghai: Shanghai Guji Press. [李行道撰，「包待制智賺灰闌記雜劇」，臧懋循輯，陶宗儀等撰，《續修四庫全書・集部戲劇類》第1760冊，元曲選一百卷，上海：上海古籍出版社，2014，第1–49頁].

Mair, Victor H. (1993), 'The Linguistic and Textual Antecedents of *The Sūtra of the Wise and the Foolish*', *Sino-Platonic Papers*, 38. Retrieved from http://sino-platonic.org/complete/spp038_sutra_wise_foolish.pdf (accessed 30 August 2019).

Miller, R. D. (2011), 'Solomon the Trickster', *Biblical Interpretation* 19: 496–504.

Qian, Zhongshu. (2007) *Guanzhui Bian*, Vol. III, Beijing: SDX Joint. [錢鍾書，《管錐編》（三），北京：三聯書店，2007].

Ying, Shao (ed.) (1980), *Fengsu tongyi jiaoshi*, Shuping Wu commented, Tianjin: Tianjin Renmin. [應劭撰，《風俗通義校釋》，吳樹平校釋，天津：天津人民出版社，1980].

THE GOLDEN AGE OF ELIJAH THE PROPHET AS CULTURE HERO IN ZIONIST EDUCATION

Tamar Lammfromm

Introduction

The *TaNaKh* (as the Hebrew Bible is commonly called in Israel) has been omnipresent in the life and culture of contemporary Israel, ever since the pre-State waves of Jewish return to the Homeland at the end of the nineteenth century. This is so in political and practical life, for the Orthodox and the traditionalist and the secular-secularist alike, from birth to death and beyond. *TaNaKh* and halakhic regulations govern life in this ostensibly Western-style democracy, for Jews at least.

Among other things, every Israeli child who went through the non-religious system of education that was developed by Zionist instruction and continued after the establishment of the State, will attest to the copious presence of *TaNaKh* teaching in all levels of basic education (from kindergarten on to the end of high school); and to the upgrading of many *TaNaKh* figures to a contemporary useful paradigm. Such figures are often transformed, diverging from their original *TaNaKh* signification(s), so that they are useful for contemporaneous ideologies that incorporate and rework post-biblical concepts as they appear in the *TaNaKh*, Aggadah, Midrash and Talmud. Elijah the prophet is one such figure.

As the herald of the Jewish people's national redemption in *Eretz Israel*, the figure of Elijah played a significant role in non-Orthodox Zionist education in the pre-State Jewish *Yishuv* (Heb. 'Settlement'), especially during the British Mandate period (summer 1920 to May 1948, following the British military regime which had started in 1917),[1] after the founding (1948) of the Israeli State and

---

1. '... in 1917, during World War I, the Zionists persuaded the British government to issue the Balfour Declaration, a document that committed Britain to facilitate the establishment of a "Jewish homeland" in Palestine. Amid considerable controversy over conflicting wartime promises to the Arabs and French, Britain succeeded in gaining the endorsement of the declaration by the new League of Nations, which placed Palestine under British mandate. This achievement reflected a heady mixture of religious and imperial motivations that Britain would find difficult to reconcile in the troubled years ahead'. https://www.britannica.com/place/Israel/History#ref105326

until the 1960s. In essence, we can speak of several Elijahs: one, the fanatical prophet portrayed in the book of Kings (1 Kgs 17–19, 21 [cf. 2 Chron. 21.12]; 2 Kgs 1–2]; the other(s), the precursor of redemption (emanating from the interpretation given to Mal. 3.23-24 [KJV 4.5-6]), whom God will send to the people before enacting His horrific Day of Judgement. This messenger figure evolves, in post-biblical times, into a figure of infinite kindness, a miracle worker who assists those in need, as found in rabbinic literature and folktales. This study focuses on the latter figure of Elijah: not on the biblical prophet who opposes idolatry, but rather on 'his' redemptive and beneficial roles. In Zionist literature, such roles were expanded to include that of the herald of national redemption.

This role, which was also reflected in new stories and poems for children written in Hebrew at the time (Ofek 1985: 2.555–7, 643), was influenced by the national values that gained in strength in the second half of the nineteenth century. Then, the Jewish national movements returned to ancient heroes who were now given a new, nationalistic garb. This return is also related to the Bible's role in shaping the unique Zionist culture: the Bible was viewed as an important component of national identity and constitutive book that embodied the collective memory of the Jewish people, in addition to providing a historical basis for the national aspirations of the Zionist movement and historical legitimacy of the renewed political organization (Ben Amos 2002: 9, Mathias 2002: 22).

Accordingly, Hebrew-Zionist culture emphasized the Bible far more than it did other sanctified Jewish texts, such as the Mishnah and the Talmud, which in the eyes of the Zionists in the *Yishuv* represented Diaspora culture (Lammfromm Lederson 2016: 24–9; Simon 2002: 23–32). At the same time, however, Modern Hebrew literature did not show any commitment to the traditional approach towards biblical heroes (Zerubavel 2013: 760; Shaked 2005: 9–18), viewing them in a different light; and that was also the case with Elijah's image.

The British Mandate period and Israel's early years of statehood saw a revival in Elijah's popularity in Hebrew elementary school education (ages 6–13). In order to understand the importance attributed to Elijah and the characteristics elementary-school teachers ascribed to him during this period, I will focus on the approaches and motivations to teaching Elijah as based mainly on writings by teachers, curricula, articles in professional journals and the daily press, books, and scholarly research on the period. In the discussion, I will distinguish between the teaching of the poems and stories about Elijah in Hebrew literature classes that began in the lower grades; and the teaching of stories about Elijah in Bible classes, taught in elementary schools from the fifth grade (age 10–11) onwards. I will explore the changes that occurred in Elijah's character in Bible lessons as well as why such importance in young children's eyes was attributed to him. The connection between Elijah's varied features and his traditional roles, according to the Bible as well as the shapes assumed in the popular mind following midrashim, folkloristic tales, and Modern Hebrew literature, merit a separate study.

Elijah the Prophet – The Herald of Zionist National Redemption

One of my childhood memories is hearing repeatedly the *piyyut* (liturgical poem, usually sung) 'Elijah the Prophet' (author unknown), whose first stanza was sung on Israel radio every week on Saturday night, after Shabbat.[2]

Elijah the Prophet	אליהו הנביא
Elijah of Tishbi	אליהו התשבי
Elijah of Gilead	אליהו הגלעדי
May he soon come to us	במהרה יבוא אלינו
With the Messiah, son of David.	עם משיח בן דוד

The special place accorded to Elijah in the liturgical hymns recited at the end of the Sabbath, on Saturday night, was part of the tradition as it developed over the years and the belief among Diaspora Jews that Elijah would herald the Messiah. This created the feeling that the return to mundane weekdays and their attendant anxieties was an opportune time to mention the anticipation of redemption and to pray for its realization (Shinan 1999: 219–22).

Israeli children of secular/ist, traditional, and Orthodox families alike were familiar with an Elijah figure from an early age. They – like me, a girl from a secular home with an affinity to tradition – had often heard the *piyyut* every week ever since the British Mandate period. However, they were mainly exposed to the properties of Elijah figures that carried no resemblance to the biblical zealous prophet of God.[3]

Songs about Elijah the Prophet were sung in the *Yishuv* in the 1920s at major events, such as the inauguration of the Hebrew University, as part of the notion that the idea of national redemption, of the people and the land, was being realized. These things were related, writes Hacohen, to the hope stirred up by the Balfour Declaration[4] (November 1917) and General Allenby's arrival in Jerusalem as a

---

2. For the full *piyyut* see https://web.nli.org.il/sites/nlis/he/song/pages/song.aspx?SongID=188#3,138,1204,356

3. The *piyyut* was sung by the *chazan* Ephraim Di-Zahav, and began to be played on *Kol Israel* ('Voice of Israel') Radio during the Mandate period. It was apparently first performed live and later recorded in 1953.

4. 'The Balfour Declaration was a letter written by British Foreign Secretary Arthur Balfour to Lionel Walter Rothschild, in which he expressed the British government's support for a Jewish homeland in Palestine. The long-term effects of the Balfour Declaration, and the British government's involvement in Palestinian affairs, are felt even today. Britain's acknowledgement and support of Zionism, and Zionism's focus on establishing a Jewish homeland in Palestine, emerged from growing concerns about the direction of the First World War; see https://www.history.com/topics/middle-east/balfour-declaration#section_3

conqueror of Ottoman Jerusalem (December 1917). These developments, Hacohen notes, inspired Levin Kipnis (an Israeli author for children, 1894–1990) to write his poem 'The Messiah', based on a Jewish folk song. The poem describes Elijah's arrival in Eretz Israel to herald the coming of the Messiah, who would soon arrive in Jerusalem riding on a white donkey.[5]

In a collection edited by Shlomo Rozowsky (1929), *From the Songs of the Land*, which documents the songs that were popular in Eretz Israel in the 1920s, the Elijah poems were placed in two categories: The *piyyut* 'Elijah the Prophet' was assigned to the category of 'Religious Folk Songs', which also includes other traditional songs that the Jewish Pioneers remembered from their childhood. A new poem that Zalman Shneur (1887–1959) wrote, 'Elijah the Prophet', was placed in the category of 'Children's Songs'. Shneur's poem presents Elijah as entering the home on Passover *Seder* night, when the door is opened to him (so as part of the Haggadah home ceremony) as the one who will redeem all the far-flung of Israel 'when the Messiah is revealed' (Rozowsky 1929: 81, 144–5).

In accordance with the Zionist ambience, Elijah brings parents and children to the land of Israel (perhaps a new nationalist midrash on Mal. 3.23-24):[6]

He will cry out in great cheer	בקול חדוה קרוא יקרא
To those most far and near,	אל כל נדחי העם,
Fathers and sons he will then gather	אבות בנים אז יקבץ
From every distant world corner.	מכל כנפות עולם.
To our land he will lead us very soon,	אלי ארצנו חיש יוליך
This old man of ours.	אותנו זה השב.
In a joyous voice, a rejoicing crowd,	בקול שמחה, המון חוגג,
A multitude will throng.	קהל גדול ורב.

The new poems which expressed anticipation for Elijah's arrival were set to music and sung at community singsongs along with the traditional songs that the Zionist pioneers had learned as children in their parents' homes. The new stories and poems, the *piyyutim* and traditional folksongs about Elijah were also included in the collections of songs published by schools, such as the booklet *Tslilei Hanina* (Heb. *Sounds of Hanina*) published in 1927 in memory of Hanina Karchevsky, a

---

5. Hacohen 2003: 476–7, 493–4. In Shapira's booklet *From the Songs of the Second Aliya*, the Saturday night *piyyut* 'Elijah the Prophet' was included under the 'Shabbat songs' category (Shapira 1948: 30), whereas Levin Kipnis's poem 'The Messiah' was placed in the 'folk songs' category (23).

6. הנה אנכי שלח לכם את אליהו הנביא לפני בוא יום יהוה הגדול והנורא והשיב לב אבות על בנים ולב בנים על אבותם פן אבוא והכיתי את הארץ חרם

'Lo, I will send the prophet Elijah to you before the coming of the awesome, fearful day of the LORD. He shall reconcile parents with children and children with their parents [lit. 'fathers' and 'sons'], so that, when I come, I do not strike the whole land with utter destruction' (JPS 1985).

music teacher at the Gimnasia Herzliya high school,[7] which included songs he had taught in the school's music classes. Its purpose – as Haim Bograshov, one of the headmasters of the Gimnasia Herzliya, explained in the preface to the booklet – was to strengthen the students' national sentiments and attachment to the land of Israel (Karchevsky 1927).

While modern Hebrew authors tried to discard supernatural features found in the Elijah tales, they also sought to emulate folkloristic Jewish texts. This was part of the intention to create authentic, popular national folklore that was taking shape, an addendum to cultural heritage and affiliation with Jewish tradition, in order to reinforce a unique national character (Berlovitz 1994: 103–6, Grossman 2008).

How and why did Elijah assume a pivotal role in Zionist national education? One explanation is related to the stories about him that had been circulating in Diaspora Jewish communities, which gave people hope of redemption and turned him into a symbol of and testimony to the Jewish people's vitality and belief in its regeneration (Raz 1986: 32). Allusions to the ancient sources recharged not only children, but also grownups, with new strength. One example is the use made by the Israeli poet Nathan Alterman (1910–70) in his newspaper column 'The Night of Elijah the Prophet', on Passover – Elijah's visit to the Passover *Seder* held in a combat unit in 1948 during Israel's War of Independence.[8] In this poem Elijah, the herald of redemption, learns about the revival of the nation and blesses the 'newborn' nation and its fighters:

Bless each squadron whether resting or moving.	יברך את כל הפלוגה אם חונה ואם ניידת
He will bless the rising force of the nation	יברך את הכוח הקם לאומה
That with the festival of its birth	שעם חג ראשיתה
Is reborn.	בשנית היא נולדת.

The choice to valorize Elijah is aimed at revitalizing the spirit of loyalty to and acceptance of the Zionist cause (Cohen-Levinovsky 2012: 617–618).

Another explanation for the choice of Elijah that is put forth by scholars was that his image 'restored' a dimension of sanctity to the nation's political aspirations, which had got lost in the process of secularization: it was felt that Elijah's legendary image, back to the land of Israel, could impart sacredness to the past, present and future. In accordance with this approach Elijah, who returned to Eretz Israel in the new national songs, restored a sense of sacredness and eternity to the places

---

7. The first high school in Eretz Israel (and the world at large) to have Hebrew as its instruction language. Established in Jaffa 1905 and then moved to Tel Aviv. Still active as a six-year high school, with a stellar reputation, today.

8. Alterman's column appeared in the Labour Movement's newspaper *Davar* under the name *The Seventh Column* in the years 1943–67. The poems in the column dealt with actual topics and most were later incorporated into books. This entry is from a poem that was published on 23 April 1948.

mentioned in them.⁹ Thus children's anticipation of Elijah's coming on Passover *Seder* night was meaningful, as we shall also see below.

The Non-Biblical Elijah

The conceptual development of Elijah's image, which is different from the Elijah that appears in 1 Kgs 17–19, 21 and 2 Kgs 1 and 2.1-18,[10] is often associated with the verse in 2 Kings (2.11) that tells us that Elijah 'ascended to the heavens in a whirlwind'. This comes, as noted, in addition to what is stated about him in the final verses of Mal. 3.23-24 (KJV 4.6; there is some disagreement among scholars as to whether these verses are an integral part of Malachi's prophecy, or a later addition).[11] Elijah's alternative image is of a gentle, compassionate, forgiving and benevolent old man, the messenger of good news. He is a saviour who appears to people in various disguises, intervenes and works miracles to help those who await him in times of trouble (Ginzberg 2003: 1000–6). Such an image was developed in Christianity and Islam too.[12]

A full analysis of Elijah's alternative image is beyond the scope of this article, and this is not the place to expand on its various features and development. These features can be found in the many midrashim about him and in folktales told in Jewish communities across the globe.[13] However, we can underscore certain general features of his character, and relate to two of them: Elijah who provides material aid, such as food, to people in distress; and Elijah the saviour, the man of eternal kindness, who appears to and helps sufferers wherever they may be, provides assistance in times of trouble, and rescues Jews from blood libels. In the new songs and stories associated with Elijah that were composed in Eretz Israel, some of which were geared toward children, his redemptive characteristics were most commonly noted. In some, Elijah saved a person at home (such as Levin Kipnis' poem 'Elijah the Prophet'), and in others, as we have seen, he helped to bring redemption to the Land of Israel.

---

9. Naor 2009: 199–200. An example can be found in Jacob Fichman's poem 'Legend', in which Elijah teaches a boy Torah in the 'castle' on the banks of Lake Kinneret (Hever 2004: 77–78;), a poem that was later included in the State schools curriculum for sixth grades (Curriculum 1954: 2.108).

10. Some scholars consider 2 Kgs 2.1-18 as part of the Elijah stories, while others take the view that chapter 2 belongs to the Elisha stories (see Cogan and Tadmor 1988: 33; Rofé 1988a: 44; Uffenheimer 1984: 186–7; Shemesh 1997: 15–16).

11. For more on this subject, see Haran 2008: 3: 390, n8; 655 n115; Assis 2011: 207–8, nn2–7, 209; Rofé 1992: 82; Kaufman 1964: 4. 376.

12. On traditions associated with Elijah in Christianity, see e.g. Thrall 1970; Miller 2007; Nir 1991. For his image in Islam, see Wensinck 1978.

13. For studies on Elijah in rabbinic literature, post-talmudic literature and in folktales, see Greenwald 2003; Lindbeck 2010; Wiener 1978; Hoshen 2012: 237; Peli 1986; Amorai 1973. For a traditional approach to the prophecy in Malachi, see Gevaryahu 1963.

Some of the stories and poems written in the twentieth century also add aspects of social solidarity and an aspiration for equality to Elijah's character as herald of national redemption. Children awaited his arrival on Passover *Seder* night, with the full goblet of wine designated for him on the table, based on the tradition the *Seder* night would be the time of redemption heralded by him. Perhaps children also recalled Elijah's name from stories about the traditional chair kept for him at circumcision ceremonies. The anticipation for Elijah's arrival on the *Seder* night is part of the tradition that developed over the years, which combined Elijah's role as helper and consoler with that of his role as herald of redemption.[14] Even the Passover *Haggadot* written in the (mostly secular) *kibbutzim* mentioned Elijah as one who 'when his wandering comes to an end, the redemption will come to Israel' (Shua 2011: 440): even in the *kibbutzim*, *Seder* nights included songs about Elijah, as well as the ingathering of the exiles and peace.

The Hebrew-Zionist writers, who themselves grew up on yearnings for redemption and who nostalgically remembered their childhood anticipation of Elijah's arrival on *Seder* night, also wrote stories and poems on Passover-related topics. These, in turn, were included in elementary school textbooks under the category of 'holidays and festivals'. Thus, for example, a second-grade textbook included a story by Levin Kipnis called 'The Secret', in which a little girl sees Elijah in a dream. He appears to her as a kindly old man with a snow-white beard, wearing a 'grand mantle with a broad belt around his waist'. The latter detail is consistent with his description in 2 Kgs 1.8. The special emphasis given to Elijah as a saviour who helps destitute people celebrate the Passover *Seder* with lavish amounts of food and fine clothing can also be found in new stories that were based on folk traditions (e.g. Shir 1961, *Passover Stories for Children*; and see p. 131 here for the discussion of the story 'The Magician').

Approaches to Teaching Elijah Stories in Bible Classes in the Pre-State Period

In the pre-State period (up to 1948), most teachers in the *Yishuv* education system belonged to one of the two non-Orthodox ideological vectors: General, which promoted traditional national education and was defined as addressing all parts of the population, with an eye to national unity and Zionist fulfilment in a general Zionist direction; and Socialist, the Schools of the Labour and Kibbutz Movements, which promoted a social, agricultural, pioneering and idealistic approach. Bible study at schools served to reinforce those goals, shape the children's identity and inspire them. During this period, it was widely accepted among many teachers that it was not appropriate to introduce young students in elementary school to the conclusions of academic Bible criticism.[15]

14. For more on the customs associated with Elijah on *Seder* night, see Goren 1994.

15. For approaches to academic Bible criticism in Bible school teaching in Israel, see Amit 2009.

Some of the non-religious teachers felt no commitment to the biblical view whereby the prophet is God's messenger who, in his prophecies, demands the observance of God's laws;[16] others preferred to attribute the source of prophecy to the prophet himself, whom they portrayed as a man fighting for his ideas. The latter approach, which did not appear in official curricula, enabled teachers to empower the visionary prophet as a role model. The focus on the prophet Elijah as a man fighting for his principles reinforced this educational value of fighting for a cause, the instilling of which in students was important as part of the national/nationalistic education.

The teachers were deeply impressed by Elijah's personality in the stories of Kings. Benzion Mossinson (1878–1942), who taught Bible at the Gymnasia Herzliya high school, particularly related to Elijah's courage in standing all alone and risking his life in his demand that the people recognize the God of Israel as the one and only God (Mossinson 1919: 160). Mossinson added that Elijah embodied a new type of prophet, one who was not a court prophet but forcefully demanded of the people and the king that they obey God's laws uncompromisingly. Of Elijah's words to Ahab, 'Would you murder and take possession' (הרצחת וגם ירשת, 1 Kgs 21.19), Mossinson wrote that this 'was the most vigorous protest ever spoken to a despotic ruler in the name of justice and integrity to this day'. Moshe Sister, a teacher in the Labour Movement schools and member of the Kibbutz movement, a Marxist in his approach, taught Bible as secular-realistic literature (Schoneveld 1976: 86–8, Dror 2007: 180, 183). Sister wrote that Elijah, who fought for ideals of justice and national authenticity, stood up for what he believed even when he occasionally fell into despair and was disheartened (Sister 1955: 167–77).

Such teachers emphasized that Elijah was different from his surroundings – he was a man who had come from the eastern bank of the Jordan River, from a place that was not yet affected by the influence of Jezebel, and who zealously fought for the exclusive worship of the Hebrew God. They pointed to Elijah's multifaceted nature and to the fact that he did not reside in a permanent abode, but rather appeared and disappeared intermittently like a whirlwind.[17] Sister distinguished between Elijah as a historical figure and Elijah as a legendary figure, and compared the forging of Elijah's image to that of Moses.[18] When teaching younger students, the teachers preferred not to offer rational explanations for miracles performed,

---

16. For more on the biblical prophet, see Seeligmann 1996: 188; Kaufmann 1964: 246–50.

17. Scholars of biblical criticism too assumed that Elijah impressed his contemporaries with his courage and spiritual strength. To this was added his foreignness, frequent disappearances and sudden appearances which, according to Rofé, created the impression that 'Elijah divided his time between the human world and the divine world'. For more on Elijah and his war against the Ba'al, see Rofé 1988a: 183–96 and Garsiel (2014: 187–92), who wrote about the forging of Elijah's image in Kings.

18. Sister 1955: 177. For a discussion of the distinction between a literary figure and a historical figure, see Shemesh 1997: 6–7. Biblical criticism scholars viewed the Elijah stories as of a legendary nature (Rofé 1988a), at the centre of which lies the figure of the Man of God; see Cogan 2000: 485–6 on 1 Kgs 21.1-29; and Kaufmann 1964: 4.227, 245.

although they were aware of the miracles' legendary nature. Nevertheless, when teaching older students (10th grade, 15–16 years old), the teachers sought to develop a critical awareness of the distinction in Elijah stories between the legendary and miraculous on the one hand; and the historical on the other hand (Ha-Levi 1960: 31).

The teachers also noted the unique appearance of Elijah, 'a hairy man, with a leather belt tied around his waist' (2 Kgs 1.8, and see Zech. 13.4), which they attributed to his being a nomad (Mossinson 1919: 154–7). It may be assumed that the prophet's unique appearance captivated the imagination of the Zionist teachers, perhaps also because it was so different from that of Eastern European Diaspora Jews.

Only some of the teachers taught the Bible stories against a contemporary backdrop (Amit 2009). One of them was Benzion Mossinson, who included the conclusions of biblical criticism in his Bible teaching. When introducing 1 Kings 21, Mossinsohn taught the historical and political context of Ahab and Jezebel's marriage, whose religious and social consequences led to Elijah's prophetic activities (Mossinsohn 1919: 152, 157). According to Mossinson, Elijah inveighed against idol worship, which was reinforced in the wake of Ahab's marriage to Jezebel and practised in addition to Yhwh worship, as well as against social injustice.

Teaching the Elijah Stories: A Social Perspective

Because of Elijah's actions and endeavours, some viewed him as part of a movement that fought for the character of government in ancient Israel (Sister 1955: 178–9; see Kaufmann, 1964: 4.255).

Many Bible teachers related to how Elijah courageously fought to purge society of its evils (Schoneveld 1976: 96). In Labour Movement schools in the cities, *kibbutzim* and *moshavim*, Bible study involved a dialogue between students and the biblical text that was focused on biblical ethical values (Dror 2007: 179, 192). In this spirit, some teachers in the Labour Movement schools interpreted Elijah's struggle against idolatry as a national-social struggle against imperialistic forces that influenced culture. Elijah, they claimed, was one of the first prophets to understand the connection between idolatry and social sins, who foresaw the danger that the lust of idolatry and its abominations posed to society and fought against them. Idolatry was explained in this context as a feature of the despotic regime that was initiated with Ahab and Jezebel's marriage, since Jezebel used her influence to make idolatry an integral part of the kingdom of Israel.

Jacob Banai, who taught Bible in Labour Movement schools according to a national moralistic approach, presented Elijah as a prophet whose prophecies deal mainly with social issues (Schoneveld 1976: 94–6; Dror 2007: 180–1). He maintained that Elijah decided to redeem his people from the harmful pursuit of worthless beliefs and the worship of silver and gold idols because those eroded the nation's integrity and moved it toward decay and decline. Banai (1964: 83; 1952: 4) added from his own experience that the children would understand the battle of Elijah and the Yhwh prophets against Jezebel, who was responsible for Naboth's execution, and Elijah's zeal and his war to purge Eretz Israel from the contamination of idolatry, if they were told that the case of Naboth the Jezreelite (1 Kings 21) was indicative of the many injustices perpetrated by the tyrannical regime. In this way, they would learn to distinguish between the rites of Ba'al and Asherah, which Banai explained were associated with a life of lawlessness and debauchery, with those close to the monarchy getting rich at the expense of the enslaved masses who lived in hunger and disease, on the one hand; and the demands made by Elijah and the other prophets to live an honest life of virtue, on the other.[19]

When Banai (1952: 84) and similarly Sister (1955: 158–60, 166–72) emphasized Elijah's struggle for social features in their teaching of Naboth's vineyard story, they did not relate to the fact that Elijah's mission was prophetic and was commanded by God. Because they made Elijah's battle for social justice the story's central focus, Elijah's criticism of Ba'al worship and the actions that emanated from his zeal for God were given only minor attention, despite the centrality of these themes in Elijah stories in Kings (Shapira 2005: 10-11).

Notably, the emphasis on the social aspects of Elijah's activities and his compassion were based on chapters that, in the view of biblical scholars, were the result of later redaction,[20] but were consistent with the approach of Bible commentators regarding Elijah's character in these chapters. Elijah's representation as a prophet whose singular focus was on social justice, mainly in the story of Naboth's vineyard,[21] is inconsistent with the conclusions of some scholars, who considered the story to be a very late adaptation that differed from the events described in 2 Kgs 9.25-26.[22] This is also the case in regard to the story of the resurrection of the widow's son (1 Kgs 17.17-24) about which commentators wrote that it marked the change in the prophet's heart in the direction of compassion and pity (Bachrach 1984: 129). However, scholars are divided as to whether the story belongs to the sequence of the stories of the drought or is in fact a late addition (Simon 1997: 204, 278; Rofé 1988a: 132–5; Cogan, 2000: 93).

In this period, then, Labour Movement Bible teachers endowed Elijah's character with qualities that stemmed from their own philosophy and the ideology that underlay it, as well as from Elijah's image in the midrashim and folktales that presented his more compassionate side, and with the hope of fostering a swift

---

19. Joseph Klausner (1912: 18–19) had already written about the possible connection between class tension created as a result of social disparities, and the religio-ideological struggle between the Yhwh and Ba'al cults, which in the teachers' view symbolized the influence of Canaanite culture.

20. For a discussion of the redaction process of Kings, see Haran 2008: 2.31 n.11 and pp. 184, 216; Yeivin in Gevaryahu 1963: 33–5.

21. Sister 1995: 167–79; Bloch 1953; and see Buber 1942: 73–6.

22. Seeligman 1996: 209–11; Rofé 1988b; Amit 2015: 31, n35. For more on this subject see Cogan 2000: 485–6.

redemption. It may also be assumed that in the teachers' desire to bring the biblical stories closer to their young students' worlds, knowing that the subject of idolatry was not something the children were familiar with, they did not dwell on idolatry when teaching the book of Kings, so as not to 'disturb' the learning experience and to more strongly implement their educational goals.

The story of Naboth's vineyard was part of the nationalistic education in both the General and the Labour Movement schools, and was aimed at bolstering the Zionist approach to holding onto the land, feeling connected to the homeland by farming it. Therefore Naboth was portrayed as a simple, innocent vine-grower connected heart and soul to his ancestors' land inheritance, to the point of self-sacrifice, and unwilling to hand it over even for a fair price, who was crushed by the brute force of the government (Oryanowski 1938: 87–8). Some teachers in the General schools, such as Gavrieli (1954: 229), considered the teaching of the story an educational opportunity. Gavrieli suggested teaching the story as a lesson in moral education, to reinforce the students' ability to make moral judgements. According to his proposal, the problem would be presented in class and its features explored in order to draw conclusions that include moral principles.

For students aged 16–18 in the Labour Movement schools, when studying the book of Kings for the second time, the trend we saw in the fifth grade did not change. This time too, the profound changes in society caused by the monarchy, the growing disparities between social classes, the fate of helpless and hopeless individuals, in their view prepared the ground for the appearance of the Latter Prophets (Bloch 1954: 221). However, this time the Elijah stories were studied as part of the interdisciplinary subject, 'the formation of class society', which included discussions of themes such as the manifestation of tyranny in the days of Ahab and the opposition to it on the part of the Rechabites and prophets; the classification of kings as either 'good' or 'evil'; the social background of the war against the worship of the Ba'al; the social nature of Elijah's prophecies; and the change in the status of the Elders (Bloch 1953: 166; Alon 1954).

The Importance Attributed to Elijah During the Mandate Period and the Early Years after the Establishment of the Israeli State

The children's acquaintance with Elijah's image in the *Aggadah* and his figure as the herald of national redemption, before they studied the book of Kings in fifth-grade Bible classes, appears to have influenced how he was taught in such lessons. That is why, and in accordance with the children's age, some teachers downplayed his more zealous aspects, toning his image down to make it gentler and kinder. When one of the teachers, Benjamin Ha-Levi, tried to explain Elijah's biblical behaviour, he wrote (1960: 32) that the killing of the many Ba'al prophets was a response on the part of the servants of God oppressed by Jezebel and led by Elijah. It is reasonable to assume that this gentler version of Elijah mitigated the contrast between the various aspects of Elijah's character, making it easier to conflate them.

As Amitai wrote in a teacher's guide: 'In the *Aggadah*, what remains is the Elijah who saved the widow and her son rather than the zealous and raging Elijah' (Amitai 1953: 449).

The veteran teacher Haim Aryeh Zuta explicitly addressed the question of whether to discuss the contrast between the two Elijahs in the lessons, and recommended that teachers not enter into a discussion about the contradictions unless the students asked about them (Zuta 1935: 122–3). In the latter case, Zuta proposed that a contrived explanation be given that Elijah's reproofs and wrath were aimed at the kingdom of Israel (which had murdered the prophets of God and established the worship of the Ba'al). For the kingdom of Judah, on the other hand, the railing, zealous Elijah had become a symbol of salvation, comfort and redemption, the herald of good news, hero of living legends that circulated throughout the generations. Furthermore, in order to reconcile the contradiction between the biblical Elijah and Elijah the herald of the redemption in the *Aggadot*, Zuta suggested that teachers present the miracles associated with stories about Elijah as a mythical element that was preserved over the years in legends of Israel's history.

The reason teachers made such efforts to preserve this image of Elijah was related to the importance attributed to Elijah's hope-inspiring figure, and the fear that criticism of him would 'spoil' this image. Zuta explained that it was better for Elijah to become a symbol of zealous truth and honesty for children, of a Judaism that has persevered miraculously throughout its entire lifetime and of the rebirth of Israel as an independent nation. Like the nation, Elijah lives in eternity: he reveals himself at times of trial and tribulations, brings salvation to both society as a whole and the individual, and in the future will appear to herald the Messiah. In a newspaper article offering guidance to parents, the parents were entreated not to destroy the children's faith that Elijah would come to visit them at the *Seder*, taste from his wine goblet and bless them, for fear that disillusioning them would be harmful to their spirit ('Let the Children welcome Elijah the Prophet', *Yedioth Ahronoth*, 23 March 1956). In another article, Esther Avisar ('Give to the children after sitting at the Seder', *Yediot Ahronot*, 8 April 1960) explained the need in this way: 'The wondrous image of Elijah the Prophet who symbolizes the good-hearted redeemer and savior, who honors each and every Jewish home with his presence on *Seder* night, lifts the child from reality to hidden, remote worlds, filled with imagination and visions, a dimension that children so lack in their day-to-day lives'.

Elijah in the National Curricula for Israeli State Education, Written in 1954

The years following the establishment of the Israeli state saw a continuation of some of the trends noted here in reference to Elijah in earlier periods. In elementary schools, children studied songs and stories about Elijah that appeared in their textbooks. New and traditional songs that portrayed him as the herald of redemption were also included in the musical education state curriculum for the fourth grade.[23]

In the curricula for Israeli State education written in 1954, students were given the opportunity to gain significant acquaintance with Elijah as they learned about him in the fifth grade in three different study subjects: *Divre ha-Yamim* (history), Hebrew literature and Bible. Studying the Elijah theme concurrently in a number of different subjects was not a complete innovation. Even in the curriculum of at least one Labour Movement school in the pre-State years, fifth-graders had learned about Elijah in two subjects: Hebrew literature and Bible.[24]

The Hebrew literature State curriculum included the story *Oseh ha-Nifla'ot*, 'The Magician' by I. L. Peretz,[25] which is based on midrashim and folktales that developed in their wake (Peretz 1948: 14–19; see Berlovitz, 1994: 99–100). In the story, a 'magician' reveals himself to a poor couple and fills their home with everything needed for the Passover *Seder*. At the end of the story, we are told that 'only then – realizing that their guest had been the Tishbite [the Prophet Elijah] – did they sit down to have a merry *Seder*'.

In the State curriculum for *Divre ha-Yamim*, in the context of the theme 'prophecy',[26] a number of lessons were dedicated to the topic of 'The prophets, their struggle for social justice and against foreign influences'; the war against Ba'al worship was emphasized in addition to the demand to enforce social justice.

In the fifth-grade Bible curriculum, similar to the trends that prevailed in earlier periods, emphasis was placed on the social aspects of Elijah's prophecy.[27] Nevertheless, the programme explicitly attributed the source of prophecy to God, in line with the trend – in the first decade of the Israeli State – to restore 'tradition' to the general State educational system, including in its Bible classes. The claim was that the Bible's influence grew weaker when its binding aspect as being the word of God was expunged from it (Lammfromm Lederson 2016: 155–8). Accordingly, in the points emphasized in teaching 1 Kings 17–19 and 21 (studied in abbreviated form from a secondary rewrite, not from the actual biblical text) Elijah was described as 'a messenger of God and miracle worker' who endangered his life as he reproved the king, a 'troubler of Israel', and who in his zeal for God killed the Ba'al prophets. In the context of Naboth's vineyard story, it was noted, Elijah exemplified extraordinary moral strength by rebuking the king for seizing the vineyard. A similar formulation can be found in the points of emphasis for the teaching of 2 Kings 1,[28] where it is noted that in his zeal for the God of Israel Elijah rebuked King Ahaziah of Israel, who followed Ba'al.

---

23. Curriculum 1954.1: 127, 178.
24. For the curriculum, see Reshef 1985: 204.
25. I. L Peretz (1852–1915; Warsaw, Poland. One of the greatest Jewish writers of the Jewish Renaissance in the nineteenth century. Peretz wrote in Yiddish and Hebrew.
26. Curriculum 1954: 2: 30.
27. Curriculum 1954: 2: 7.
28. Curriculum 1954: 2: 8.

A comparison of the students' familiarity with the Elijah figure across the various fifth-grade study subjects shows that the contrast between the 'biblical' Elijah – the religious zealot – and the other Elijah children had come to know from new Hebrew literature and folktales was not presented in full. The students were familiar with Elijah as God's messenger who castigated kings in his struggle for morality. This portrayal of Elijah, which mainly emphasized the struggle for social justice, was aimed at strengthening education towards social values through the image of the biblical Elijah, and could serve as a bridge for getting to know him as the herald of the redemption in such a way as to give additional moral strength to nationalist-Zionist values. Here too, an effort was apparently made to 'fuse' Elijah's different images and to encourage students to follow the prophet's example of courage and determination.

The State Bible curriculum for the eighth grade (ages 13–14) included the study of a second, abbreviated cycle of the books of the early Prophets. This time the subject studied was 'Elijah the Prophet and his war against the Baʻal and foreign culture' (1 Kings 17–19; 2 Kings 1–2).[29] The changes in the points to be emphasized in the teaching of Elijah stories, and the positioning of his war against the Baʻal as the central focus of study, may indicate the possibility that when older students were involved, a discussion was held on the fundamental aspects of Elijah's prophecy that was ignored when they were younger.

Summary

The image of Elijah the Prophet, which took on unique features as the national herald of redemption, achieved a pivotal role in the Hebrew Zionist culture of the *Yishuv*. For many, Elijah represented hope – an important role when hope is for salvation, in a belief that salvation will come in our time. His character also preserved the connection to traditional Judaism and to the sanctity of various sites in Eretz Israel.

This Zionist Elijah, who was completely different from the zealous biblical Elijah, arose from his portrayal in rabbinic literature and folktales that developed in their wake. This was the image projected to Israeli children from a young age and in the stories and poems studied at school in Hebrew literature classes and at the Passover *Seder*.

National-ideological aspects were also highly present in Bible study, and Bible teaching was enlisted for the moral education of both individual and society. In Bible classes, Elijah was portrayed as a person who risked his life to fight for his principles. Most of the teachers whose writings are reviewed here did not directly address the contradictions between the two different Elijahs or dispel the myth surrounding his character, which they considered educationally crucial. Some tried to reconcile the two images by providing justification for his zealotry, thereby

---

29. Curriculum 1954: 2: 164.

mitigating the contradiction between them. Accordingly and in order to adapt the teaching of the Elijah stories to young children, to whom the subject of idolatry was unfamiliar, Elijah's zealousness was moderated. Teachers, mainly from the Labour Movement Schools and in accordance with their socialist ideology attributed to Elijah primarily mercy and a willingness to fight for social justice. Apparently, they assumed that through such teaching they would be able to make the children appreciate and enjoy the Elijah stories, while being raised as ethical individuals. These goals appear to have been more important to those teachers than teaching the biblical text as it was, or than considering (scholarly) biblical criticism for the relevant chapters.

In later years, after the establishment of the State of Israel, elementary school children grew less familiar with the different versions of Elijah the Prophet. His image as the herald of national redemption was gradually phased out of the curriculum. The number of texts that have focused on him in recent years in Hebrew Literature studies totals no more than one or two stories or one poem on an average in each school year, in most cases in association with his appearance during Passover. Over the years, Elijah occasionally makes a fleeting appearance in the textbooks for the third and fourth graders in poems such as in the poem *Gingi* ('Redhead'), by Miriam Yalan-Shteklis (1900–84, an Israeli poet and writer famous for her children's books). This poem has been included in the curriculum in recent years too.[30]

Elijah, the herald of national redemption, has been replaced by new cultural heroes as part of processes that Israeli society has been undergoing in recent years (Simon 2002; Shapira 2005: 23–33).

In recent years Elijah, the herald of national redemption, has been replaced by new cultural heroes as part of the processes affecting Israeli society (Simon 2002; Shapira 2005: 23–33). Even in Bible classes in State schools, only some of the students are familiar with this figure, because according to the new curriculum (2019), the Elijah stories are only studied once, in the eighth grade (age 14); they are no longer taught in elementary school. Neither are the Elijah stories included in the matriculation exams.[31]

Today, unlike in previous periods, the likelihood that Israeli children in elementary schools will become acquainted with the different images of Elijah the Prophet is very small. What remains is the legendary old man for whom they wait on *Seder* night.

30. In this poem a child suffers because he is a redhead. At night Elijah takes the child to heaven, where he meets King David who, according to tradition, is a redhead too, and thus consoles the child. Rather than glorify Elijah's figure, the poem is used to promote the acceptance of the 'other' or different.

31. For the new curriculum (2019) see: http://meyda.education.gov.il/files/Mazkirut_Pedagogit/tanach/TochnitTashat.pdf.

Bibliography

[Editors' note. The subject matter of this essay dictates that most of the references are to Hebrew language bibliographical items. The titles are supplied here in an approximate English translation. Consultation with the original items in Hebrew can be accessed by reference to the Hebrew publication venue/periodical.]

Alon, M. (1954), 'Biblical Society', *Ha-Hinukh* 26.3-4: 248–57 [Heb.].
Amit, Y. (2009), 'Biblical Criticism in the Teaching of the Hebrew Bible', *Studies in Jewish Education* 9: 101–13 [Heb.].
Amit, Y. (2015), 'Shaping and Meaning in the Story of Naboth's Vineyard (1Kgs 21)', *Beit Mikra* 60.1: 19–36 [Heb.].
Amitai, O. (1953), *Teaching the Former Prophets in Elementary School*, Tel Aviv: Histadrut ha-Morim be-Yisrael [Heb.].
Amorai, Y. (1973), 'On the Figure of the Prophet Elijah in the Midrash and Talmudic Aggadah', in *Vehinei Ein Yosef*, Tel Aviv: Ofek, 175–82 [Heb.].
Assis, E. (2011), 'Moses, Elijah and the Messianic Hope: A New Reading of Malachi 3, 22-24', *ZAW* 123.2: 207–20.
Bachrach, Y. (1984), *Jonah Son of Amitai and Elijah,* Jerusalem: Israel Jewish Agency [Heb.].
Banai, J. (1952), 'Ideological and Didactic Principles of the teaching of the Bible', *Hed ha-Hinukh* 26.5: 4. [Heb.].
Banai, J. (1964), 'The Story of Elijah the Prophet', *Urim Lahorim* 12.4: 83–5 [Heb.].
Ben Amos, A. (ed.) (2002), 'Introduction', 7–13 in *History, Identity and Memory: Images of the Past in Israeli Education*, Tel Aviv: Tel Aviv University Press [Heb.].
Ben-Yehuda, N. (1990), *Autobiography in Song (Israeli Folksongs)*, Jerusalem: Keter [Heb.].
Berlovitz, Y. (1994), 'Zibn gute Johr (Seven Good Years)', *Bikoret Uparshanut* 30: 99–120 [Heb.].
Bloch, M. (1953), 'On Teaching the Bible', 158–70 in *Horisons of Education and Culture*, edited by Tsevi Zohar, Merhavya: Hakibbutz ha-Artzi Hashomer Hatzair [Heb.].
Bloch, M. (1954), 'Bible Teaching in Highschool', *Ha-Hinukh* 26: 218–25 [Heb.].
Buber, M. (1942), *The Prophetic Faith*, Tel Aviv: Bialik Institute [Heb.].
Cogan, M. (2000), *1 Kings*. AB 10; New York: Doubleday.
Cogan, M. and H. Tadmor (1988), *2 Kings*, AB 11; New York: Doubleday.
Cohen-Levinovsky, N. (2012), 'From Passover 1948 to Passover 1949: Festivals and Festivities during the War of Independence', 609–39 in *Culture, Memory, and History: Essays in Honor of Anita Shapira, II. Israeli Culture and Memory*, Jerusalem: Tel Aviv University and The Zalman Shazar Center for Jewish History [Heb.].
Curriculum (1954), *Curriculum for the Elementary School (State school and Religious State School)*, Vol. 1 (Grades 1–4); Vol 2 (Grades 5–8), Jerusalem: Israel Ministry of Education and Culture [Heb.].
Dror, Y. (2007), 'Teaching the Bible in the Schools of the Labor and the Kibbutz Movements, 1921–1953', *Jewish History* 21: 179–97.
Garsiel, M. (2014), *From Earth to Heaven: A Literary study of Elijah Stories in the Book of Kings*. Bethesda, MD: CDL Press.
Gavrieli, N. (1954), 'Bible Teaching in Elementary School (An Attempt at Fixing a Method)', *Ha-Hinukh*, 26: 225–31 [Heb.].
Gevaryahu, H. (ed.) (1963), 'Elijah the Prophet: Memorandum of Lectures and Discussions at the Israel Bible Society Meetings', Jerusalem: The Israel Bible Society [Heb.].

Ginzberg, L. (2003), *Legends of the Jews*, vol. 2, Philadelphia: Jewish Publication Society.
Goren, Z. (1994), '"Pour Thy Wrath" and the Prophet Elijah's Cup in Non-Orthodox *Haggadot*', *Mehkere Hag* 6: 94–105 [Heb.].
Greenwald, I. (2003), 'Elijah in Talmudic and Extra-Talmudic Sources', *Pathways Through Aggadah* 6: 41–7 [Heb.].
Grossman, H. (2008), 'The Prophet Elijah: A Zionist Hero', *Kesher Eyin* 178: 20–1 [Heb.].
Hacohen, E. (2003), 'Jerusalem in Hebrew Songs, 1917–1928', 473–98 in *Jerusalem and the British Mandate*, edited by Yehoshua Ben-Arieh, Jerusalem: Yad Yizhak Ben Zvi [Heb.].
Ha-Levy, B. (1960), *The Prophecy: A Proposal for a Biblical Subject for the 10th Grade*, Merhavya: Department of Education of the Kibbutz ha-Artzi [Heb.].
Haran, M. (2008), *The Biblical Canon: Its Consolidation to the End of the Second Temple Times and Changes of the Form to the End of the Middle Ages*, v. 3 (Jerusalem: Magnes) [Heb.].
Hever, H. (2004), 'The Kinneret: The Holiness of Place and Nation', 74–107 in *Maelstrom of Identities: A Critical Look at Religion and Secularity in Israel*, edited by Yossi Yonah and Yehuda Goodman, Jerusalem: The Van Leer Institute [Heb.].
Hoshen, D. (2012), *Fire and Water: Philosophical Models in the Bible and the Sages*, Jerusalem: Hebrew Readings Press [Heb.].
Karchevsky, H. (1927), *Hanina Sounds*, Tel Aviv: ha-Gimnasyah ha-Ivrit Herzliya [Heb.].
Kaufmann, Y. (1964), *The Religion of Israel*, vols. 3–4, Tel Aviv: Bialik Institute [Heb.].
Kipnis, L. (1957), 'Hasod', in *Bait*, 95–6, Tel Aviv: Karni [Heb.].
Klausner, J. (1912), *Our Scriptures*, Jaffa: A. Atin [Heb.].
Lammfromm Lederson, T. (2016), 'On Teaching the Latter Prophets in Non-Orthodox Hebrew Education in the Pre-State and in the State of Israel', PhD diss., Tel Aviv University [Heb.].
Lindbeck, K. H, (2010), *Elijah and the Rabbis: Story and Theology*, New York: Columbia University Press.
Margalit, S. (1989), 'The Prophet from Tishbe in the Gilead', *Beit Mikra* 34.3: 216–22.
Mathias, Y. (2002), 'Nationalizing Education: The Emergence of a State History Curriculum', 15–46 in *History, Identity and Memory: Images of the Past in Israeli Education*, edited by Avner Ben-Amos, Tel Aviv: Tel Aviv University Press [Heb.].
Miller, D. M. (2007), 'The Messenger, the Lord, and the Coming Judgment in the Reception History of Malachi 3', *NTS* 53.1: 1–16.
Mossinson, B.-Z. (1919), 'Eliyahu', *Moledet* 7.3-4: 152–61 [Heb.].
Naor, A. (2009), 'Four Models of Political Theology: Supporting Greater Israel Ideology by Labor Zionists Thinkers', 170–203 in *God Will Not Stand Still: Jewish Modernity and Political Theology*, edited by Christoph Schmidt, The Van Leer Institute [Heb.].
Nir, R. (1991), 'John the Baptist in Elijah's Image: Aspects of a Christian Tradition', *Katedra* 139: 55–78 [Heb.].
Ofek, U. (1985), *The Who's Who of Children's Literature*, Tel Aviv: Zmora Bitan [Heb.].
Oryanowski, A. (1938), 'Planning the Teaching of Tanakh', *Shorashim* 1.2: 6–17 [Heb.].
Peli, P. (1986), 'The Prophet Elijah and the Sages', 141–68 in *Aharon Mirsky Jubilee Volume: Essays on Jewish Culture*, edited by Zvi Malachi, Lod: Habermann Institute for Literary Research [Heb.].
Peretz, I. L. (1948), 'The Magician', in Peretz, *Mipi ha-Am*, vol. 1; Tel Aviv: Dvir [Heb.].
Raz, H. (1986), 'Transformations in the Prophet Elijah's Image', *Sifrut Yeladim Vanoar* 12.3: 28–32 [Heb.].
Reshef, S. (1985), *Progressive Education in Eretz-Israel (Palestine) 1915–1929*. Tel-Aviv: Sifriyat Poalim [Heb.].

Rofé, A. (1988a), *The Prophetical Stories: The Narratives about the Prophets in the Hebrew Bible, Their Literary Types and History* (Jerusalem: Magnes).

Rofé, A. (1988b), 'The vineyard of Naboth: The origin and message of the story', *VT* 38: 89–104.

Rofé, A. (1992), *Introduction to Prophetic Literature*, Jerusalem: Academon [Heb.].

Rozowsky, S. (1929), *From the Songs of the Land: A Collection of Yisraeli Songs, with Music Notes* (Warsaw: The World Committee of Hebrew Youth and the Keren ha-Kayemet le-Yisrael [Heb.].

Schoneveld, J. (1976), *The Bible in Israeli Education*, Assen/Amsterdam: Van Gorcum.

Seeligman, I. L. (1996), *Studies in Biblical Literature*, edited by Avi Hurvitz, Sara Japhet and Emanuel Tov, Jerusalem: Magnes [Heb.].

Shaked, M. (2005), *I'll Play You Forever: The Bible in Modern Hebrew Poetry – Readings* (Tel-Aviv: Yediot Ahronot Books) [Heb.].

Shamir Z. (2013), *The Minstrel, The Mistress and the Maid: Bialik Between Hebrew and Yiddish*, Tel Aviv: Safra Books [Heb.].

Shapira, A. (2005), *The Bible and Israeli Identity*, Jerusalem: Magnes [Heb.].

Shapira, S. (ed.) (1948), *Songs of the Aliyah ha-Sheniya*, Tel Aviv: Ha-Merkaz le-tarbut [Heb.].

Shemesh, Y. (1997), 'The Stories of Elisha: A Literary Analysis', Ph.D. diss., Ramat-Gan: Bar-Ilan University [Heb.].

Shinan, A. (1999), *Siddur Avi Chai*, Tel Aviv: Yediot Ahronot [Heb.].

Shinan, A. and Y. Zakovitch (2004), *That's Not What the Good Book Says*, Tel Aviv: Yediot Ahronot [Heb.].

Shinan, A. and Y. Zakovitch (2012), *From Gods to God: How the Bible Debunked, Suppressed, or Changed Ancient Myths and Legends,* Philadelphia: Jewish Publication Society.

Shir, M. (ed) (1961), *Passover Stories for Children*, Tel Aviv: 'Etsbeoni [Heb.].

Shua, Z. (2011), *The History of the Kibbutz Haggadah,* Beit Hashita: Machon ha-Chagim [Heb.].

Simon, U. (1997), *Reading Prophetic Narratives*, The Biblical Encyclopaedia Library, vol. 15; Ramat Gan: Bar-Ilan University Press [Heb.].

Simon, U. (2002), 'The Status of the Bible in Israeli Society, From National Interpretation to Existential Contingency', 23–46 in Simon, *Seek Peace and Pursue it: Topical Issues in the Light of the Bible, The Bible in the Light of Topical Issues*, Tel Aviv: Yediot Aharonot [Heb.].

Sister, M. (1955), *Problems in Biblical Literature*, Tel Aviv: Hakibbutz Hameuchad [Heb.].

Sitton, S. (1998), *Education in the Spirit of the Homeland': The Curriculum of the Teachers' Council for the Keren Kayemet 1925–1953. Dor Ledor* 14 [Heb.].

Thrall, M. E. (1970), 'Elijah and Moses in Mark's account of the Transfiguration', *NTS* 16: 305–17.

Uffenheimer, B. (1984), *Ancient Prophecy in Israel*, Jerusalem: Magnes.

Wensinck, A.J. (1978), 'Al-Khadir', in *Encylopaedia of Islam*, new edition, Leiden: E. J. Brill. 4. 902–5 (https://referenceworks.brillonline.com/entries/encyclopaedia-of-islam-2/al-khadir-al-khidr-COM_0483?s.num=16)

Wiener, A. (1978), *The Prophet Elijah in the Development of Judaism: A Depth-Psychological Study*, London: Routledge & Kegan Paul.

Zakovitch, Y. (1982), 'A Still Small Voice: Form and Contents in 1 Kings 19', *Tarbiz* 51: 329–46 [Heb.].

Zakovitch, Y. (2000), 'Elijah and Elisha in the "Praise of Israel's Great Ancestors" (Ben Sira 47:36–48:19)', 163–77 in *Studies in Bible and Exegesis*, vol 5, edited by Moshe Garsiel et al., Ramat Gan: Bar-Ilan University Press [Heb.].

Zerubavel, Y. (2013), '"The Bible Now": Contemporization, Political Satire and National Memory', *Jerusalem Studies in Jewish Folklore* 28.1: 755–73.

Zuta, H. A. (1935), *Ways of Teaching the Bible, with Examples*, Jerusalem: R. Mas [Heb.].

Zuta, H. A. (1938), *A Teacher's Journey: Memories, Reviews and Essays,* Jerusalem: R. Mas [Heb.].

SANCTIFIED ASSASSINATIONS – QUEEN ATHALIAH OF JUDAH AND ISRAEL'S PRIME MINISTER RABIN: A COMPARISON OF TWO POLITICAL-RELIGIOUS MURDERS

Ora Brison

Introduction[1]

This essay focuses on two politically and religiously motivated murders: The assassination of biblical Queen Athaliah[2] in the Kingdom of Judah of the eighth century BCE (2 Kgs 11.13-16; 2 Chron. 23.12-15),[3] and the assassination of the Prime Minister of the State of Israel, Yitzhak Rabin, on 4 November 1995. By comparing these two murder stories I aim to show how, though these assassinations happened 2,700 years apart, in different circumstances, different cultures and different peoples/societies, they share some significant similar motifs and characteristics. Moreover, the aftermaths of both events indicate that the murderers and their followers did accomplish their goals, bringing about a politico-religious transformation of national and historical significance. Or did they?

Athaliah's assassination is the first account of a murder and consequent replacement of a reigning ruler in the Kingdom of Judah by Yahweh's Temple

---

1. This essay, first presented as a paper at the SBL International Meeting in Buenos Aires, Argentina (July 2015), is dedicated to the memory of my late friend Rachel Maori, and to my cousin and friend Rachel Ashkenazi (may she be blessed with long life – תיבדל לחיים ארוכים), whose insightful comments on an earlier draft were invaluable .

2. Athaliah's name contains the theophoric suffix *ya* and the prefix *'athal*, which is defined as related to the Akkadian noun *etellu*, 'great, exalted, master.' The meaning of her name is 'God is great, God is master' (Zadok 1999); otherwise, the root *'-t-l* is unknown in Hebrew.

3. Unless otherwise indicated, I refer to the NKJV Bible translation.

priests.⁴ Her murder was an attempt to achieve objectives and aspirations of the priestly elite, as supported by military groups and 'the people of the land'.

Yitzhak Rabin's assassination is considered politically and nationalistically motivated. Nonetheless I propose that, essentially, the assassination was religiously and theologically motivated.⁵ The murderer and his supporters – fanatical right-wing, highly Orthodox Jewish rabbis and their disciples – as well as the murderer's background, objectives and moral justification all originated in the religio-theological ideology of the so-called Settlement Movement in the West Bank Occupied Territories.⁶ Both Athaliah and Rabin were perceived by their religious-political opposition as illegitimate (sinful) leaders who must be replaced. Rabin's murder was performed by a single person; Athaliah's was a collective effort. Nevertheless, the similarities between the two are many, and highly disturbing.

Let us examine first the story of Queen Athaliah, the political and religious background of her time, and the participants in her consequent assassination.

Athaliah: Status and Characteristics

Athaliah is introduced in the Bible as a princess of the Omride dynasty who ruled over the Kingdom of Israel. Her parentage is presented in two versions: as the daughter of Ahab, King of Israel (in 2 Kgs 8.18; 2 Chron. 21.6); and (in 2 Kgs 8.26; 2 Chron. 22.2) as the daughter of Omri, Ahab's father.⁷ Her marriage to King Jehoram of Judah was probably aimed at strengthening ties and reaffirming military treaties between the northern and southern kingdoms (1 Kgs 22.4; 2 Kgs 3.7; 2 Chron. 18.1-3; 20.35-36) (Brenner-Idan 2014: 29).

Athaliah's story is part of the larger narrative about the Omride dynasty and the Elijah/Elisha cycle. The attitude towards her is critical and negative, and the biblical

---

4. While this was the first murder of a queen regent/ruler in Judah, the biblical books (1 and 2 Samuel, 1 and 2 Kings and 1 and 2 Chronicles) refer to at least fifteen cases of uprising/coups against a king regent or his decendants in the Kingdom of Israel: For example Nadab, son of Jeroboam, was killed by Baasha (1 Kgs 15.27-8); Jehu killed members of the House of Ahab: Jehoram son of Ahab (2 Kgs 9.24), Jezebel (2 Kgs 9.33) and Ahaziah king of Judah, son of Athaliah (2 Kgs 9.27). Shalum (2 Kgs 15.14) and Pekahiah (2 Kgs 15.30) were assassinated by those who succeeded them. After the assassination of Athaliah, the rulers Joash (2 Kgs 12.21), Amon (2 Kgs 21.23) and Gedaliah (2 Kgs 25.25) were also murdered in the Kingdom of Judah (Cohen 2000: 2).

5. My objective in this essay is to examine the prime motives for these two assassinations. Obviously, there were other motives and reasons (of secondary nature: economic, cultural etc.) for those murders which can also be considered.

6. See, for example, Ravitzky 1993; Freedman 1995; Karpin & Friedman 1998; Inbari 2012; Sagi 2015.

7. The Peshitta to Chronicles suggests that she was Ahab's sister. The NRSV translates 'Omri's granddaughter'. See also Katzenstein 1955; 1971.

authors connect her to the evil doings perpetrated by the House of Ahab. Jehoram's greatest sin is his marriage to her: 'And he walked in the way of the kings of Israel, just as the house of Ahab had done, for the daughter of Ahab was his wife; and he did evil in the sight of the LORD' (2 Kgs 8:18).[8] Notably, there is no mention in Kings of any evil deeds carried out by Jehoram that are referred to in 2 Chron. 21.4. After the death of his father, King Jehoshaphat, Jehoram kills all his brothers in order to secure his rule. After Jehoram's death and the murder of his sons by Jehu (2 Kgs 10.13-14 = 2 Chron. 21.16-17; 22.1), his and Athaliah's son, Ahaziah, is enthroned (2 Kgs 8.24-25; 9.29) by the people of Jerusalem (2 Chron. 22.1).[9]

Although the text does not specify it, many commentators assign the building of a Ba'al temple and the promotion of Canaanite Ba'al cult in Judah to Athaliah's reign.[10] As a result of supporting the Ba'al cult and giving it an official state status, Canaanite religion became the main rival to the Yahwistic cult (Morgenstern 1938; Montgomery 1951: 424; Gray 1970: 569).[11]

Similar to the negative reference relating to Jehoram's reign (2 Kgs 8.18), the biblical author sums up the rule of his son Ahaziah by blaming his mother Athaliah's bad influence : 'He too followed the practices of the house of Ahab, for his mother counseled him to do evil' (2 Chron. 22.3). After just one year on the throne, while on a visit to his relative King Joram of Israel in Jezreel, Ahaziah too is killed by Jehu (2 Kgs 9.27-28; 2 Chron. 22.9).

Upon learning of her son's death, Athaliah murders all other remaining royal heirs[12] except Ahaziah's youngest son Joash, rescued from the massacre by Jehosheba. Athaliah then seizes the throne and reigns as monarch of Judah for six or seven years until her grandson Joash – who has been hidden in the Temple and raised by priests – is crowned king in an uprising against her that is led by the High Priest Jehoiada. Consequently, Athaliah is killed (2 Kgs 11.16, 20; 2 Chron. 23.15, 21). These descriptions are probably intended to demonstrate the religio-political threat that Athaliah was thought to pose to the kingdom's cultural/religious norms (Dutcher-Walls 1996: 7, 70).

---

8. Brenner-Idan (2014: 115–18) claims that similar accusations are directed at foreign women associated with idolatry: the 'women of Moab' (Num. 25.1-3; 15-18) 'King Solomon's wives' (1 Kgs 11.1-10) and Jezebel (1 Kgs 16.31).

9. The different groups that participated in the coup against Athaliah are discussed in the following chapter.

10. On the Ba'al Temple in Samaria and Judah, see Yadin 1978: 127–9.

11. It is difficult to date the introduction of the Phoenician Ba'al cult into the Kingdom of Israel. However, Ahab was probably responsible for the dissemination of Phoenician Ba'al worship, influenced by his wife Jezebel, daughter of Ethba'al king of Sidon (1 Kgs 16.31). By building a temple for Ba'al in Samaria (1 Kgs 16.32) and giving the Ba'al's prophets a legal royal status, Ahab established the Ba'al cult and granted it formal status.

12. This statement is in contrast to former references telling us that the royal family was murdered by Jehoram, Athaliah's husband, when he came to power (2 Chron. 21.4), and that those who remained were later killed by Jehu (2 Kgs 10.13-14; 2 Chron. 22.8).

Athaliah is the only reigning monarch of Judah not a direct descendant of the Davidic line. She is the only woman who rules as a sole sovereign over the Kingdom of Judah. This is a singular situation, considering that in biblical Israelite society a woman could not attain an institutional position of authority and influence in the royal court unless she was the queen mother like Bathsheba (1 Kgs 1.15-31), Maacah (1 Kgs 15.13) or Nehushta (2 Kgs 24.8, 12; also referred to in Jer. 13.18; 29.2), or if she was the king's wife like Jezebel (1 Kgs 21.8-14). We may assume that during the last years of her husband's illness and in her son's absence, Athaliah acted as a coregent (Ashman 2004: 183), thereby strengthening her position in the court.

When looking at Athaliah's story, it is notable that it lacks all the formulaic features that characterize the pragmatic framework of the book of Kings – formulas that appear in the descriptions of all the kings, including Zimri who reigned for only seven days (1 Kgs 16.15-20) (Kochman 1999). The Bible offers neither details about her reign or about her relations with the elite or with other influential classes in the kingdom, nor her connections with Tyre and the Northern Kingdom. All references and adjectives describing Athaliah present her negatively, so as to influence the reader's view by emphasizing the illegitimacy of her reign.

We do not learn of any confrontation between Athaliah and her subjects, her ministers or the priests of Yahweh's temple during her reign. However, as the narrative unfolds, the perceptive reader may infer from Athaliah's portrayal, the accusations against her and the inevitable comparison of her story with that of Queen Jezebel, that she will end up being deposed and murdered (Dutcher-Walls 1996: 70). The predictive words delivered by the prophets Elijah and Elisha (1 Kgs 21.21-23; 2 Kgs 9.7-10), prophesying the destruction of her family, the House of Ahab (Morgenstern 1967), echo throughout her story.

Although Athaliah is portrayed as a powerful figure and a cruel murderess, it seems that she is not a very authoritative and mighty ruler. She does not surround herself with an entourage of court personnel that would remain loyal to her over time; and apparently she is neither aware nor informed of the growing strength of groups opposing her. Her unawareness may have also reflected her underestimation of the growing strength of the Yahwistic religious cult ideologies – or, at the very least, even if she was careful, we are not told about it.

Athaliah's apparent disregard of her risky situation and the weakening of the court elites enables Yahweh's temple priests (loyal to the House of David) who are hiding Joash, the heir to the throne, to gain power and eventually challenge her right to rule over the kingdom. Eventually the priests of Yahweh's temple in Jerusalem fight against the worship of other gods, assemble and organize with other religious/political groups to jointly overthrow Athaliah.[13] Indeed, two of the main Deuteronomistic theological themes communicated in Kings, which revolve around the twin themes of securing and perpetuating the Davidic line's rule and

---

13. Reviv suggests that the coup against Athaliah constituted a 'religious revolt' (1971: 542-3).

the struggle between Yahweh and the Canaanite god Ba'al, are illuminated in Athaliah's story.[14]

We now turn to a short description of the other main characters and religious/military groups involved in Athaliah's story and the conspiracy against her.

Individual Figures and Groups Participating in Athaliah's Story

Jehosheba

Jehosheba is King Jehoram's daughter who saves her nephew Joash, Ahaziah's son, from Athaliah's massacre (2 Kgs 11.2-3 = 2 Chron. 22.11-12). In Chronicles Jehosheba (also named Jehoshabeath) is described as the wife of the priest Jehoiada, the prime conspirator against Athaliah who hides Joash in the Temple.[15]

Jehoiada the High Priest

The Jerusalem Temple chief priest Jehoiada is the initiator and central active figure in the conspiracy against the reigning queen. When first mentioned in the text, he is already deeply involved in this conspiracy, strengthening his power by aligning with several military leaders (2 Kgs 11.4; 2 Chron. 23.1). Jehoiada's personal connection to the royal family is revealed only in Chronicles (2 Chron. 22.11), where it is mentioned that he is married to Jehosheba. He is presented as 'the high priest' in 2 Kgs 12.10 and alternately as 'chief priest' and 'high priest' in 2 Chron. 24.6, 11 – titles granted only to one other priest in Kings, Hilkiah, during the reign of King Josiah (2 Kgs 22.4; 23.4, 24),[16] and to several other priests in Chronicles.[17]

Unlike other coup planners, Jehoiada does not beseech divine sanction and approval of a prominent, independent religious figure (generally a prophet). He decides to initiate the coup against Queen Athaliah because apparently he considers

---

14. Smith (1971: 23–8) maintains that it is misleading to consider Israelite religion 'as a unique entity' in both the Kingdom of Israel and the Kingdom of Judah. The people officially worshipped other gods at the many different sanctuaries of the major cities and in many small communities (29). The demand that the Israelites should worship Yahweh alone and none other began, writes Smith, in the period following Queen Athaliah's death. In spite of prophets who denounced the worship of other gods, this kind of worship remained not only common, but dominant throughout the monarchic period.

15. The use of plural ויסתרו in the description of her action (2 Kgs 11.2) might indicate that, at that time, other people had already been involved in the conspiracy against Athaliah (Montgomery 1951: 424; Gray 1970: 569).

16. Notably, during these periods an extreme religious reform/change was carried out under the leadership of the priestly circles (Sweeney 2007: 345).

17. The other priests are Seraiah (2 Kgs 25.18); Amariah (2 Chron. 19.11); Azariah (2 Chron. 26.20) and another Azariah (2 Chron. 31.10). Aaron is mentioned with the title 'chief priest' in Ezra 7.5.

himself a supreme religious authority. His powerful position is apparent when he sends for various military groups that guard the palace and the temple: 'the captains of the hundreds', 'the body guards' (the Carites) and 'the escorts' (2 Kgs 11.4). They all swear allegiance and show immediate obedience to him. Jehoiada anoints Joash (who is still a child) king in a cultic coronation ceremony, surrounded by the priests, the different military groups and 'the people of the land'. This is the first time the Bible describes the anointing of a new king solely by a priest: until then kings are anointed by prophets – except for Solomon, who is anointed jointly by the priest Zadok and the prophet Nathan (1 Kgs 1.34, 39, 45).[18] Jehoiada's acts show a shift of power within the elite groups of the Judahite Kingdom. While the prophets act in God's name as individuals without much personal political power, the priests constitute a strong, prosperous, influential group to be reckoned with. All the participants pledge allegiance to Jehoiada's protégé Prince Joash in the House of God: taking this oath in the temple endows it with moral and religious validity. Jehoiada then assumes the role of military leader by giving tactical military orders, instructing Athaliah's execution to be carried out outside the temple's sacred premises. Jehoiada emphasizes his religious status as Head Priest by accompanying all his political actions with ritualistic cultic symbols, thus claiming divine sanction for them. In his behaviour and actions Jehoiada resembles the prophets Elijah and Elisha, and King Jehu in the narrative about the annihilation of Ahab's House.

Once Athaliah is murdered, all the participants in the coup enter the palace and perform another symbolic ceremonial act by having Joash sit on the throne of the King of Judah.

King Joash

The third figure participating in the coup against Athaliah is Joash, presented in the biblical story as a child reared and influenced by the Temple priests. Despite being the son of Ahaziah, he is considered the legitimate descendant of the Davidic line and, therefore, the only legitimate heir to the Judahite throne. His rise to power, although achieved in a violent coup following the murder of the reigning Queen Athaliah (his grandmother), is considered legal, and his anointment and coronation intentionally performed in the Temple – by Jehoiada the High Priest – in order to emphasize this legitimacy (Dutcher-Walls 1996: 74; Sweeney 2007: 343–4).

---

18. According to Deut. 17.15, the king is chosen by God to rule over Israel; he is anointed (in Hebrew *Mashiach*, Messiah) by God's messenger (a prophet or a priest), and thus his reign becomes sanctified by God. There is a special emphasis in the Bible on the covenant between God and the king and between the king and the people (1 Sam. 10.1, 25; 16.13; Liver 1962: 1088–90). Kingship in Israel was promised and guaranteed by God to David and his descendants. We do not have details concerning the crowning of each of the kings of Israel and Judah; however, it can be assumed that the covenant of Mizpah (1 Sam. 10.25) became the model of kingship for the Israelite kings (Ben-Barak 1976: 407–8).

Religious/Military Groups Participating in the Coup

The temple priests In Yahwistic cult and religion, priests inherit their positions and enjoy a unique status in society. Notably, however, throughout Kings (in both kingdoms) the priests are not mentioned as an influential group within the ruling classes until the coup against Athaliah.[19] The growing power of the Yahwistic priestly groups during her reign was a new situation that might be explained as a consequence of the weakening of the royal elite classes, caused by the assassination of King Ahaziah's sons and ministers by Jehu and the subsequent change of regime. After Athaliah's assassination and Joash's coronation, Jehoiada and the priests were highly involved in state matters. I suggest that similar contextual characteristics are seen also in the growing influence and role of the priesthood in the time of King Josiah's reform/reign, about two centuries later.

The Military Groups and the Royal Guards (2 Kgs 11.4)

The military groups mentioned in this story are 'the captains of the hundreds' (שָׂרֵי הַמֵּאוֹת), the 'Carites' (כרי),[20] the bodyguards and the 'escorts' (רצים)[21] who run before the king's chariot. They all join Jehoiada, becoming the executive arm in the coup against the queen. This group is associated with the king's personal protection and was probably under his direct command and authority (1 Kgs 14.27-28).[22] The escorts in Athaliah's story are described as having a central role in the coup against her.

The People of the Land Besides the temple priests and the military groups, another most important group that participated in the coup against Athaliah was 'the people of the land' (עַם הָאָרֶץ). The meaning of this term changes in different biblical (and later) periods (Talmon 1967).[23] Van Seters interprets the term as denoting the leaders

---

19. The only reference is to the priests Zadok and Abiathar in relation to the succession struggle over David's throne in 1 Kgs 1 (Zadok in verses 8, 26, 32, 34, 38, 44-45; Abiathar in verses 7, 19, 25, 42).

20. It is not clear who are the biblical Carites that Jehoiada brings to the temple as guards. Most commentators identify them with the group named the Cherethites (הַכְּרֵתִי), mentioned among the military groups faithful and supportive to David and Solomon (2 Sam. 8.18; 20.23). This probably refers to a foreign mercenary unit, presumably an ethnic group from southwestern Asia employed by the foreign armies of Egypt and Lydia (Loewenshtamm 1962; Cogan and Tadmor 1988: 126).

21. BDB 930: the outrunners, the royal escorts, royal bodyguards. See also 1 Sam. 22.17; 2 Sam. 15.1; 1 Kgs 14.27-28 = 2 Chron. 12.10-11; 1 Kgs 1.5 (according to the MT).

22. In the story of Jehu's violent coup he, as the new king, commands his guards-escorts to kill the Ba'al priests and worshippers (2 Kgs 10.25). They are also described as guarding Joash during the coronation: 'Then the escorts stood, every man with his weapons in his hand, all around the king' (2 Kgs 11.11).

23. In the singular form (as opposed to its plural form, peoples of the land) it occurs about fifty times (BDB: 766).

of the tribes (2007: 97). The reference to 'the people of the land' occurs in Kings several times in the context of the changing of a ruler (Joash – 2 Kgs 11.14, 18, 19, 20; Yotam – 2 Kgs 15.5; Josiah – 2 Kgs 21.24; Yehoahaz – 2 Kgs 23.30). Some scholars suggest that in the First Temple period the term 'the people of the land' probably referred to a group of supporters and loyalists of the House of David (perhaps from the tribe of Judah). This group operated within the city of Jerusalem and its purpose was to ensure the continuity of the Davidic line (Tsevat 1956: 116; Talmon 1967: 71).

This specific group also joins the temple priests after Joash's coronation, participates in the destruction of Ba'al temples, altars and statues and in killing Matan, Ba'al's priest. 'The people of the land' have a similar role in Josiah's reform two centuries later. They are mentioned for the most part as a group that accompanies the removal of Ba'al worship and priests of the high altars in Judahite territory outside of Jerusalem.[24]

The Murder of a Queen (2 Kgs 11.13-16; 2 Chron. 22.12-15)

The loud noises of the celebration of Joash's coronation in the temple draw Athaliah's attention. Rather than staying in her palace and asking her men to inquire what the commotion is about, she enters the temple area that is within the palace-temple building complex.[25] There, unprepared for what she sees, she is utterly taken by surprise, shocked as she recognizes the proceedings as a coronation and tears her clothes, shouting 'Treason! Treason!' (קשר קשר).[26] Notably, this is the only instance in Athaliah's story that we hear her voice and get a glimpse of her reaction in this traumatic situation.

Athaliah's murder and replacement have most probably been carefully planned and intended to be performed openly rather than clandestinely. The date chosen for the coup was the New Year festival, when many people come to Jerusalem to celebrate in the temple. Joash's coronation and enthronement are performed in public before a crowd and accompanied by a religious covenant-making ritual carried out by Jehoiada. The intention is to emphasize Joash's legitimacy as heir to the Davidic throne.[27] Athaliah is removed by force from the sanctified temple

---

24. On 'the people of the land' see Soggin 1963; Vaux 1964; Nicholson 1965; Loewenshtamm 1971: 239–40; Ben-Barak 1976; Cogan and Tadmor 1988: 129–30; Talmon 1999; Van Seters 2007: 97.

25. On the architecture and ideology of the palace and temple compound, see Meyers 1983.

26. The tearing of clothes is a mourning custom, but in this context it carries clear overtones symbolizing the removal of the monarchy from the reigning ruler (see 1 Sam. 15.27-28; 1 Kgs 29–31) (Cohen 2000: 27).

27. Joash's silence throughout the story is striking. Dutcher-Walls maintains that this literary device is intended to emphasize that, while his status is vital to the story, his personal character is not (Dutcher-Walls 1996: 31).

premises and executed in public per Jehoiada's instructions to the captains of hundreds (Cogan and Tadmor 1988: 130).

The coup achieves the aims of its initiators and supporters. The foreign illegitimate ruler, a woman, a follower of Ba'al, is murdered and replaced by a legitimate Davidic descendant. The Ba'al temple is destroyed, its priest Matan is killed, and the absolute superiority of Yahweh's worship is asserted. The newly established governance of the kingdom would, from here on, be carried out under priestly guidance and influence.

Notably, while most of the uprisings/coups against rulers or their decendants in the Kingdom of Israel were generally executed by usurpers for personal political, social and economic goals, the primary motives for Athaliah's assassination seem to be theological/ideological. Throughout Athaliah's story resonates the theological/ eschatological idea expressed in 1 Chron. 17.11-15 that kingship would be besowed at all times upon the house of David by God himself, which is emphasized by her violent replacement.

The Assassination of a Prime Minister

Yitzhak Rabin, then prime minister of Israel, was assassinated in Tel Aviv on 4 November 1995, by an extreme right-wing, Orthodox Jewish activist, at the end of a rally supporting the Oslo Accords. This murder was one of the most traumatizing and formative events for the Israeli State since its establishment in 1948: an occurrence that left a deep imprint and has significant consequences for the political, social, cultural and moral values of the Israeli people, as well as for the continuation of the peace process between Israel, the Palestinians and the Arab World.[28]

The Oslo Accords, signed between the Israeli government and the Palestinian leadership in August and September 1993, offered a geographical and political solution to the Israeli–Palestinian conflict. They were based on a worldview centered on liberal and civil human rights ideologies, with pragmatic political comprehension regarding the needs of the various populations in the region. The perspectives expressed in the Oslo Accords propose Israel's withdrawal from Palestinian occupied territories in exchange for a peace agreement between Israel and the Arab World, and the establishment of a Palestinian state in the West Bank and the Gaza Strip.[29] Those ideas and understandings stood in stark contrast not only to the ideologies, standpoints and perspectives of various extreme nationalistic secular people, but mainly to the ideologies of extreme religious groups in Israel.

---

28. On Rabin's assassination, see Peri 2000; Ephron 2015.

29. On the peace negotiations and the signing of the Oslo Accords, see Freedman 1998; Beilin 1999; Buchanan 2000; Eran 2002.

The Sociopolitical-religious Background of Rabin's Assassination

To try and understand the aspects, perspectives, motives and atmosphere that led to Rabin's murder, and in order to substantiate my argument that the religious aspect has major significance for this murder, we must describe the sociopolitical-religious circumstances/background in Israel at the time of the murder. It is also important that we go back to the history of the Zionist movement, the establishment of the State of Israel and the 1967 Six-Day War and the religious-political groups that rose following this military victory. But first, I would like to describe briefly Yitzhak Rabin's personal background, his career and his political standpoint.

Yitzhak Rabin (1922–95)[30]

Rabin was born in Jerusalem in 1922 to a family of Russian-Ukrainian Jewish Immigrants. Both his parents were socialist activists for most of their lives.[31] When Rabin was sixteen years old he joined the *Palmach*, a commando unit of the *Haganah* (the pre-State, mainstream Jewish defence organization in the then British mandate called Palestina/Eretz Israel). After the establishment of the state he served in the *IDF* (Israel Defence Forces) for twenty-seven years, and moved up the military hierarchy until he was appointed Chief of Staff in 1964. Under his command the *IDF* achieved victory over the neighbouring Arab states (Egypt, Syria and Jordan) in the Six-Day War (1967). After his retirement from military service Rabin served as Israel's ambassador to the United States from 1968 to 1973.

Rabin was politically aligned with the socialist, left-wing political parties. He was appointed prime minister in 1974 and resigned in 1977. He was the first Israeli-born prime minister of Israel, as well as the first military veteran in this position. From 1984 to 1990 he served in several national unity governments as Minister of Defence, until he was reelected for a second term as prime minister in 1992. During this term, secret negotiations took place between Israeli left-wing political leaders (among whom was Shimon Peres, Rabin's political rival) and PLO (Palestinian Liberation Organization) leader Yasser Arafat. These negotiations eventually led to the Oslo Accords. For most of his career, Rabin did not regard the PLO as a legitimate partner for any kind of peace agreement. But the bitter experience of the bloody years of the Palestinian first *intifada* (uprising) in Israel (1987–93) seems to have convinced him that the status quo was unsustainable, and that Israel could not rule by force over one and a half million Palestinians. Although he was not involved in the first stages of the negotiations, Rabin accepted the

---

30. For Rabin's biography, see Goldstein 2006; Rabinovich 2017.

31. His father, Nehemiah, born in the Ukraine, moved to the United States and immigrated to Palestina/EI after joining the Jewish Legion during the First World War. His mother, Rosa Cohen, was among the first members of the *Haganah* and known for her socialist activities as 'Red Rosa' - a tribute to Rosa Luxemburg, the Jewish Polish-German revolutionary (1871–1919), commemorated for her actions during the anti-Jewish pogroms in the Old City of Jerusalem. On Rosa Luxemburg, see Evans 2015.

proposals and decisions that were made in these meetings, and signed several historic agreements with the Palestinian leaders as part of the Accords. He also signed the peace treaty with Jordan. In 1994 Rabin was awarded the Nobel Peace Prize, together with Shimon Peres and Yasser Arafat, following the signing of the Oslo Accords.[32] The Oslo Accords created the Palestinian National Authority and granted it partial control over parts of the Gaza Strip and the West Bank.

The Accords greatly polarized Rabin's image in Israeli society: some saw him as a hero for advancing the cause of peace; some considered him a traitor for giving away land they saw as rightfully belonging to Israel. Although many right-wing protests were held in Israel against the agreements, Rabin continued on the path of the Oslo Accords.[33]

Rabin's Assassination

The opposition to and demonstrations against the Oslo Accords were mostly directed personally against Rabin, who had been turned by some into a symbol of a traitor. On 4 November 1995 Rabin attended a mass rally at the Kings of Israel Square (now Rabin Square) in Tel Aviv, held in support of the Oslo Accords. When the rally ended, Rabin was shot while walking towards his car. Rabin was rushed to a nearby hospital where he died shortly afterwards. The assassin, immediately seized by Rabin's bodyguards, was later charged with murder, found guilty and sentenced to solitary life imprisonment. Shortly after the assassination Israel's minister of foreign affairs, Shimon Peres, was appointed acting prime minister. Peres lost this position seven months later in the 1996 elections, when the right-wing parties won and formed a coalition with the religious parties. Rabin's murder enabled the return to power of a right-wing government headed by Benjamin Netanyahu, and greatly intensified the power of religion and nationalism in Israeli politics.

Between State and Religion in Israel

Israel is a democracy; and yet, it is unique in not having an official separation between religion and state. The State of Israel was established on liberal, democratic ideas of human rights and equality, on the one hand; and on Jewish tradition rooted in biblical and postbiblical law, on the other (Elior 2015:80). Due to historical, national, social and political complexities, the founding leaders of the State refrained from defining the separation in the Declaration of the Establishment of the State of Israel. They believed that the foundational document – known as the Declaration (or Scroll) of Independence – based on humanistic, secular, liberal and democratic ideals of freedom, justice and peace, would sufficiently ensure

---

32. The Nobel Peace Prize 1994; see https://www.nobelprize.org/nobel_prizes/peace/laureates/1994/press.html.

33. Freedman 1995; Rabinovich 2017.

complete equality of social and political rights to all the state's citizens irrespective of religion, race or sex. However, the *Knesset* (the Israeli Parliament) maintained that the Declaration was neither a law nor an ordinary legal document. Over the years, significant concessions were made by secular Israeli governments to the religious parties. These resulted in no national consensus that allows drawing up a proper constitution that would, among other issues, regulate the relations between religion and state. The problem of the separation of religion and state had already started at the founding of the Zionist movements.

The Zionist Movement and the Establishment of the State of Israel[34]

The Zionist movement emerged as a Jewish national revival movement in Central and Eastern Europe at the end of the nineteenth century. The European enlightment and Emancipation brought about a major change in the position and status of the Jews in Western European countries. The Emancipation led to the cancellation of legal restrictions to Jewish citizenship in Europe. The Jews were recognized as equal citizens, granted the rights and duties of citizenship and enabled organized Jewish communities and individuals to radically change their relations with the official institutions of various European countries.[35] The Zionist movement is considered to be the product of this overall epoch of European liberalism. From its beginning, the goals of Zionism were the return to Zion, to secure a national home for Jews by the gathering of Jews from diasporas, establishing of an independent Jewish sovereignty and the revival of Hebrew culture and language. Apart from these general principles, the Zionist movement was never homogenous. The yearning for the return of the Jewish people to its 'old-new land' was expressed in diverse ideologies and philosophies within the different groups of the Zionist movement. There were several attitudes towards Zionism, which can be divided roughly into three main streams of Judaism: secular Zionist Judaism, religious Zionist Judaism and ultra-Orthodox Judaism.[36]

Under the influence of the political and social changes of the European Emancipation, the American Bill of Rights and the Constitution as well as the French Revolution, the secular Zionist stream rejected the religious/faith dimension of Judaism and defined Judaism as a nation, ethnos and culture rather than a religion. Its purpose was to establish a homeland (on a defined territory) for a Hebrew/Jewish nation and to create a national entity and a people detached from the burden of the Jewish past of Diaspora generations. This was to be achieved by separating religion

---

34. This short summary of the Zionist movements, the establishment of the State of Israel and Gush Emunim movement is based on Elior 2015 and Simon 2002: 229–73. See also Shapira 2004; Persico 2017.

35. On Emancipation, Jewish Emancipation and Self-Emancipation see Katz 1986; Birnbaum and Katznelson 1995.

36. Most of the Jewish people were not particularly interested in Zionism in general and embraced ideologies like socialism, communism and local-nationalism; for example, the Jewish Labour Bund (Blatman 2003; Zimmerman, 2004; also http://www.bundism.net/bibliography).

from state and creating a secular nation state. Secular Zionism succeeded in its main mission, which was the establishment of a secular state for the Jewish people in 1948 – the State of Israel. The newly established Israeli government decided not to enforce a secular constitution on its citizens, leaving the Declaration of Independence as a formative, yet not strictly binding document, loosely outlining the notion of an ideal, perhaps unrealistic society in the new state. Today, decades later, there exist only a handful of 'basic laws', only two of which are aimed at protecting human rights. Israel is far from a national consensus for a proper constitution that could, among other issues, regulate the balance between religion and state.

Until 1967 some equilibrium existed between state politics and the religious aspirations of most religious groups. Most of the biblical holy sites were inaccessible, and Messianic dreams of conquest and settlement were subdued. In 1967 this changed.

Rabin's assassination is, therefore, connected to thousands of years of Jewish mythical/religious beliefs in God's covenant and the divine promise to Abraham and his descendants that the Land of Israel is given to the people of Israel, and the notion that the Bible is the founding document of the people of Israel throughout its generations: 'To your descendants I have given this land, from the river of Egypt to the great river, the River Euphrates' (Gen. 15.18). The establishment of the State of Israel is understood as the expression of the Messianic Jewish ideal, the realization of the eschatological prophecy of the End of Days. Uriel Simon writes that the background for Rabin's assassination can be explained on the basis of the central aspect of Judaism: 'Holiness is at the heart of the religion of Israel' (Simon 2002: 238). According to Simon, the definition of 'holiness' consists of two elements: sacred place and holy time, while the relative importance of each element is connected to time/period and situations/circumstances. As long as the Jerusalem temple existed, the sanctity of the place was foremost; when the Second Temple was destroyed, the significance of holy time increased, and it became possible to worship God even without a sanctuary and far from holy places. The establishment of the State of Israel changed this equation which existed for thousands of years.

The majority of the Israeli State's Jewish citizens consider themselves secular and traditionally-observant Zionists. However and for many reasons, there is a constant drift to the political nationalistic right. But most Israelis also understand that there is a realistic need to compromise and be flexible on the issue of Israel's state borders, and to accept that there is another people within these territories who also have rights by virtue of their generation-long residence in this land. Recent polls show that slightly more than 50% of Israeli citizens support a two-state solution.[37]

---

37. A joint poll conducted in 2017 by the Tami Steinmetz Center for Peace Research (TSC) at Tel Aviv University and the Palestinian Center for Policy and Survey Research (PSR) shows that the support for a comprehensive peace agreement among Israeli Jews has dropped, but remains unchanged among Palestinians. There is also a decline among Israeli Jews' support of the two-state solution (53%) and a rise among Palestinians (52%): http://www.pcpsr.org/en/node/696

The ultra-Orthodox groups regard the Land of Israel as part of the holy land's territory and most consider the return to it as a sovereign state to have been initiated divinely as a 'sacred time'. But, for them, God's promise will be realized only upon the physical arrival of the Davidic Messiah. Those groups neither consider themselves nor are considered Zionist. There were (and still are) additional groups, mostly religious right-wing ones (although not self-defined as ultra-orthodox) that did not (and do not) recognize the authority of a secular government with regard to state laws which, in their opinion, contradict religious laws. Some actively oppose the goverment (Elior 2015: 88–91; Sagi 2015: 317–20; 388–9). Regrettably, these conflicting beliefs and ideologies culminated in the murder of a prime minister.

Modern Orthodox Zionist Judaism is a political movement with ideologies that are very different from those held by the ultra-Orthodox. In contrast to the latter, modern-Orthodox national Zionism expresses the biblical ethos in unequivocal historical terminology. Its goal is to bring about the coming of the Messiah 'here and now' and to actively fulfil the biblical divine promise. In the pursuit of messianic redemption, some members of this movement are quite ruthless (Keshev and Ir Amim 2013: 45–51; Elior 2015: 86–91).

Religious nationalism accepted the theology formulated by Rabbi Avraham Yitzchak Hacohen Kook and his son Rabbi Zvi Yehuda Kook, who regarded the Jewish state as a divine instrument that would bring about the final redemption, claiming that after a period of democratic rule the state will be transformed into a religious state that will be organized and operate according to Jewish law (Ravitzky 1993; Fischer 2007: 215–69; Aran 2013). After the Six-Day War (1967), it seemed as if the divine promise was being fulfilled in the form of Israeli/Jewish sovereignty over the greater part of the historic Land of Israel.

Following Israel's victory in the 1967 war, the *Gush Emunim* (Heb.: Bloc of the Faithful) movement was established – an offspring of the Israeli national-religious, and Zionist, political party. Its leaders promoted and unofficially directed the Jewish settlement activity in the territories occupied during the war: the West Bank (Judea and Samaria), Gaza Strip and Golan Heights. The goal was to colonize as much of these areas and establish Israeli settlements as quickly as possible. Within the religious nationalist community, Israel's wars are identified with God's battles. For this community, the victory and conquest of the West Bank in the Six-Day War were a clear indication that the messianic process of redemption was underway. This community regards the settling and inhabiting of biblical Canaan, the Promised Land, by Jews as a fundamental political objective that is religiously sanctioned, even sanctified. This belief rejects all territorial compromises and assigns the solution of the conflict with the Palestinians to the creation of a single-state (with diminished civil rights for its Palestinian inhabitants).

Fanatics, both Jewish and Palestinian, totally rejected the Oslo Accords and actively tried everything to sabotage their application. Rabin's assassination took place during a wave of terrorist activities against Israeli civilians and settlers in the Occupied Territories. Palestinian terrorist acts significantly increased the polarization between Jewish Israeli left- and right-wing voters. Having signed the Oslo Accords, Prime Minister Rabin was often portrayed in religious national media as an illegitimate leader, and accused of being a traitor and even a murderer. His positions regarding the Oslo Accords were described as acts of treason. These groups, led by fanatical rabbis, sanctified the land, and the Occupied Territories became sacred in their eyes. Submitting sacred land to non-Jews, as had been agreed to in the Oslo Accords, thus became a mortal sin. Rabin's photos in military uniform were manipulated to show him in Nazi uniform. He was labelled not only a traitor but also a heretic. The violent demonstrations against Rabin, and his denunciation and excommunication by the religious extremists, culminated in a bizarre (pseudo-Kabbalistic) cursing ritual, the *Pulsa' [or Pulsi] de Nura'* (Aramaic: lash[es] of fire), conducted by a radical right-wing activist and intended to stop Rabin and the peace process. Although Israeli security forces were aware of these groups and their ideologies, these forces failed to assess how deep was their commitment to those beliefs. In November 1993, the Union of Rabbis for the People of Israel and Eretz Israel issued the first דין רודף (Heb. *din rodef*, the 'law of the pursuer'), and דין מוסר (Heb. *din moser*, the 'law of the informant'), in connection with the plan to surrender of (parts of) the Land of Israel. According to the halakha, it is a religious duty to kill Jews who actively endanger the life of other Jews by pursuing or informing on them. Therefore, any person may act within the framework of this law even without an order from an authorized court, when the circumstances so require.[38]

A halakhic ruling prohibiting the evacuation of West Bank settlement areas was published in July1995.[39] On 4 November 1995 Rabin was assassinated (B. Michael 2016).

Two Assassinations: A Comparison

The assassinations of Athaliah and Rabin happened 2,700 years apart in different cultures. Still, they share central characteristics and similar motifs.

---

38. These Jewish religious principles stem from the midrash to Exod. 22.1 in the *Talmud Bavli Sanhedrin 72a*: 'if someone comes to kill you, rise up and kill him first' (Inbari 2012: 139). The purpose of the killing is not punishment but rather prevention. See also Karpin and Friedman 1998; Fischer 2007: 363–6.

39. In 1977 Rabbi Zvi Yehuda Kook (a prominent spiritual/religious leader of Religious Zionism) ruled that there was no possibility of discussing the giving away of the Land of Israel under any political-security circumstance, and called for civil war in connection with plans for withdrawal: 'On this land and its borders, we are committed to self-sacrifice' (Rosnak 2013: 116). Rabbi Zvi Yehuda Kook forbade the return of territories or withdrawal from them; and Rabbi Menachem Mendel Schneerson, the Lubavitcher Rebbe, firmly supported the policy of 'not an inch'. In their opinion, the territorial expansion following the Six-Day War and the settlement throughout the Occupied Territories were an expression of God's will to redeem his people (Elior 2015: 86–90). See also Fischer 2007: 168–88.

Both murders present a struggle between religious ideologies. Let us state the obvious: in Rabin's case, secularism is a religious system as well. The main resemblance between Athaliah's murder and Rabin's assassination is the identity of the religious, ideological, political and theological motives behind both. The situation in which religious groups refuse to recognize the authority of a secularist, non-religious government or monarch, or another (religious or otherwise) ideology, but also try to overthrow them by illegal means is similar in both cases.

The two assassinations depart from the conventional model of a ruler's murder (in ancient and modern times), initiated and carried out by a military leader and/or military troops who wish to seize power and replace the former regime. Notably, in Athaliah's case, the participation of military groups plays an instrumental role in the coup, rather than as its instigator. Indeed, the texts are emphatic that Jehoiada, 'the chief priest', is throughout the entire enterprise the *metteur en scène* (Cohen 2000: 6). In Rabin's case the military was not involved at all.

The opposition to Athaliah's rule came mainly from a Yahwhistic priestly group and House of David supporters. Rabin's opposition came mainly from ideological religious and non-religious nationalistic groups. The purpose of the assassinations of both Athaliah and Rabin was to initiate a fundamental sociopolitical and religio-theological change. Both murders may be perceived as part of the theological link to the biblical covenant between God and his people and to the belief in God's promise to give the Land of Canaan to the Israelites.

Rabin's murderer and the group he belonged to were totally immersed in religious and eschatological-messianic ideas, as evident from their discourse, writings and conduct.[40] Athaliah's murder was instigated by a Yahwistic priestly group headed by the High/Chief Priest who opposed the syncretic Ba'al cult that had been favoured during Athaliah's reign in Judah. The priests fought to ensure the preponderance of Yahweh's cult and the rule of his chosen Davidic king. Rabin's murderer was obsessed with the idea of putting an end to the implementation of the Oslo Accords and breaking the Oslo spirit. This could be considered similar to destroying Ba'al's temple and the attempts to end Ba'al's cult and worship in Judah. In both cases, the assassinations were the starting point for religious upheaval and the strengthening of religious dogma. Athaliah's murder and Joash's coronation represent the reestablishing of legitimacy, with God's chosen Davidic descendant winning the throne. But, in fact, the most significant change brought about by this assassination is that Jehoiada and the temple priests become the most influential and authorized political power in the kingdom.

In contemporary Israel, the ultimate goal of fundamentalist and radical religious groups has been and still is to strengthen their covenant with the God of Israel and thus bring about a greater Israel and, eventually, redemption. Some of these groups actually discuss the renewal of a Davidic monarchy (Fischer 2009).

The issue of the sovereign's divine legitimacy is a significant aspect/motif in the story of Athaliah, and it is also expressed in the opposition against Prime Minister Rabin's governing and actions: he was perceived, from a religious point of view, as

---

40. Ravitzky 1993; Inbari 2008; Rosnak 2013.

a heretic and unauthorized/illegitimate leader for agreeing to give up some Land of Israel territories and turn them over to the Palestinians. This was perceived as offensive sacrilege.

The shared characteristics between the two assassinations can be seen also in other aspects. The date chosen for the coup against Athaliah was the New Year festival, when many pilgrims come to Jerusalem. The date chosen for Rabin's assassination was during a peace rally in which tens of thousands of people participated. Both murders were perpetrated in public, in front of crowds. Neither murder was a spontaneous act; rather, both were planned carefully and intended to be performed and presented openly. More similarities are evident in the outcome of the events. After Athaliah's murder, even though Joash becomes king, Jehoiada and the priests are very much involved in state matters. This was so significant that when, later on in his reign, Joash dares to sound different ideas concerning the management of the temple, opposing those of the priestly class, he too is murdered (story in 2 Chron. 24; only a short notice in 2 Kgs 12.21; and see further below). These aims are made obvious by the replacement of the monarch (Joash instead of Athaliah) and the religious reform that took place immediately after her murder. As mentioned above, after Rabin's assassination and short period in which Shimon Peres was Israel's acting prime minister, the leftist government was replaced (through democratic elections!) by Benjamin Netanyahu's right-wing party, in coalition with the religious parties. Several short-lived left-wing and centre-line coalition governments that tried to revive the peace talks and reach interim agreements with the Palestinian Authority failed.[41] Since Rabin's murder, coalitions of right-wing and religious parties have been in power for most of the time. The religious parties are strengthening their hold on the Israeli secular life by legislating halakhic-based laws, and by introducing religious changes and restrictions into the Israeli Army (*IDF*)'s regulations. Indeed, the similarities between the two murders extends to the aftermath and consequences during subsequent years.[42]

Conclusion

I have argued that Athaliah's [ostensibly] religiously motivated murder put an end to the separation between kingdom and priesthood in Judah. The texts about Joash's rule after Athaliah's murder provide additional data on the relationship between the priesthood and the king during this period, and shed light on the motives for Athaliah's murder. Joash's forty years as king are characterized mostly by the influence of Jehoiada and Yahweh's temple priests. In 2 Chron. 24.17, 20-25 we see how only after Jehoiada's death Joash seizes the opportunity to diminish the priests' privileges. He reduces priestly rights, limiting priests to engage in temple

---

41. The twenty-eighth government (1999–2001); the thirtieth government (2003–6); the thirty-first government (2006–9). https://www.knesset.gov.il/govt/heb/GovtByMinistry.asp

42. On the prospects of peace after Rabin's assassination, see Filkins 2015.

matters, and restores the status of traditional, 'secular' royal court personnel, to which the king's ministers belong. Once again the change is not accepted by the priests; the opposition against Joash increases and he is later murdered. One cannot rule out the possibility that Joash's servants, who conspire and murder him, come (again) from priestly circles (Kochman 1999: 98). If one thought that Athaliah's murder was prompted predominantly by her gender, her foreignness, her being a daughter of the House of Ahab, and by non-religious political reasons, Joash's murder strengthens the assertion that the overarching motivation for her murder was religious, born out of religious fanaticism and the intolerance of self-styled Yahweh messengers.

Over two decades have passed since Rabin's assassination. The political and religious situation in Israel and in the region has changed dramatically. Rabin's assassination almost certainly stopped Israel's withdrawal from the Palestinian Occupied Territories and the implementation of the Oslo Accords. New settlements were built also under left-wing-centre-line governments, but mainly under Benjamin Netanyahu's governments.

It would be too simplistic to blame and associate the situation and relations between Israel and the Palestinians today solely on the murder. Nevertheless, before Rabin's assassination, even though there were few chances for a comprehensive peace agreement in the 1990s, Israelis and Palestinians still hoped that peace would eventually come. Since Rabin's assassination there have been waves of organized terrorist acts by Palestinians, climaxing with the outbreak of a second Palestinian uprising against Israel (the Al-Aqsa *Intifada* of 2000–2005); and peace talks have stagnated. The 2007 split in the Palestinian Authority, the rise of Hamas and the strengthening of Palestinian extremist groups that are against any agreement with Israel whatever, also contributed to the almost complete break in negotiations. Moreover, the failure of the USA and European countries to renew the peace talks, and the chaotic events in the Middle East, can promise no positive solution in the foreseeable future.

As for the political, cultural and ideological changes in Israeli society that occurred following these events, there is no doubt that Rabin's assassination is the fault line between a realistic Israel based on secular liberal rationalism; and a setting whereby religious myths and fanaticism take over. The State of Israel today is much more religiously and nationalistically oriented than it was almost twenty-five years ago when Rabin was murdered. Today, the thought of another religio-political murder is no longer inconceivable.

Epilogue (February 2021)

In January 2020, the former US President Trump presented, in Washington, a peace plan for Israel and the Palestinians, nicknamed 'deal of the century'. Benjamin Netanyahu, Israel's prime minister (still), was in attendance; the Palestinians were not. The plan, in its general frame, was biased in Israel's favour; it got immediate rave reviews from Netanyahu and the Jewish crowd present. They were ecstatic, even though a quick scrunity showed that it contained a plan for 'two states for two people', 'two lands for two people' – almost exactly in terms of conditions and territory as in the Oslo Accords, for the support of which Rabin was declared a traitor and eventually murdered.

Trump's plan is Pro-Israeli, but nevertheless includes the return of West Bank territories to Palestinian rule. Fifty Jewish Rabbis, of *Gush Emunim* and other West Bank settlers, object to the plan on religious and territorial grounds. The Israeli political Right that hated the Oslo Accords more or less accepts its twin, the Trump Plan, especially since it is accompanied by peace accords with countries that do not have land borders with Israel, such as the United Arab Emirates and Morroco.

So now we wait.

Bibiography

Ackerman, S. (1993), 'The Queen Mother and the Cult in Ancient Israel', *JBL* 112: 385–401.

Aran, G. (2013), *Kookism: The Roots of Gush Emunim, the Settlers' Culture, Zionist Theology, Messianism in our Time* Jerusalem: Carmel Publishing [Heb.].

Ashman, A. (2004), '"And Athaliah Did Reign over the Land" (2 Kgs 11.3): On the Israelite Queens in the Bible', *Beit Mikra* 49.2: 178–93 [Heb.].

B. Michael (2016), 'Rabin's Death Wasn't a Political Murder – It Was a Religious One', *Ha'aretz*, 15 November. Available online: http://www.haaretz.com/opinion/. premium-1.753157 [Heb.]. [Accessed June 2020]

Beilin, Y. (1999), *Touching Peace: From the Oslo Accord to a Final Agreement*, London: Weidenfeld & Nicolson.

Ben-Barak, Z. (1976), 'The Mizpah Covenant as the Source of the Israelite Monarchic Covenant', *Beit Mikra* 3: 402–11 [Heb.].

Ben-Barak, Z. (1991), 'The Status and Right of the Gebira', *JBL* 110: 23–34.

Birnbaum, P. and Katznelson, I. (eds.) (1995), *Paths of Emancipation: Jews, States, and Citizenship,* Princeton: Princeton University Press.

Blatman, D. (2003), *For Our Freedom and Yours: The Jewish Labour Bund in Poland 1939-1949*, London; Portland.

Bowen, N. R. (2001), 'The Quest for the Historical *Gébîrâ*', *CBQ* 64: 597–618.

Brenner-Idan, A. (2014), *The Israelite Woman: Social Role and Literary Type in Biblical Narrative*, London and Oxford: Bloomsbury T&T Clark.

Brenner-Idan, A. (2015), 'Male Royals and Their Ethnically Foreign Mothers: The Implications for Textual Politics,' 25–33 in I. Douglas Wilson and D. V. Edelman (eds.), *History, Memory, Hebrew Scriptures A Festschrift for Ehud Ben Zvi*, Winona Lake, IN: Eisenbrauns.

Buchanan, A. S. (2000), *Peace with Justice: A History of the Israeli-Palestinian Declaration of Principles on Interim Self-Government Arrangements*, Basingstoke: Palgrave Macmillan.

Cogan, M. and H. Tadmor (1988), *II Kings: A New Translation with Introduction and Commentary*, AB 11, New York: Doubleday.

Cohen S. A. (2000), 'How to Mount a Successful Coup d'Etat: Lessons from the Bible (II Kings 11, II Chronicles 23)', *Diplomacy & Statecraft* 11.3: 1–28.

Dutcher-Walls, P. (1996), *Narrative Art, Political Rhetoric: The Case of Athaliah and Joash*, Journal for the Study of the Old Testament Supplementary Series 209, Sheffield: Sheffield Academic Press.

Elior, R. (2015), 'What Kind of a Religion is Judaism?, *Part 2*', *Odyssey* 29: 76–91 [Heb.].
Ephron, D. (2015), *Killing a King: The Assassination of Yitzhak Rabin and the Remaking of Israel*, New York: W.W. Norton & Company.
Eran, O. (2002), 'Arab–Israel Peacemaking', 121–47 in A. Sela (ed.), *The Continuum Political Encyclopedia of the Middle East*, New York: Continuum.
Evans, K. (2015), *Red Rosa: A Graphic Biography of Rosa Luxemburg*. Edited by. P. Buhle. London and New York: Verso.
Filkins, D. (2015), 'Shot in the Heart: When Yitzhak Rabin Was Killed, Did the Prospects for Peace Perish, Too?', *The New Yorker*, 26 October: 9–38.
Fischer, S. (2007), 'Self-Expression and Democracy in Radical Religious Zionist Ideology', PhD diss., The Hebrew University, Jerusalem.
Fischer, S. (2009), 'Religious Zionism on the Brink of the Third Millennium: Two Faith Cultures', *Akdmot* 22: 9–38 [Heb.].
Freedman, R. O. (1995), *Israel under Rabin*, Boulder, CO: Westview Press.
Freedman, R. O. (1998), *The Middle East and the Peace Process: The Impact of the Oslo Accords*, Gainesville, FL: University Press of Florida.
Goldstein, J. (2006), *Rabin: A Biography*, Tel Aviv: Schocken [Heb.].
Gray, J. (1970), *I & II Kings: A Commentary*, 2nd edn, OTL, Philadelphia: Westminster.
Inbari, M. (2008), *Jewish Fundamentalism and the Temple Mount*. Edited by K. Metzer, Jerusalem: Magnes [Heb.].
Inbari, M. (2012), *Messianic Religious Zionism Confronts Israeli Territorial Compromises*, New York: Cambridge Univerity Press.
Karpin, M. and Friedman, I. (1998), *Murder in the Name of God: The Plot to Kill Yitzhak Rabin*, New York: Henry Holt & Co.
Katz, J. (1986), *Jewish Emancipation and Self- Emancipation*, Philadelphia-New York: The Jewish Publication Society.
Katzenstein, J. H. (1955), 'Who Were the Parents of Athaliah?', *IEJ* 5: 194–7.
Katzenstein, J. H. (1971), 'Athaliah, Athaliahu' in M. D. Cassuto et al. (eds), *Encyclopaedia Biblica*, VI: 430–1, Jerusalem: The Bialik Institute [Heb.].
Keshev and Ir Amim (2013), *Dangerous Liaison: The Dynamics of the Rise of the Temple Movements and Their Implications*, March 1. Researched and written by Y. Be'er, Y and edited by T. Persico. http://www.ir-amim.org.il/sites/default/files/Dangerous%20 Liaison-Dynamics%20of%20the%20Temple%20Movements.pdf
Kochman, M. (1999), 'Jehoiada's Revolt', in M. Haran (ed), *Olam Hatanach, 2 Kings*, 88–9, Tel Aviv: Divrei Ha'yamim Publication [Heb.].
Kochman, M. (1999), 'The Murder of King Joash of Judah', in M. Haran (ed.), *Olam Hatanach, 2 Kings*, 98, Tel Aviv: Divrei Ha'yamim Publication [Heb.].
Liver, J. (1962), 'King, Kingship (Heb. מלך,מלוכה)' in M. D. Cassuto et al. (eds.), *Encyclopaedia Biblica*, IV: 1080–1112, Jerusalem: The Bialik Institute [Heb.].
Loewenshtamm, E. (1962), 'Carites (Heb. כרי)' in M. D. Cassuto et al. (eds), *Encyclopaedia Biblica*, IV: 310–12, Jerusalem: The Bialik Institute [Heb.].
Loewenshtamm, E. (1971), 'People of the Land (Heb. עם הארץ)' in M. D. Cassuto et al. (eds), *Encyclopaedia Biblica*, VI: 239–42, Jerusalem: The Bialik Institute [Heb.].
Meyers, C. L. (1983), 'Jachin and Boaz in Religious and Political Perspective', *CBQ* 45: 167–78.
Montgomery, J. A. (1951), *A Critical and Exegetical Commentary on the Books of Kings*. Edited by H. Snyder Gehman. Edinburgh: T&T Clark.
Morgenstern, J. (1938), 'A Chapter in the History of the High-Priesthood', *AJSL* 55: 1–24, 183–97, 360–77.

Morgenstern, J. (1967), 'The Fall of the House of Ahab', *VT* 17.3: 307–24.
Nicholson, E. W. (1965), 'The Meaning of the Expression *Am-Ha'aretz* in the Old Testament', *JSS* 10: 59–66.
Peri, Y. (2000), *The Assassination of Yitzhak Rabin*, Stanford: Stanford University Press.
Persico, T. (2017), 'How the Last Jewish Attempt to Oppose the Secularization Process Failed', *Ha'aretz*, 22 June: 44–8 [Heb.].
Rabinovich, I. (2017), *Yitzhak Rabin: Soldier, Leader, Statesman*, New Haven, CT: Yale University Press.
Ravitzky, A. (1993), *Messianism, Zionism and Jewish Religious Radicalism*, Chicago & London: University of Chicago Press.
Reviv, H. (1971), 'On the Days of Athaliah and Joash', *Beit Mikra* 17 (4): 541–8 [Heb.].
Rosnak, A. (2013), *Cracks: Unity of Opposites, the Political and Rabbi Kook's Disciples* Tel Aviv: Resling [Heb.].
Sagi, R. (2015), *Messianic Radicalism in the State of Israel: Chapters in the Secret of the Messianic Reform in the Thought of Rabbi Yitzhak Ginzburg*, Tel Aviv: Gvanim [Heb.].
Shapira, A. (2004), 'The Bible and Israeli Identity', *Journal of the Association for Jewish Studies* 28.1: 11–42.
Simon, U. (2002), *Seek Peace and Pursue It: Topical Issues in the Light of the Bible: The Bible in Light of Topical Issues*, Tel Aviv: Yedioth Aharonot [Heb.].
Smith, M. (1971), *Palestinian Parties and Politics that Shaped the Old Testament*, New York & London: Columbia University Press.
Soggin, A. J. (1963), 'Der Judäische Am-Ha'arets und Das Königtum Juda ein Beitrag zum Studium der Deuteronomistischen Geshichtsschreibung', *VT* 8: 187–95.
Sweeney, M. A. (2007), *I & II Kings: A Commentary,* Louisville & London: Westminster John Knox Press.
Talmon, S. (1967), 'The History of Am Ha'arez in the Kingdom of Judah', *Beit Mikra* 12.3: 27–55 [Heb.].
Talmon, S. (1999), 'Am Ha'aretz', in M. Haran (ed), *Olam Hatanach, 2 Kings*, 91–3, Tel Aviv: Divrei Ha'yamim Publication [Heb.].
Tsevat, M. (1956), 'Sociological and Historical Observations on Zechariah XII', *Tarbiz* 1.25: 111–17.
Van Seters, J. (2007), *The Origins of the Hebrew Bible: Some New Answers to Old Questions*, Leiden: Knninklijke Brill NV.
Vaux, R. de (1964), 'Le sens de l'expression « peuple du pays » dans l'Ancien Testament et le role politique du peuple en Israël', *Revue d'assyriologie et d'archéologie orientale* 58.4: 167–72.
Yadin, Y. (1978), 'The "House of Ba'al" of Ahab and Jezebel in Samaria, and that of Athaliah in Judah', 127–35 in R. Moorey and P. Parr (eds.), *Archaeology in the Levant: Kathleen Kenyon Festschrift*, Warminster: Aris & Phillips.
Zadok, R. (1999), 'Athaliah', in M. Haran (ed.), *Olam Hatanach, 2 Kings*, 89, Tel Aviv: Divrei Ha'yamim Publication [Heb.].
Zimmerman, J.D. (2004), *Poles, Jews, and the Politics of Nationality*, Madison, Wisconsin: University of Wisconsin Press.

Part III

CHRONICLES-EZRA-NEHEMIAH

MANASSEH AS PERPETRATOR IN KINGS AND CHRONICLES: A VIEW ON VULNERABILITY

Gerrie F. Snyman

Perpetrators in the Biblical Text

In encountering villains and perpetrators of the worst kind in the Old Testament / Hebrew Bible (OT/HB) the following come to mind:

1. The evil perpetrated by the villain or wrongdoer is of such a nature that no redemption seems possible. The character is physically removed from the scene.
2. The villain or perpetrator is portrayed in such a way that the reader fails to empathize with them, ultimately feeling they get their just deserts. There is a link between the nature of the evil act and the manner of the character's downfall.
3. In some instances, the justification of the evil act, which functions as the last straw, has a ring of truth around it, implicating the victim or protagonist against whom the wrongdoer is acting.
4. In most cases, the remorse shown by the evildoer or perpetrator is believed to be inadequate and fails to alter the outcome of the evil perpetrated.
5. In popular reception of these stories, the villain becomes the hallstand for an external force (Satan, devil, snake) that drives the character to destruction.

The last two aspects, the inadequacy of remorse and the attribution to an external force, uncovered for me the failure and hopelessness I experience in the current South African discourse about the apartheid past. Whiteness as the evil Other has no idea how to act in the face of the several presentations and expositions of trauma black people suffered, and the hardships they endured because of racism. In short, we as whites have no idea how to play our role as perpetrators of racism in the face of revelations of such contemptuous behaviour. Instead of becoming vulnerable, we become fragile. Fragility relates to an inability to realize that one's position of power (and, with race, racial superiority) has had an impact on the life and perceptions of others. Subsequently, when taken to task, even at a very minimum level, the racial stress becomes unbearable, resulting in the expression of certain defense mechanisms – for example anger, fear, guilt, silence, or simply removal of oneself from the situation (cf. DiAngelo 2012: 54, 126).

Vulnerability follows from the ethical moment in the face-to-face meeting between two persons, crying out to each other not to be killed. The ensuing metaphorical naked countenance radically obliges each to not destroy or violate the other (Levinas 1990: 8). Vulnerability is a basic human condition in which harm is as possible as being open and affective (Gilson 2016: 96). In reality, it is the negative view of vulnerability as harm that drowns the epistemic nature of vulnerability in focusing on the link between it and violence. Vulnerability is understood as weakness, harm and injury, pertaining to only vulnerable victims in contrast to invulnerable perpetrators. Understood in this way, vulnerability presupposes a hierarchical and inequitable distribution of exposure to weakness, harm and injury, resulting in a disposition and treatment of others that is patronizing, oppressive, paternalistic, controlling, stigmatizing and exclusionary (Gilson 2016: 129).[1] Vulnerability is seen as a negative state that should be avoided at all costs, since it is stigmatizing and oppressive. It symbolizes powerlessness par excellence: weakness and lack of autonomy.

In the book of Esther, the Jews are portrayed as vulnerable. They are still in exile and very exposed to harm and injury, as the planned genocide by their arch nemesis Haman the Amalekite shows. In order to survive, the Jews need to get access to power, which they receive via Esther, queen to the Persian king and cousin to Mordecai, the staunch believer who is the cause of all the mayhem against the Jews. To survive, the roles of power has to be reversed. As a result, Haman becomes the perpetrator who is removed with his head covered and is hanged immediately on the gallows he has intended for Mordecai (Esth. 7.9-10). Given the influence of wisdom in the book of Esther, Haman's fall from grace is mostly seen as the epitome of foolishness: he falls into his own trap when he has to take Mordecai on a horse around the city of Susa (Esth. 6.11). But he has been very clever and rhetorically depicted the Jewish people with a ring of some truth (Esth. 3.8-9) to win over the king's consent to a genocide: according to him, the Jews were separate, following their own laws. In fact, that was part of Persian strategy in the colonies. Once caught out, Haman seeks a pardon from the queen (7.7); but it appears to be misconstrued by the king who left the scene and returns, finding Haman in close proximity of Esther. Haman is immediately removed from the premises (7.8).

In at least two popular receptions (sermons within the South African, Christian orthodox reformed traditions) Haman's personal liability or responsibility is put on the shoulder of an external evil force, Satan. Boon (2016) argues that God

---

1. For a full discussion on the issue of vulnerability and its negative as well as positive understanding with regard to biblical perpetrating characters, see Snyman 2017.

allows Satan to make his move by getting Haman's plan of destruction of the Jews accepted by the king. Haman, being an Agagite and thus from Amalek (Esth. 3.1), is but a pawn in the larger war between God and Satan. He does not appear to act out of a free will. He is preprogrammed to do evil. Thinus du Plessis (2011) calls Haman's plans to destroy the Jews (which he links to Mordecai's refusal to bow before Haman) a satanic ruse. He too links Haman to the devil but declares that God is more powerful than Satan: Haman goes too far by tempting the deity in trying to destroy his people.

Let us now move from how a 'foreign' unsavoury character of royalty is depicted to the description of another unsavoury yet native 'perpetrator' with royal credentials.

Manasseh as Perpetrator in 2 Kings 21.1-18 and 2 Chronicles 33.1-20

In the royal history of Manasseh as king of Judah, in the books of Kings as well as in Chronicles, Manasseh is portrayed as the villain, with the kingdom of Judah bearing the brunt of his iniquities as defined in terms of deuteronomistic law.[2] The Judahites' military defeat, the destruction of the cult and their eventual deportation with king Josiah's death are linked to Manasseh's idolatry and wickedness in Kings (cf. Ohm 2010: 252). In Kings, readers receive Manasseh with a strong sense of blackballing:[3] not a particularly successful Manasseh is presented as Judah's own Ahab, the symbol of depravity of the Northern Kingdom, in shedding innocent blood (2 Kgs 21.16).

In blackballing Manasseh, the Kings version effectively disassociates Manasseh from Judah in connecting him to the Northern Kingdom in at least three ways: identification with Ahab, connection with foreign cults, and his name.

The reference to Ahab (2 Kgs 21.3) in which Manasseh was re-erecting the altars and sacred poles for the host of heaven which his father Hezekiah destroyed, and which Ahab during his reign once served, alludes to those sins of the Northern Kingdom that led to its downfall and exile. Like Ahab before him and the Amorites, Manasseh acted with abomination in going after idols and drawing his subjects with him (v. 10). He parallels Jeroboam, another evil king of Israel, who caused the downfall of his people (cf. Stravakopoulou 2007: 252). Manasseh's wickedness has the same result as the evil of Jeroboam: the people suffer and are taken captive. In fact, Jeroboam, Ahab and Manasseh are portayed as the evilest kings. Manasseh shares the evil of the worst kings of the Northern Kingdom and stands opposite

---

2. Thomas Römer (2014: 250-1) names six instances where Manasseh is accused of breaking the law: Deut. 12.29-30 and 2 Kgs 21.2 = 2 Chron. 33.2; Deut. 12.2-4 / 16.21 and 2 Kgs 21.3 = 2 Chron. 33.3; Deut. 17.3 and 2 Kgs 21.3 = 2 Chron. 33.3, 5 and 7; Deut. 19.19-14 and 2 Kgs 21.6 = 2 Chron. 33.6; Deut. 19.10 and 2 Kgs 21.16 (no parallel in Chronicles).

3. Blackballing refers to adverse views of someone to the point of shunning the person or expelling the person from a particular group. See Stavrakopoulou 2007: 248.

those depicted as the best (Van Keulen 1995: 145). Manasseh's evil outweighed Josiah's piety and cultic reforms. The latter could not thwart the destruction of the temple and Jerusalem as well as the exile. It was as if Manasseh's evil neutralized beforehand any later reforms (Halpern 1998: 489).

Surely, Manasseh is not the only king of Judah who committed idolatry but his cultic wrongdoing, measured against deuteronomistic laws, places him apart from the rest, turning him into a scapegoat in order to explain the exile and catastrophe the audience of the book of Kings is confronted with (Lasine 1993: 166). In the end, Manasseh is associated with the abominable practices of the Canaanites to the point of surpassing them, because he led his people astray. For this reason, the story identifies him with the Northern Kingdom whose following of foreign nations' cults led to their demise.

The identification with the Northern Kingdom is also manifested in his name, which appears to be of Northern Kingdom origin in 1 Kgs 4.13, thereby playing on an anti-Manasseh sentiment (Stavrakopoulou 2007: 253). He is singled out as a religious deviant. Subsequently, the book of Kings, in listing all his crimes and alluding to an association of his name with the Northern Kingdom, is in effect asking the readers what they expect of a man of this caliber (cf. Stavrakopoulou 2007: 256). Nonetheless, the outcome of Manasseh's portrayal in Kings is twofold: firstly, Manasseh is a king whose reign was fifty-five years long – in terms of deuteronomistic theology quite a successful king, yet he is vilified; and secondly, the inhabitants of the kingdom are depicted with no responsibility about future events: Manasseh is presented as responsible for their exile much later on.

2 Chron. 33.1-9 resembles 2 Kgs 21.1-9, except that here there is no reference to Ahab or the killing of innocent people. The story in verses 10-17 differs considerably, with a building project, a military strategy and a spiritual renewal that justify Manasseh's reign of fifty-five years. His story actually resembles that of Asa in 2 Chronicles 14-16 to a large extent in noting successful building projects, cultic reforms and military victories. Like Asa, he is not faultless: he fails to listen to the deity who, in reaction, sent the Assyrians to humiliate them. Retribution is immediate in Chronicles whereas punishment in King's arrives only a few generations later. They also took him captive to Babylon.[4] His capturing is quite public and humiliating, but mild and disproportionate to his wrongdoing when compared to Jehoram's bowel disease in 2 Chron. 21.18 (Japhet 1993: 1009).

Manasseh experiences a conversion in captivity and is sent back to Jerusalem, in effect restored to his original position, as was the case with Necho I in Egypt (Kelly 2002: 142). His repentance consists of humility and prayer; he humbles himself before Yahweh and prays. Prayer was important, even in Persian and Hellenistic circles (Handy 2013: 231). The Chronicler refers to it twice and in the Hasmonean period an apocryphal text was produced containing Manasseh's

---

4. The reference to Babylon is strange, as one would expect Nineveh, the capital of the Assyrians. Kelly (2002: 141) argues the possibility that the Chronicler thinks about the eventual exile of Judah to Babylon.

prayer (see Page 2010; Nodet 2010) in which he appears without a shred of evil or iniquity.[5]

The repentance provides a reason for his long reign, an aspect the Chronicler could not deny (Becker 1988: 111; Japhet 1993: 1002; Lasine 1993: 179). What would a repentance imply at the time of writing? According to Handy (2013: 228), in the Persian period Jews who participated in the cult of foreign gods were no longer regarded as Jews. In terms of the audience, Manasseh would not have been part of Judah any more. He would be regarded as one of the Diaspora who returned with foreign cultic practices. Deuteronomistic history required him to leave these foreign cults in favour of the God of Abraham, Isaac and Jacob.

Upon return to Jerusalem, and backing his repentance, Manasseh restores the Yahweh cult and initiates building projects, securing a long reign. His building of the wall in Jerusalem not only suggests Jerusalem as an administrative centre for the (Persian) empire but also alludes to Nehemiah's own wall-building in the restoration project. After all, Jerusalem is mentioned five times in the Chronicler's version (cf. Handy 2013: 226).

Kings and Chronicles represent two traditions about Manasseh:

> The wonderful, temple-restoring, good king Manasseh developed in Yehud under Persian imperial rule. The Manasseh of irredeemable evil, incorporating the entire notion of Satan as the embodiment of evil, seems, as a working hypothesis, to have originated during the Hasmonean wars and rule. (Handy 2013: 234)

It is the latter negative interpretation that appears to have stuck. Readers usually side with biblical heroes like David, Solomon, Hezekiah or Josiah. Manasseh remains a villain. In *The Martyrdom of Isaiah,* Manasseh's evil has him to chop Isaiah in two. In 1 Enoch 89.56 it looks as if Manasseh is portrayed abandoning his flock of sheep to wild beasts under the influence of Satan. In rabbinic literature his portrayal is a bit more ambiguous. The Talmud makes him a Torah scholar interpreting Leviticus in thirty-five ways (Liss 2002: 207). *B. Sanh.* 102b refuses to judge him since Yahweh is the only one who judges. Although his evil is seen as being great, it is also tied to his greatness as scholar of the Torah according to the Talmud (Feldman 1991: 2–8). His repentance in Chronicles saves him from losing out on his share of the world to come. Josephus saw his transgressions as an internal affair and ascribed the loss of the kingdom to Jeroboam (*Ant.* 9.282; Feldman 1991: 12).

---

5. The Prayer of Manasseh, largely composed of biblical terms and phrases, is thought to have been originally composed in Greek in the late first century BCE, after which it was translated into Latin and Syriac. Verses 1-7 praise the deity providing a list of his deeds and promises. The second section (verses 8-10) serves as Manasseh's confession of his numerous sins (defined in the most general terms in v. 9), and the prayer concludes with verses 11-15 as a petition for forgiveness. Nodet (2010: 346–8) provides a different structure.

Manasseh and Vulnerability

In 2 Kings 21 Manasseh gets off scot-free. Moreover, his reign is long and quite successful when compared to that of Solomon. As king, he does not suffer the consequences of his wrongful acts. It is as if he is invulnerable. The inhabitants of Jerusalem are the ones to become vulnerable enough, although chronologically later in Zedekiah's time, when they suffer the destruction of their city and temple as well as eventual captivity. Nonetheless, their plight gives credence to a negative understanding of vulnerability: the infliction of harm, suffering, injury and weakness.

Indeed, vulnerability as a negative state can also be read into 2 Chronicles 33 with Manasseh's physical suffering: he is put in hooks and bronze chains and taken into captivity. He becomes a failed autonomous subject. His vulnerability as a deficit of autonomy assigns to him a particular inferiority, weakness and dependency on the Assyrians (and on Yahweh). The antidote to this vulnerability is power, sovereignty, well-being and competence – someone stronger, an invulnerable saviour. But since the vulnerable lacks agency to overcome his or her own vulnerability, he or she needs to open up to such a saviour, acknowledging his or her own subordination and unequal status. This makes vulnerability stigmatizing and oppressive, and perhaps the reason why Manasseh's reception in interpretive history is of a character who is weak and without real autonomy. The hallmark of evil remains, despite the positive evaluation given in 2 Chronicles 33.

In 2 Chronicles 33, the deity acts as the invulnerable saviour, with the king as the vulnerable subject. Although Manasseh's captivity suggests a negative vulnerability, I am of the opinion that he reveals a vulnerability that is part of the human condition. The deity reveals how susceptible Manasseh could be to harm, but his own action reveals perhaps his exposure to the gaze of others (emperors and their officials), creating a political community in which Manasseh is forced to participate and, as a result, becoming open to the ambivalences created by the political ideologies and decrees of his overlords. Manasseh stands accused of idolatry in both stories (of Kings and of Chronicles), but historically one needs to ask whether his actions as king of Judah and the assumed openness to other forms of worship are not a case of diplomacy and tactical interaction with a new context, which was in the process of developing with the Assyrian presence nearby. This is Römer's opinion: for him, Manasseh was a loyal vassal who merely reinforced those cultic symbols that related to Assyrian culture and politics (Römer 2014: 251).

In fact, does his openness to other ways of divine veneration not constitute vulnerability as likely, with the deity Yahweh as the invulnerable opposite other? Buchner (2008: 488) sees Manasseh as steering a safe course between his Assyrian masters and the inhabitants of Judah and their religious leaders: he maintains the official Yahweh cult to sooth the latter but placates the Assyrians by allowing bolder expressions of folk religion. Morrow (2013: 73) refers to indigenous practices Manasseh introduces without disturbing Assyrian cultic practices (goddesses and Assyrian astral deities) that Judah started to incorporate as an Assyrian vassal.

Yahweh becomes angry and lashes out at the people in the book of Kings, and at Manasseh in the book of Chronicles. His anger results in vulnerability as harm and injury. Does the deity's anger reflect his defeat as national deity and his rejection of Judah as his favorites? In Kings, it is as if the author appears to provide clarification for the eventual destruction of Jerusalem and the temple, as well as the exile of Judah. Manasseh's idolatry and evildoing are the reasons, but he is not made to suffer the consequences; his subjects are (Sweeney 2007: 266). Manasseh's transgressions constitute the reason for the fall of the kingdom and temple – the misdeeds of a *single* king resulted in the demise of an *entire* kingdom. In the case of the Northern Kingdom, it was the evil deeds of all the kings that led to its demise (Sweeney 2007: 268). But it is Yahweh who evokes the Babylonian invasion to punish his people. He is not conquered by the Babylonian deities or decommissioned as the god of Judah (Römer 2014: 286). The exile, the loss of land, and the destruction of Jerusalem are all the result of Yahweh's anger against Jerusalem and its leaders, in typical deuteronomistic style, without any chance of escaping the Babylonian invasion.

In effect, it is Yahweh who controls the Babylonian deities. The latter argument introduces monotheism into the discussion. An unintended consequence is that the deity is rendered invulnerable, and his worshippers extremely vulnerable and susceptible to harm and injury. But the biblical text has multiple layers of traditions which sometimes confront readers with mutually exclusive portrayals of Yahweh. Anderson (2016: 10-11) refers to various references to Yahweh as the only and universal deity as well as Yahweh as one amongst many, albeit then as the head of a pantheon or divine council. He thinks that, in post exilic Judaism, the discordant and incongruous view on Yahweh is deliberate because of a particular power configuration that came into being (2016: 15):

> A nascent, monotheistic community in the Persian province of Beyond the River would have had a vested interest in both approaches – one more subtle and the other more direct, to critique old orthodoxy and orthopraxy of the monarchic era that still existed in Yehud. They wished to rebuff the understanding of Yahweh as the head of a pantheon, replacing it with a monotheistic Yahwism that allowed for angelic, messenger-type beings.

It is clear that in the new evolving ideology the ways of the past are wrong and attributed to the captivity of Judah or rather Jerusalem. The exile was the result of a certain belief system and behaviour in which Yahweh played a role as the main deity with a few gods under his control. The worshipping of Yahweh as part of a pantheon led directly to the destruction of the temple. But since it is a new assessment and interpretation, it has to be presented very cautiously because the old view was still offered and followed by some leaders. The new scribal class within the priesthood would have received economic benefit in propagating this new view, but they had to be careful not to alienate those who pay taxes. As Anderson states:

> The [new form of Yahwism] was essentially used to state more openly and directly that the old position, though still around, where Yahweh was the head of

a pantheon, was a bad one. Look what happened – Yahweh allowed us and our ancestors to suffer and be subjugated and taken into captivity because of our apostasy in worshipping him incorrectly.

The process already started with the writing of Kings, hence the specific portrayal of Manasseh as idolatrous. Two separate invulnerabilities were set up against each other with neither giving sway. Philip Davies (2016: 26) draws a link between the political development of the monarchy from a national institution to an imperial one, and the religious development towards monotheism in the Persian Period. He makes the following remarks:

1. Monarchy in the Ancient Near East is an autonomous locus of power with the ability to impose taxes, engage in war and require personal loyalty.
2. The emergence of an organized and centralized state with a monarch at its helm encouraged a parallel religious development with a centralized cult.
3. The kingship on earth reflected the divine kingship in heaven.
4. The royal god lived in a palace or temple with priestly servants as worshippers seeing the face of the deity as they also saw the face of the king.
5. The deity cared for the people through the agency of the earthly monarch.
6. The presentation of the deity of a state as a king, Creator or Chair of a divine council is a statement on the nature of the state and its ruler.
7. The emergence of empire allowed for the construction of a dynastic deity that overshadowed the local or nationalistic deities of the vassal-kings and their states, sometimes causing a tension in loyalty towards either of the deities.
8. Monarchic theism became imperial theism. The imperial deity within a unified world political system is as natural a system as that of a national deity in a smaller kingdom.

According to Davies's scheme, autonomy runs parallel to invulnerability. The monarchy emerged as an autonomous locus of power with the ability to impose taxes, engage in war and require personal loyalty. In this way, the monarchy encouraged parallel religious development with a centralized cult: earthly kingship parallelled divine kingship. The monarch as well as the deity became invulnerable; any effort to render them vulnerable was met with negative sanction. Both has a designated area with designated personnel to serve them.

The emergence of empire allowed for the construction of a dynastic deity that dominated the local or nationalistic deities of the vassal-kings and their states, sometimes causing a tension in loyalty towards either of the deities. Monarchic theism became imperial theism. In Chronicles, in the last verses of the book (2 Chron. 36.22-23), the deity becomes imperial in the support for Cyrus, the new imperial ruler. In the Chronicler's eyes, Yahweh became the imperial deity: whether the Persians saw it that way is another story!

With monotheism in the background of both stories about Manasseh, what happens to vulnerability? Does monotheism link up with a reductively negative view of vulnerability? A reductively negative understanding of vulnerability implies weakness, harm and injury, and alludes to destructive violence that divides a community into victims and perpetrators. In the Kings' story Manasseh is the perpetrator, and the inhabitants of Judah become the victims suffering destructive violence. In Chronicles Manasseh, the perpetrator against Yahweh, becomes the victim of the Assyrians acting as Yahweh's surrogate. In Kings, Manasseh remains a self-sufficient master subject, independent and invulnerable. His assumed god-like position comes into conflict with the god-like position of his similarly invulnerable deity. But Manasseh harms the invulnerable deity, who consequently acts with violence. In the Kings narrative, Manasseh appears to imitate divine violence by shedding so much blood that Jerusalem is filled from end to end (2 Kgs 21.16). His actions to protect his invulnerability cause harm and injury to his subjects, who become the vulnerable victims of divine wrath. The Kings version provides the reader with a scheme of cause and effect. Actions have consequences, and vulnerability as harm and injury is projected negatively.

Is the Chronicles version much different from the Kings version? Does Manasseh, after his humiliation, return and resume his position as king, an autonomous, self-sufficient master subject? No, not quite. Manasseh is rendered vulnerable in a negative way (2 Chron. 33.11-12, NRSV):

Therefore the Lord brought against them the commanders of the army of the king of Assyria, who took Manasseh captive in manacles, bound him with fetters, and brought him to Babylon. While he was in distress, he entreated the favor of the Lord his God and humbled himself greatly before the God of his ancestors. He prayed to him, and God received his entreaty, heard his plea, and restored him again to Jerusalem and to his kingdom. Then Manasseh knew the Lord indeed was God.

The way in which Manasseh is publicly humiliated and taken captive makes him weak, harmed and prone to injury. In this condition – Manasseh recognizes his vulnerability in being in extreme discomfort and unease – he turns to his deity and humbles himself. His deity, in turn, responds positively and returns him to Jerusalem. Upon his return, he is no longer an autonomous self-sufficient master subject. He retains his position of power and privilege, but he commits himself to his deity who now becomes the autonomous self-sufficient master as monotheistic deity. He enters into an asymmetrical relationship in which the monotheistic god is in possession of not only what the vulnerable king needs but also the access to that what Manasseh needs. Manasseh is forced to seek the help of the self-sufficient invulnerable deity as his saviour.

Conclusion

It is clear Manasseh receives a better reception in Chronicles than in Kings.

In both, Manasseh as perpetrator is not treated kindly. In Kings he remains a recalcitrant king, failing to recognize his own vulnerability. In Chronicles he indeed recognizes his vulnerability, but nonetheless undergoes the treatment meted out to perpetrators. His vulnerability allows him to return. It is not a reductively negative vulnerability that we see in the end, but a particular epistemic vulnerability that enables him to be open to being wrong and to alter his beliefs and habits when he returns to Jerusalem and then experiences a long reign.

On a personal note: current socio-political discourse problematizes whiteness in post-apartheid South Africa. The critique on whiteness is very public in the link to racial privilege and black victimhood, even to the point of criminality in its association of apartheid as a crime against humanity. Whiteness used to give people a sense of invulnerability because of the colonial processes since 1652, a power and autonomy over a Black Other in a geographical space that has been colonized. Reading the biblical text from a critique on whiteness requires, from me, a unmistakable acknowledgement of my own racist upbringing and its privileges in the perpetrator culture. Instead of exercising an invulnerability, I can no longer hide. I am obliged to render myself vulnerable in order to confront my complicity. Manasseh's hooks and fetters have become my silence and my internal introspection when I am forced to look into Black eyes, feel the embarrassment and internalize the critique. Recognizing my own vulnerability helps me to dismantle that privilege and other aftereffects of apartheid. It becomes an instance for change. Failure to recognize such vulnerability makes one continue to sustain a sense of false protection and its oppressive relations.

Bibliography

Anderson, James (2016), 'Creating Dialectical Tensions: Religious Developments in Persian-Period Yehud Reflected in Biblical Texts', 10–23 in *Religion in the Achaemenid Persian Empire: Emerging Judaism and Trends*, edited by Diana Edelman, Anne Fitzpatrick-McKinley and Phillipe Guillaume. Orientalische Religionen in Der Antike 17. Tübingen: Mohr Siebeck.

Becker, Joachim (1988), *2 Chronik*. Vol. 20. Die Neue Echter Bibel. Kommentar Zum Alten Testamentum Mit Der Einheitsübersetzung. Würzburg: Echter.

Boon, Pieter G. (2016), 'God almagtig laat Satan toe om sy skuif te maak – Haman se vernietigingsplan word aanvaar'. Sermon, Pretoria, October 2. Available online: http://www.vgk.org.za/preke/24788. (Accessed 9 April 2018.)

Buchner, Dirk (2008), 'Boshet in Jeremiah 3:24: Disenfranchisement and the Role of the Goddess in Seventh-Century Judah', *Journal of Theological Studies* 59.2: 478–99.

Davies, Philip R. (2016), 'Monotheism, Empire, and the Cult(s) of Yehud in the Persian Period', 24–56 in *Religion in the Achaemenid Persian Empire: Emerging Judaism and Trends*, edited by Diana Edelman, Anne Fitzpatrick-McKinley and Phillipe Guillaume. Orientalische Religionen in Der Antike 17. Tübingen: Mohr Siebeck.

DiAngelo, Robin (2012), *What Does It Mean to Be White? Developing White Racial Literacy*. Counterpoints: Studies in Postmodern Theory of Education, 398. New York: Peter Lang.

Du Plessis, Thinus (M. J.) (2011), 'Ester 7:4'. Sermon, Gereformeerde Kerk, Bellville, 12 June 2011. Available online: https://www.gkbellville.org/preke/PAest7.pdf. (Accessed 4 March 2018.)

Feldman, Louis H. (1991), 'Josephus' Portrait of Manasseh,' *Journal for the Study of the Pseudepigrapha* 9: 3–20.

Gilson, Erinn (2016), *The Ethics of Vulnerability: A Feminist Analysis of Social Life and Practice*, Routledge Studies in Ethics and Moral Theory 26, London: Routledge.

Halpern, Baruch Lemaire (1998), 'Why Manasseh Is Blamed for the Babylonian exile: The Evolution of a Biblical Tradition', *VT* 48.4: 473–514.

Handy, Lowell K. (2013), 'Rehabilitating Manasseh: Remembering King Manasseh in the Persian and Hellenistic Periods. Social Memory and Imagination,' 221–35 in *Remembering Biblical Figures in the Late Persian & Early Hellenistic Periods*, edited by Diana Edelman and Ehud Ben Zvi. London: Oxford University Press.

Hattingh, Piet (2011), 'Wat moet jy doen as die wiele afkom', presented at the Worship Service, Middelburg, Cape, 22 May 2011. Available online: https://www.witkerk.co.za/Preke/2sam14-17.html. (Accessed 4 March 2018.)

Japhet, Sara (1993), *I & II Chronicles, A Commentary*. Old Testament Library. London: SCM Press.

Kelly, Brian (2002), 'Manasseh in the Books of Kings and Chronicles (2 Kings 21:1–18; 2 Chronicles 33: 12–20)', 131–46 in *Windows into Old Testament History: Evidence, Argument, and the Crisis of "Biblical Israel"*, ed. V. Philips Long, David W. Baker and Gordon J. Wenham, Grand Rapids: Eerdmans.

Lasine, Stuart (1993), 'Manasseh as Villain and Scapegoat', 163–83 in *The New Literary Criticism and the Hebrew Bible*, edited by Cheryl Exum and David J. A. Clines. JSOTsupp 143. Sheffield: Sheffield Academic Press.

Levinas, Emmanuel (1990), *Difficult Freedom: Essays on Judaism*, trans. Sean Hand, Baltimore: Johns Hopkins University Press.

Liss, Hanna (2002), '"The Sins of the Prophets:" Biblical Characters through Rabbinic Lenses', *Lexington Theological Quarterly* 37.4: 197–213.

Morrow, William S. (2013), 'Were There Neo-Assyrian Influences in Manasseh's Temple? Comparative Evidence from Tel-Miqne/Ekron', *CBQ* 75: 53–73.

Nodet, Etienne (2010), 'Prières de Manassé (2 Chr 33, 1*; TSK 1.144*; 4Q381)', *Revue Biblique* 117.3: 345–60.

Ohm, Andrew T. (2010), 'Manasseh and the Punishment Narrative', *Tyndale Bulletin* 61.2: 237–54.

Page, Hugh (2010), 'Prayer of Manasseh,' 316–18 in *The Africana Bible: Reading Israel's Scriptures from Africa and the African Diaspora*, edited by Hugh Page, Minneapolis: Fortress Press.

Römer, Thomas (2014), *L'invention de Dieu*. Les Livres Du Nouveau Monde. Paris: Seuil.

Snyman, Gerrie F. (2017), 'Read as/with the Perpetrator: Manasseh's vulnerability in 2 Kings 21:1–18 and 2 Chronicles 33:1–20', *Scriptura* 116.2: 188–207.

Stavrakopoulou, Francesca (2007), 'The Blackballing of Manasseh,' 248–63 in *Good Kings and Bad Kings: The Kingdom of Judah in the Seventh Century BCE*, edited by Lester Grabbe. T&T Clark Biblical Studies. London: T&T Clark.

Sweeney, Marvin A. (2007), 'King Manasseh of Judah and the Problem of Theodicy in the Deuteronomistic History,' 264–78 in *Good Kings and Bad Kings: The Kingdom of Judah in the Seventh Century BCE*, edited by Lester Grabbe. T&T Clark Biblical Studies. London: T&T Clark.

Van Keulen, Percy S. F. (1995), 'Manasseh through the Eyes of the Deuteronomists: The Manasseh Account (2 Kings 21: 1–18) and the Final Chapters of the Deuteronomistic History'. PhD, Leiden: University of Leiden.

PLUS ÇA CHANGE, PLUS C'EST LA MÊME CHOSE: RABBINIC INTERPRETATIONS OF DEUTERONOMY FROM EZRA-NEHEMIAH TO CONTEMPORARY ISRAEL'S CONVERSION CONTROVERSY

Atar Hadari

Editor's Introduction

Issues of intermarriage, or marriage outside the faith community, are treated as crucially important in the Hebrew Bible, especially in deuteronomistic literature. Attitudes to it are mostly negative, focused on marriage with foreign, non-Israelite or non-Judahite women, with the perceived danger of their religious practices involving worship of other deities. The legal opinions of the Jewish Orthodox establishments to intermarriage, as clearly seen in post biblical *halakha*, up to and including the State of Israel, has always been negative. And acceptance or rejection of intermarriage remains a key issue in Jewish life today, in and outside Israel.

A measure of correction to such socially unacceptable intermarriage is conversion to Judaism, the act of joining the faith community formally. This is seen as especially crucial in the case of women, since maternal parentage is the only deciding factor aside from conversion in determining the Jewishness of a person (male or female). With the dwindling of Jewish religious communities outside Israel, and the stream of immigrants from the former Soviet Bloc to Israel who do not come from entirely Jewish parentage, the issue of conversion has become a matter for thousands rather than single applicants for admission.

Historically, in Jewish sources, attitudes to conversion are of two kinds: strict, almost grudging; or alternatively more lenient. We can find sayings in the Talmud such as 'Converts are as difficult to Israel as [skin] scabs';[1] and the opposite view, calling for a more compassionate attitude.[2] Both are possible as legal options available to the converting judge within the *halakha*.

---

1. As for instance in *b. Kidd.* 70b, *Yeb.* 47a, *Nidd.* 13b and elsewhere: קשים גרים לישראל כספחת.
2. For instance *b. Pes.* 78b; *Tanḥuma Lech Lecha*, 6.

Performing conversions is the prerogative of the Orthodox courts and decided by Orthodox Rabbis, so by state decree in Israel and by common practice also in the Jewish Diaspora. Non-Orthodox Jewish communities – such as the Reform, Conservative or Liberal – have their own conversion procedures. However, these are not recognized by the Orthodox establishment as valid, which has practical implications for matters of parentage, marriage, divorce, property inheritance and so on. The important question is, therefore, which of the available halakhic options – stringent-maximalist or lenient-minimalist – will be adopted by the Orthodox conversion court. The full range of demands from a convert will include prior study of Jewish commandments (*mitzvot*), willingness to and demonstration of observing [all of] them in daily life, immersion (for females) and circumcision (for males), together with a proven intention to convert for the appropriate reasons.

Overview

This article will discuss varying modes of rabbinic interpretation of Jewish law and the reformulation of that law to comprehend different circumstances, and particularly the two modes that such interpretations may be formulated in. I will draw on a range of Jewish legal sources separated in historical periods by thousands of years: from the Pentateuchal codifications of Deuteronomy, to the post-exilic Ezra-Nehemiah, to the post-enlightenment responsa of Moses Schreiber (1762–1839), better known as the *Hatam Sofer,* whose rulings inaugurated a new era of Orthodox rabbinic opinion responding to the modernising tendencies of post-enlightenment European Jewry (Brown 2011: 154); and, finally, the contemporary rabbinic rulings (Heb. *piskei din*) of the Rabbinic High Court Judge Avraham Sherman and Senior Rabbinic High Court Judge Shlomo Dichovsky as they clashed over the question of conversion in contemporary Israel. While these texts originate far apart from each other in time and space, they do proceed one from the other in a consistent understanding of how Jewish law is developed.

Intermarriage in Ezra and in Deuteronomy

I will start not at the beginning – Deuteronomy – but with Ezra, and the definition given in the text of the legal mission with which he is entrusted. The dictionary definition of that mission encompasses the issues this article will discuss. I will quote from the King James Version (KJV) for familiarity but analyse its translations, and will quote the original biblical passages and other original language texts in the notes.

> For Ezra had prepared his heart to seek the law of the LORD, and to do it, and to teach in Israel statutes and judgments. (Ezra 7.10[3])

3. כי עזרא הכין לבבו לדרוש את תורת יהוה ולעשת וללמד בישראל חק ומשפט

The Hebrew word לדרוש, from *d-r-sh* Qal, which the KJV renders as 'to seek' has at least a dual meaning, which the dictionary summarises thus: resort to, seek, study, discuss, search out (a meaning), expound (*BDB* 1907: 205).

A few verses later the mission is restated thus, in Aramaic (Ezra 7.25):

> And thou, Ezra, after the wisdom of thy God, that is in thine hand, set magistrates and judges, which may judge all the people that are beyond the river, all such as know the laws of thy God; and teach ye them that know them not.[4]

This reformulation of Ezra's mission locates the authority for his legal function as deriving from the wisdom 'that is in thine hand', suggesting it is his mastery and possession of the written law and his role of scribe which gives him that authority. But the previous verse, defining his function as 'to seek', suggests that it is not the written law which is the true issue but the *interpretation* of that law. Ezra is coming back to the land of Israel post-exile to attempt to [re-]establish legal and social norms which pertain to the pre-exile; and the action of the Book will be the way he will do so.

Before proceeding to how it is that Ezra performs his function and re-interprets the laws of Deuteronomy for post-exilic conditions, it will be necessary to introduce two other concepts/terms which separate the world of Deuteronomy and Ezra from that of *Hatam Sofer* and contemporary Jewish law. Those terms derive from the Talmud and so I will give their definitions from Jastrow's dictionary. There are, in simplistic language, two basic modes of Jewish (Orthodox) legal ruling. There is a best case scenario ruling – לכתחילה (*lechatchila*, Heb. 'at the start', 'directly'; Jastrow 1903, 1661); and a best case after the fact scenario which Jastrow cites as its opposite – בדיעבד (*bediʿavad*, Aram. With the sense of 'in retrospect'). Rabbinic rulings are often formulated as what you would like the case to be, and what you can permit the case to be after your room for manoeuvre has been constrained by the case at hand. Ezra's response to the facts he finds on the ground in Jerusalem, the way he responds to them and how his ruling is enforced, demonstrates the difference between these two kinds of rabbinic ruling.

The problem Ezra is called on to address is a political one. One political faction in Jerusalem attacks another for having disobeyed the laws against intermarriage:

> And at the completion of these things, drawn nigh unto me have the heads, saying, 'The people of Israel, and the priests, and the Levites, have not been separated from the peoples of the lands, as to their abominations, even the Canaanite, the Hittite, the Perizzite, the Jebusite, the Ammonite, the Moabite, the Egyptian, and the Amorite, for they have taken of their daughters to them, and to their sons, and the holy seed have mingled themselves among the peoples of

---

4. ואנת עזרא כחכמת אלהך די בידך מני שפטין ודינין די להון דאנין [דאיניו] לכל עמה די בעבר נהרה לכל ידעי דתי אלהך ודי לא ידע תהודעון

the lands, and the hand of the heads and of the seconds have been first in this trespass... Then were assembled unto me every one that trembled at the words of the God of Israel. (Ezra 9.1-2, 4[5])

It should be noted that Ezra's only actions in Israel up to this point had been to institute readings of the law and to divest his authority as rapidly as possible onto others he finds already in Jerusalem, in what Tamara Cohn Eskenazi calls his 'communal orientation and persistent delegation of power and recognition', returning vast treasures to the temple by handing them to a prince of Judah (Ezra 1.8) and to twelve priests and Levites (8.24-30; Eskenazi 1988: 67), handing them the Temple vessels he is entrusted to return, to empower them to reinstitute the old processes of worship. This crisis, which acts as the climax of the book, is not his own enforcement of pre-exilic law on the new status quo; it is a result of internal conflicts within the post-exilic society, which he is called upon to address. But the way the crisis is framed obscures a subtlety in the pre-exilic law, which the political insurgents seek to overlook. We turn now to Deuteronomy, where the laws of intermarriage posit two different kinds of case:

> When the LORD thy God shall bring thee into the land whither thou goest to possess it, and hath cast out many nations before thee, the Hittites, and the Girgashites, and the Amorites, and the Canaanites, and the Perizzites, and the Hivites, and the Jebusites, seven nations greater and mightier than thou; And when the LORD thy God shall deliver them before thee; thou shalt smite them, and utterly destroy them; thou shalt make no covenant with them, nor show mercy unto them: Neither shalt thou make marriages with them; thy daughter thou shalt not give unto his son, nor his daughter shalt thou take unto thy son. (Deut. 7.1-3[6])

This is the basic position about intermarriage, the *lechatchila* best case scenario position, if you will. And we will return to that last line about whom one gives one's sons and daughters to in the post-enlightenment response of the *Hatam Sofer*. But later in Deuteronomy the best-case scenario position is moderated into two other positions regarding different tribes:

---

5. וככלות אלה נגשו אלי השרים לאמר לא נבדלו העם ישראל והכהנים והלוים מעמי הארצות כתועבתיהם לכנעני החתי הפרזי היבוסי העמני המאבי המצרי והאמרי: כי נשאו מבנתיהם להם ולבניהם והתערבו זרע הקדש בעמי הארצות ויד השרים והסגנים היתה במעל הזה ראשונה: ואלי יאספו כל חרד בדברי אלהי ישראל על מעל הגולה...

6. כי יביאך יהוה אלהיך אל הארץ אשר אתה בא שמה לרשתה ונשל גוים רבים מפניך החתי והגרגשי והאמרי והכנעני והפרזי והחוי והיבוסי שבעה גוים רבים ועצומים ממך: ונתנם יהוה אלהיך לפניך והכיתם החרם תחרים אתם ברית ולא תחנם: ולא תתחתן בם בתך לא תתן לבנו ובתו לא תקח לבנך

> An Ammonite or Moabite shall not enter into the congregation of the LORD; even to their tenth generation shall they not enter into the congregation of the LORD for ever. (Deut. 23.4[7])

Still, a more moderate position is offered several verses later, regarding the Egyptian or the Edomite:

> Thou shalt not abhor an Edomite; for he is thy brother: thou shalt not abhor an Egyptian; because thou wast a stranger in his land. The children that are begotten of them shall enter into the congregation of the LORD in their third generation. (Deut. 23.8-9[8])

This position too is not favourable to intermarriage; however, it may be interpreted as demonstrating – right at the very beginning of Jewish law – an acceptance of the difference between *lechatchila* and *bedi'avad*, and here offering a post-facto acceptance of some cases of intermarriage, and a less than instant but nevertheless clearly defined social path to acceptance for the offspring of such a marriage. This nuanced legal position is entirely collapsed by the apparent ruling adopted in Ezra, though crucially it is not Ezra who offers the ruling:

> And Shechaniah the son of Jehiel, one of the sons of Elam, answered and said unto Ezra, We have trespassed against our God, and have taken strange wives of the people of the land: yet now there is hope in Israel concerning this thing. Now therefore let us make a covenant with our God to put away all the wives, and such as are born of them, according to the counsel of my lord, and of those that tremble at the commandment of our God; and let it be done according to the law. Arise; for this matter belongeth unto thee: we also will be with thee: be of good courage, and do it. Then arose Ezra, and made the chief priests, the Levites, and all Israel, to swear that they should do according to this word. And they sware. (Ezra 10.2-5[9])

What Shechaniah's proposition apparently does is to entirely discount the nuanced position in Deuteronomy, and bundle the Egyptian (explicitly) and Edomite (by implication) into the previous and more stringent position which allows no path to social acceptance for either the foreign wives or for their children;

---

7. לא יבא עמוני ומואבי בקהל יהוה גם דור עשירי לא יבא להם בקהל יהוה עד עולם:
8. לא תתעב אדמי כי אחיך הוא לא תתעב מצרי כי גר היית בארצו: בנים אשר יולדו להם דור שלישי יבא להם בקהל יהוה:
9. ויען שכניה בן יחיאל מבני עולם [עילם] ויאמר לעזרא אנחנו מעלנו באלהינו ונשב נשים נכריות מעמי הארץ ועת יש מקוה לישראל על זאת: ³ ועתה נכרת ברית לאלהינו להוציא כל נשים והנולד מהם בעצת אדני והחרדים במצות אלהינו וכתורה יעשה: ⁴ קום כי עליך הדבר ואנחנו עמך חזק ועשה: ויקם עזרא וישבע את שרי הכהנים הלוים וכל ישראל לעשות כדבר הזה וישבעו:

and requires wholesale population transfer. Ezra lends this ruling his imprimatur and it appears to be given the seal of approval as official policy that all the priests, Levites and Jewish society in general commit to. Yonina Dor (2005) argued recently that this mass exile never happened; and Lisbeth Fried notes that similar legislation passed in Athens by Pericles in 451–450 BCE, requiring two Athenian parents for Athenian citizenship because 'a woman served as a conduit, conducting her father's estate to her sons . . . if these women were foreign, these non-Athenian grandsons could wind up owning land in Athens and achieving civil power there' (Fried 2014: 25). Fried also notes that the instigator of the exile, Shachaniah ben Jehiel from Elam (Ezra 10.2), appears to be the son of one of the transgressors (10.26): the question therefore arises whether the father has taken a local woman as secondary wife and her children now posed a threat to Shechaniah's inheritance (Fried 2014: 27). The latter is a plausible historical argument; but since such hypotheses are difficult to prove, we will restrict ourselves to a consideration of what the halakhic argument was, to its result according to what the text itself reports, and to the number of actual expulsions that occurred. As a contemporary editor of a scholarly edition of the book of Ezra notes:

> If we check the number of the expellers, of the four Priestly families there were seventeen wives put out, of the Levites, singers and gatekeepers ten and of the ten tribes another eighty-six: in total, one hundred and thirteen men out of a settlement of tens of thousands of men. And above it noted that there was 'great trespass' (9:13). We are left to conclude that Ezra did not succeed in putting his thought into action completely. (Zer-Kavod 1984: 68)

Another way of considering the result of Ezra's ruling is that what Ezra put his name to was a *lechatchila* ruling which insisted on no intermarriage at all, while the *bedi'avad* reality became a de facto acceptance of all but those one hundred and thirteen cases listed. In this instance the insistence on a maximalist or *lechatchila* interpretation which excluded the leniencies available within the laws of Deuteronomy resulted in an effectively much *more* lenient *bedi'avad* position, in which most intermarriages were overlooked. By insisting on a maximalist ruling Ezra handicapped the imposition of the plain meaning of the law in Deuteronomy and failed entirely to implement his own interpretation of it, which extended the ban on *seven* specific tribes to a ban on *all* non-Jewish tribes.

Toward the Present Era: The Rulings of Moses Schreiber, the Hatam Sofer

The language of Deuteronomy is a connecting thread which runs from the ruling of Ezra to that of Moses Schreiber, the *Hatam Sofer*. When the latter was asked for a ruling to permit a still wet-nursing widow to remarry a Jew within three months of her husband's death (breaching a rabbinic but not biblical prohibition of waiting for at least three months), out of consideration of the possibility that she might otherwise act on her threat to convert to Christianity and marry a non-Jew if she were not permitted to remarry a Jew, in four cases out of the seven times he was asked this question he permitted it; however, in three cases he refused. When he did permit the marriages, he made it clear that this for the sake of the Jewish child and not the mother, his priority being to avoid the possibility that the child might be raised among non-Jews following the mother's conversion (Brown 2011: 164). In all cases where it was possible to raise the child among Jews, the *Hatam Sofer* forbade the remarriage and in doing so explicitly disputed the opinion of the *RaMa* (רמ"א), Rav Moshe Isserles (1520–72), who had authoritatively permitted such remarriages (Brown 2011: 162). The language the *Hatam Sofer* uses to frame his refusal is revealing:

> And if perhaps they do what they will do – we are not responsible for them. Let a thousand such be lost, and one ruling of the sages not be cancelled out.... But that we should in the first place assist him to transgress a minor prohibition lest he transgress a major prohibition? What are we to him and to them? (Schreiber, Responsa 33, cited by Brown 2011: 169–70)

Benjamin Brown notes that the *Hatam Sofer* marks a new stage in the interpretation of Jewish law because in contrast to his predecessors, however stringently they may have ruled, they still explicitly saw even the transgressors and criminals as people 'we are responsible for'. The *Hatam Sofer* represents a stage in which the struggle to keep the marginal people, those standing with one foot outside the camp, seemed to have become an expensive luxury, which in his view the rabbinic decisor could no longer afford: an era when the main struggle would be directed to preserving those remnants who were left within the camp. Brown argues that the *Hatam Sofer* did not see this as an innovation but as the same kind of ruthless stance previously taken against heresies such as the Sabbateans, Sadducees and Karaites (Brown 2011: 158). However, the *Hatam Sofer*'s halachic policy is based, consciously or unconsciously, on the hidden premise that those marginal people were already 'lost' to Judaism, with or without any formal apostasy (Brown 2011: 170). This approach led him to resort to the language of Deuteronomy:

> Were their legal status in our hands I would be of a mind to separate them from within our borders, our sons should not be given to their daughters and our daughters should not be given to their sons ... (Responsa of Hatam Sofer 15.86, cited by Brown 2011: 170)

This implies that on an implicit level the *Hatam Sofer* did not regard those Jews who had strayed outside the fold of halakhic observance, as he defined it, as still Jews at all. Not only was he not responsible for them, what they were practising was not Judaism as he understood it.

A Detour: Back to the Second Temple Period

To put the *Hatam Sofer*'s position about marginal figures in context, one might contrast it with that of Rabbi Yochanan ben Zakkai, the leading figure in reconstituting rabbinic Judaism at Yavneh after the fall of the Second Temple (70 CE), who before moving from the village of Arav in the Galilee to the centre of decision making in Jerusalem, lived in the provinces of Galilee for eighteen years and was only asked two halakhic questions about the Sabbath:

> Rabbi Ulla said that [Rabbi Yochanan ben Zakkai] resided in Arav for eighteen years, and they asked him only these two questions. He said: 'Galilee, Galilee, you hated the Torah; you will eventually be forced by the officers'. (*Jer. Tal. Shab.* 16.15d)

While clearly irritated by the level of observance in this backwater, it did not apparently occur to Rabbi Yochanan ben Zakkai to declare those who failed to ask him questions as outside of his sphere of responsibility or, for that matter, as non-Jews. He clearly was neither delighted by their laxness nor thought that good things would result from their negligence, but Galilee remained Galilee and he did not consider its ignorance to have put it beyond his obligation to render a legal opinion there in the two cases where his opinion was sought. An even earlier contrasting figure to set next to the *Hatam Sofer* might be Yose ben Yoezer (died 161 BCE), a priestly leader of the Maccabean period whom the Talmudic sources depict as in conflict both with the encroaching influence of Hellenism within the Jewish population at large and the Sadducee influence within the Temple itself. The Talmud depicts him disinheriting his own Hellenized son (*b. Shab.* 133b), an action elsewhere defined as being permitted to a man because it is 'legally valid, but the spirit of the sages finds no delight in him' (*b. Bab. Bat.* 133b).[10] He is also depicted as engaging in disputation with his Hellenized nephew-priest in the course of his own political execution. This encounter ends with Yose ben Yoezer's rebuke, stinging the nephew into repentance and expiation by self-imposed punishment; and, as a result, with the nephew's soul ascending to heaven before that of his pious uncle (*Gen. Rab.* 65.22). Clearly, then, Yose ben Yoezer is also a rabbinic leader who considers the marginal criminal with one foot outside the camp as entirely redeemable, let alone no longer Jewish. If Yose ben Yoezer's nephew were no longer Jewish, what would be the point of stinging him to repent? On the other hand, Yose ben Yoezer's conflict with the Sadducees caused him to be depicted as not the stringent scourge of Hellenizers but rather as someone who adopts a 'lenient' position:

> Rabbi Yose the son of Yoezer of Tzereda, testified about the ayil-locust: that it is clean and that the liquid [that flows] in the slaughterhouse [of the Temple] is not

---

10. Translated by Prawer in Lau and Prawer 2010: 100.

susceptible to uncleanliness and that he who touches a corpse becomes unclean. And they called him 'Yose the Lenient'. (*m. Eduy.* 8.4[11])

Binyamin Lau contrasts this ruling with a text from the same period, the Temple Scroll, presenting the Qumran sect position on these matters which was similar if not identical to that of the Sadducees.

And you shall make a channel all around the laver along the altar ... so that the water flows and runs through it and is lost in the middle of the earth and no one should touch it because it is mixed with the blood of the burnt offering. (11Q19, 32.12-15[12])

Lau suggests that it was in the context of the Sadducee desire to 'deepen awareness of issues of purity and impurity in the Temple,' and their objection to a ruling that diminished the sanctity of the Temple and all that came from it, that the sage 'merited' the characterisation of 'Yose the Lenient'. For our purposes the key observation is that leniency is in the eye of the beholder; and a decision that does not favour one sector of the Jewish population may be depicted as lenient by that sector.

Back to the Modern Era: What to Do?

To return to the comparison with the early modern and current era. I have taken this detour through the rulings of the Second Temple Era to indicate just two of the *Hatam Sofer*'s predecessors, as Benjamin Brown would term them, whose relations with opposing opinions illustrate how an equally disputed era of social conflict and disputed authority was addressed by key rabbinic decisions that defended the rabbis' own legal boundaries without declaring either the negligent or the self-interested to be outside the broad parameters of Judaism.

The question of who is lenient and who is stringent is not a new one, therefore; and the distinction between what is a *lechatchila* ('at the start') and what a *bedi'avad* ('in retrospect') position, likewise, echoes down the centuries. Before we venture into the present era I would like to suggest, in the light of Yose ben Yoezer's sobriquet, an alternative pair of terms/concepts through which to view a legal ruling that may depend less on the eye of the beholder. Whereas I have no delusions that these terms may be absorbed into halakhic discourse, perhaps they may be of use to historians of Jewish Law. Instead of stringent or lenient, or indeed *lechatchila* and *bedi'avad*, I would ask how broad a Jewish public that ruling would address. In

---

11. Translation by Prawer in Lau and Prawer 2010: 107.
12. Cited in Lau and Prawer 2010: 108 from Martinez and Tigchelaar (eds), *The Dead Sea Scrolls Study Edition*.

that light, a ruling may therefore be characterised as State (Heb. *mamlachti*, (ממלכתי) or Sectional (Heb. *si'ati*, סיעתי).[13] I am not making any claims about the correctness, stringency, leniency, a priori or post-facto nature of either category. I am suggesting that there are two entirely different kinds of Jewish legal thinking modes: one which attempts to produce a solution applicable to the entire Jewish people, wherever they may be and however they may practise; and another which seeks to produce a ruling for one group within the people and for that group's standards. Whether a position is stringent or lenient is a slippery question, but whether the ruling attempts to include the 'criminals' in the camp or not is perhaps a more easily determined one.

It is with this issue in mind that we now move into the present era, and the disputation between two Rabbinic High Court judges in Israel over the definition of a valid Jewish conversion.

The Dispute: A Case Study

The original occasion of the dispute was an appeal by a female convert against the decision of the Ashdod (a city in southern Israel) Rabbinic Court which denied her request for a Jewish divorce on the grounds that, in their view, she did not require such a divorce as her conversion was not valid (as an Orthodox conversion). The reason given for the invalidity of her conversion was that she had not observed the Sabbath after her conversion and, therefore, had not accepted the Torah Commandments in the course of the conversion (as required) and demonstrably was not Jewish.

Rabbi Shlomo Dichovsky and Rabbi Avraham Sherman sat together on the Rabbinic High Court for the appeal. In the ruling they issued together, the appellant was sustained and the Ashdod court's ruling overruled. In that ruling, Rabbi Dichovsky was supported by Rabbi Ezra bar Shalom and therefore gave the majority ruling; Rabbi Sherman gave the minority dissenting opinion.[14]

This was not a historic ruling. It became a historic ruling only retrospectively, when Rabbi Sherman and two other high court judges arranged to try a similar case by removing it from the procedural queue in the Rabbinic High Court to sit in their own convened *Beit Din* (Orthodox court), with Rabbi Sherman as the senior judge in place of Rabbi Dichovsky. In that subsequent ruling Rabbi Sherman's previously minority opinion became the majority ruling and the lengthy legal opinion he published engaged at length with the opinion given in the previous case by Rabbi Dichovsky. Because this ruling quotes the previous one and is the more famous document, I will cite the second ruling, not least because it was this second ruling which proposed that not only the appelant's conversion, but all 6000 conversions effected by the Rabbinic Courts for Conversion under the State of

---

13. Professor Naftali Lowenthal suggested the translation 'enclavist' instead of 'sectional' when I proposed this term to him.

14. Rabbinic High Court Decision 1-11-3939, 08.03.2001.

Israel Conversion Authority headed by Rabbi Chaim Druckman,[15] should be retroactively revoked[16]. It is here that the parallel with Ezra's maximalist ruling becomes relevant, whereas the disputation in the previous ruling is the informing legal precedent but not the event itself. In the context of the present argument Rabbi Dichovsky's position, which is cited by Rabbi Sherman, represents an explicit and self-defined *bedi'avad* position to which Rabbi Sherman offers a *lechatchila* rebuttal. Rabbi Sherman introduces Rabbi Dichovsky's ruling thus:

> The appellant, in the grounds for her appeal against the decision of the esteemed judge Attia that he was mistaken in his decision to register the woman and her children in the category of those prohibited from marriage, based her claim on the remarks of Rabbi Dichovsky who wrote in his opinion for the ruling in the appeal of case number 9363-12-1 ... in which he wrote the following: 'The test of the acceptance of commandments is measured wherever it may be, in the moment when the convert immerses for the purpose of conversion.[17] If at that moment his acceptance was complete one may not revoke the conversion even if afterwards he does not stand by it. How can the regional rabbinic court judge what occurred at that moment when it was not personally there but instead the *Beit Din* [court] for Conversion was'; and Rabbi Dichovsky's conclusion there was: 'We are dealing here with something that occurred years ago in a matter of minutes, and to be precise in the interval of less than a minute. In that same miniscule period of time it is necessary to determine what was in the mind and heart of the female convert, how is it possible to determine for certain what the convert was thinking at that crucial instant? At most it is possible to raise a doubt but our doubt cannot drive out the certainty of the *Beit Din* for Conversion ... There is no escaping the conclusion that a post-facto is not an a priori; and it is not possible to revoke a conversion post facto, after it has been performed.[18]

So far Rabbi Sherman's reference to Rabbi Dichovsky's ruling in the previous case. But to this position Rabbi Sherman offers an entirely different mode of assessment, relying not on a consideration of what was in the convert's mind at the

---

15. Rabbi Druckman was appointed the head of the Israeli State Conversion Authority in 1990 and oversaw thousands of Orthodox conversions. His work was subject to continual objections from the ultraorthodox rabbinic institutions as well as parts of the state rabbinic establishment, which occasionally necessitated intervention by Israel's Supreme Court. The most serious attack on Druckman's conversions occurred in 2008, and the legal opinions aired in that clash still define the topic.

16. Sherman, Eiserer and Sheinfeld 2008 (*Psak Din* [{verdict} Regarding the Annulment of Conversions], 4 Adar I 5768, February 10, 2008, 53 pp. (in Hebrew). http://www.nevo.co.il/

17. Immersion in a *miqve,* consecrated water source, is a mandatory part of the Jewish conversion process for women.

18. Sherman et al. 2008: 31 (Heb.)

instant of immersion; but, rather, what was her level of Jewish practise *before* conversion and what was her level of Jewish practise *after*. If there was no change, he argues, there was no intention to accept the commandments.[19] What is interesting about Rabbi Sherman's argument, however, is not the argument itself but the language he employs, which conjures up the previous views of the *Hatam Sofer*:

> There is no sense in and it is inconceivable to take this certain moment from the context of a secular life, entirely detached from a religious life of law and commandments, and to say that at that moment there was a revolutionary turning point of entry to the Jewish religion, its principles, beliefs and commandments, when immediately after the passing of 'the one instant' there is no expression or expression of the religious turning point which supposedly occurred in her [the convert's] heart; and that, even according to her own remarks and those of her partner immediately after that moment 'when she declared acceptance of commandments', they did not observe the Sabbath and did not observe the laws of family purity at all. They continued living without Jewish marriage for months after that one instant [of immersion], and even the appellant's testimony that she kept the Commandments as best as she could expresses – at best – *traditional superficial modes of behaviour and not religious behaviour* [author's emphasis, AH], as would have had to be reflected by her declaration of acceptance of commandments at the point of immersing and before the *Beit Din* [conversion court].[20]

The Dispute: An Assessment

The connection to the *Hatam Sofer* is in the final sentence, which reveals the problem with Rabbi Sherman's position. It is not my place to argue with Rabbi Sherman's ruling as a reflection of halakhic literature. There are major opinions to support Rabbi Sherman; on the other hand, there are also major opinions to support Rabbi Dichovsky. For the purposes of this study the problem of Rabbi Sherman's position is not that he does not consider the convert wife to be Jewish. The problem is that, in that final sentence, it is eminently clear that he does not consider her secular husband as Jewish either. If the husband's life and whatever religious behaviour she exhibited as part of it are 'at best traditional, superficial modes of behaviour and not religious behaviour', then we are clearly dealing here with the sort of person the *Hatam Sofer* declared he would not marry his son or daughter to; and Rabbi Sherman's ruling is clearly one for a particular group within the people who exhibit religious behaviour as he defines it, a Sectional and not a State ruling.

19. Sherman et al. 2008: 33.
20. Sherman et al. 2008: 33.

One hole I would note in Rabbi Sherman's halakhic argument is that he says no change occurred and therefore nothing happened. He goes on however to quote further from the appellant's testimony:

> Four months after the conversion the appellant declares before the regional religious court that she switches on lights on the Sabbath, and to the religious court's question whether she knew at her conversion that she had to observe the Sabbath, her reply was yes but it's difficult to do over one Sabbath. At the same meeting her Jewish partner declares, 'we switch on lights on the Sabbath', and added: 'my wife converted three months ago and there's no substantial change since the conversion apart from laws of family purity'.[21]

Neither Rabbi Sherman nor the Jewish husband appear to see this detail as what Rabbi Sherman would term a revolutionary entry into the Jewish religion, its principles, beliefs and commandments. But, according to the simple test of Rabbi Sherman's definition of a change of behaviour, something did occur: the convert had not kept the laws of family purity before the conversion, and after the conversion she began to do so. Again, it is entirely up to Rabbi Sherman what number of commandments that are kept constitute truly religious behaviour, and how much of the Jewish people he is addressing in his ruling. Nevertheless, by the terms of his own test a particular change did occur and it cannot be dismissed as entirely superficial: observing the Sabbath requires at most four days a month, where in contrast observing the laws of family purity can require two or more weeks of the month.

The view that only Sabbath observance is the decisive test is considered a relatively recent halakhic position, dating back only to 1876.

> Rabbi Schmelkes wrote: 'The basic principle with regard to proselytes in our times is to ensure that they truly take upon themselves to perform the central beliefs of religion, the other commandments, and the Sabbath, which is a central principle because a Sabbath desecrator is an idolater. If he undergoes conversion but does not accept upon himself to observe the Sabbath and the commandments, as mandated by religion, he is not a proselyte'. He ruled: 'If he undergoes conversion and accepts upon himself the yoke of the commandments, while in his heart he does not intend to perform them – it is the heart that God wants and [therefore] he has not become a proselyte'. (Schmelkes as cited in Angel 2009: 28)

I note this only because Schmelkes's view that Sabbath observance is the acid test of conversion appears to have become the standard view, and one which Rabbi Sherman feels no need to remark on. So widely accepted has this view become that it is taken as implicit in texts that predate it; and a dispute in the pages of the

---

21. Sherman et al 2008: 37–8.

journal *Hakirah*, consisting of Rabbi Marc Angel's essay and an essay in rebuttal resulted in a response to the rebuttal by Rabbi Angel in which he urged the reader to go to the original sources and read what they actually said.

> We must also keep in mind what the halakha *prefers*, and what the halakha *allows*. Obviously, the halakha prefers ideal converts who are motivated by pure love of God and Torah, and who fully desire to live a life of Torah and mitzvoth. Yet, the halakha allows conversions of individuals who do not fulfil the ideal qualifications. (Angel 2010: 47)

By Way of Conclusion

I have attempted to draw a historical line from Ezra's ruling to expel all foreign wives and their children to Rabbi Sherman's ruling to revoke 6000 conversions. The similarity between the two lies not just in the way they relate to less-observant members of the Jewish community, but also in the way the ruling fared. Just as Ezra's ruling appears to have been followed only by 137 Jewish men, Rabbi Sherman's ruling was overturned by the Supreme Court of Israel on procedural grounds and by the Sephardi Chief Rabbi of Israel, Rabbi Shlomo Amar. The significance of their rulings, however, is not in their immediate impact but in their halakhic afterlife. Anyone who picks up a page of the *Shulchan Aruch*[22] and follows the trail of opinions upon it will readily observe a certain tendency in Jewish law. A question will be raised and it will be thoroughly discussed. Then there will be an opinion rendered, often a *bedi'avad* opinion, followed by a *lechatchila* opinion which is sometimes suggested as preferable but not obligatory. That is the top line of opinion given in the language of the *Shulchan Aruch*'s author Joseph Caro himself, and the commentary of Rabbi Moses Isserles which made the book universally accepted by both Ashkenazi and Sephardi communities. In the commentaries of subsequent generations around the page however you may see a general trend to question the *bedi'avad* ruling and to prefer a shift to the *lechatchila*. That is, what the *halakha* defined in the top line as permissible is rejected over time

---

22. The *Shulchan Aruch* (Heb. 'Set Table') is a code of Jewish law that lays out practical and concise instructions distilled from Talmudic deliberation and the rabbinic commentaries attached to it. Its current form is a hybrid, initially written by Rabbi Yosef Caro (1488–1575), a Sephardi Rabbi who lived in Safed (northern Israel), with additional commentary and amendments by Rabbi Moshe Isserles (and subsequent further commentators). The First printing of Caro's work (in the 1560s) in Venice was a decade later followed by the Cracow edition, including Isserles' work, which was accepted as so uniquely authoritative by both Sephardi and Ashkenazi communities, that other halachic opinions are categorised as either *Rishonim* (prior ones) or *Achronim* (later ones) depending on their relationship to this one code.

and the minority or *lechatchila* view is adopted as the only reasonable starting point. We may see a very rapid demonstration of this principle in action by observing that despite his ruling being overturned Rabbi Sherman has become the halakhic authority of choice to whom the current Ashkenazi Chief Rabbi David Lau thought it prudent to promise his allegiance in order to secure that office.[23] Rabbi Sherman's *lechatchila* ruling has therefore been rejected as the minority view; but it remains for subsequent generations to take up as their banner.

At the risk of indulging in theology rather than in religious history, I would suggest a metaphor to define whether Judaism is a religious or an ethnic phenomenon. You might compare the Jewish people to a clam which has a pearl inside it. The religious community whom Ezra, the *Hatam Sofer* and Rabbi Sherman made rules for may be compared to the pearl. The pearl cannot exist, however, without the shell. The shell is the Jewish people, who do not necessarily practise much of anything, or at least perform quite a variety of practises in different times and places. Rabbi Yochanan ben Zakkai and Rabbi Yose ben Yoezer were acutely aware of that. Benjamin Brown also goes to great lengths to modify his portrait of the *Hatam Sofer* to note that later in his career as a rabbinic leader, and in the light of his experience of social change, he moved from his earlier attachment to stringent positions; and a more conservative-rabbinic normative tendency emerged, which tended more to keep his flock to the letter of the law 'no more and no less' rather than attempt to impose his earlier more stringent rulings (Brown 2011: 176). That is to say, the *Hatam Sofer* may have said that were their legal status in his power he would have expelled the marginal figures; but it may be asked whether, later in life at least, he would have indeed done so should that power have been given to him. Rabbi Sherman exercises considerably more power over more people than the *Hatam Sofer* ever did, but as with Ezra's ruling, his maximalist position is so far confined to the realms of the *lechatchila*. It is in the hands of generations of rabbis to come whether they choose to follow the example of Ezra, who rededicated the Temple at considerable social cost and perhaps ineffectually – or Rabbi Yochanan ben Zakkai, who opposed Sadducee purity laws and insisted the Almighty could still be worshipped even though the Temple fell.

Bibliography

Angel, Marc D. (2009), 'Conversion to Judaism: Halakha, Hashkafa, and Historic Challenge', *Hakirah: The Flatbush Journal of Jewish Law and Thought*, 7: 25–49.
Angel, Marc D. (2010), 'Response to Rabbi Eliezer ben Porat', *Hakirah* 8: 41–5.
Brown, Benjamin (2011), 'Stringency: Five Modern Era Types', 125–237 in *Studies in Jewish Law in Honour of Professor Aharon Kirschenbaum,* ed. Aryeh Edrei, Tel Aviv: Buchman Faculty of Law (Heb.).

---

23. Jewish Press, August 5 2013, story accessed 18/04/2018 at http://www.jewishpress.com/news/breaking-news/r-lau-to-submit-conversion-rulings-to-haredi-review-in-vote-deal/2013/08/05/

Dor, Yonina (2005), *Have the Foreign Women Really Been Expelled?*, Jerusalem: Magnes Press (Heb.).

Eskenazi, Tamara Cohn (1988), *In an Age of Prose: A Literary Approach to Ezra-Nehemiah*, Society of Biblical Literature Monograph Series 36, Atlanta: Scholars Press.

Fried, Lisbeth S. (2014), *Ezra & The Law in History and Tradition*, Columbia: University of South Carolina.

Jastrow, Marcus (1903), *Dictionary of the Targumim, the Talmud and Midrashic Literature*, New York: Putnam.

Lau, Binyamin and Michael Prawer (authors and translators) (2010), *The Sages: The Second Temple Period*, Jerusalem: Maggid 2010.

Sherman, Avraham, Hagai Eiserer and Avraham Sheinfeld (2008), *Psak Din [Regarding the Annulment of Conversions]*, 4 Adar I 5768, February 10, 2008, 53 pp. (Heb.), http://www.nevo.co.il/

Zer-Kavod, Mordechai (1984), *Ezra-Nehemia*, Jerusalem: Mossad Harav Kook (Heb.).

SUKKOT AS RESISTANCE IN THE DAYS OF NEHEMIAH

Lisbeth S. Fried

Nehemiah 8–10 forms the climax of the book *Ezra-Nehemiah,* and has been called a 'covenant renewal ceremony' (Baltzer 1971: 43–8; Duggan 2001: 5–7). In Nehemiah 8, Ezra reads the torah of Moses to all the people who weep when they hear it. He admonishes them to be glad, for joy in Yhwh is strength. The people celebrate, eat, drink, and send gifts. In Nehemiah 9, the Levites recount God's miracles on their behalf from the time he brought them out of Egypt, until the present, and they confess that in spite of everything God has done for them they have been disobedient. Now, because Yhwh is a just god, he has handed them over to the peoples of the lands, making them slaves in their own country to the kings that God has set over them. According to Nehemiah 10, it is because of all this that we, the undersigned, make a firm agreement, swearing to keep the torah of Yhwh and not to abandon his temple.

In Nehemiah 8, when Ezra reads the law to them, the people learn for the first time of the holiday of Sukkot:

> **8.13.** The heads of the patriarchal families of all the people, the priests, and the Levites, gathered to Ezra the scribe in order to gain insight into the words of the Torah. **8.14.** And they found written in the Torah which Yhwh commanded by the hand of Moses that the people of Israel should dwell in booths (*sūkkôt*), for the holiday of the seventh month **8.15.** and that they should proclaim [it] and send out a herald into all their cities and in Jerusalem saying: 'Go out to the hills and bring leaves of the olive tree, leaves of [pine]oil trees, and myrtle leaves, and leaves of date palms and leafy tree branches in order to make booths, as it is written'. [All translations of the Hebrew are the author's.]

We then read how they celebrated it.

> **8.16.** So the people went out and brought [them] and they made for themselves booths each on his roof, in their courtyards, as well as in the temple courtyards,

in the square of the Water Gate, and in the square of the Gate of Ephraim. **8.17.** And all the assembly of those who had returned from the captivity made booths and lived in them.

Which Text Was It That They Found Written in the Torah?

The holiday of Sukkot is described differently in the different books of our current Torah, and it is difficult to say which passage it was – if any – that Ezra read that led the people to go to the hills and gather branches to build booths on the roofs of their own houses and in their own courtyards and to live in them for the eight days of the holiday.

Sukkot in Exodus

Exodus has two holiday calendars – Exodus 23 and 34. Both command pilgrimage festivals to Yhwh three times a year. The third pilgrimage is called 'The Festival of Gathering' (defective, חג האסף [Exod. 23.16] and plene, חג האסיף [Exod. 34.22]). There is no mention of constructing or living in booths, nor of gathering branches, nor is the holiday called *Sŭkkôt*, or 'booths' ['tents' in the Greek and Latin translations]; it is simply the holiday of 'gathering'. With no reference to living in booths, neither passage in Exodus could be the passage that Ezra read.

Sukkot in Numbers

Numbers 29 does not name the holiday of the seventh month, it is simply a 'festival to Yhwh' (v. 12); nor does it command gathering branches of leafy trees, or constructing and living in 'booths'. It does provide precise dates for the holiday, however, from the fifteenth to the twenty-second day of the seventh month (Num. 29.12-38), something that is conspicuously absent in Nehemiah. The thrust of the passage is to outline the number of animals to be sacrificed on each of the seven days of the holiday – two rams, fourteen lambs and one goat each day; plus thirteen bulls on the first day, twelve on the second, eleven on the third, and so on in decreasing order until seven bulls are sacrificed on the seventh day. The total number of bulls sacrificed is seventy, and this corresponds to either the number 'of the sons of Israel' (Deut. 32.8), the number of the 'angels of God' (LXX Deut. 32.8) or perhaps, the number of the gods themselves (4QDeut. 32.8; Ayali-Darshan 2015). This does not explain why the number decreases each day, or why seven of the gods would have to wait until the seventh day of the holiday to receive their sacrifice. More likely is the idea that the diminishing number of bulls sacrificed reflects the waning moon, from full moon on the first day of the holiday (the fifteenth of the month) to the half-moon on the twenty-first day (Ulfgard 1998: 90). In any case, Numbers prescribes only a temple observance, and so it cannot be the passage that Ezra is described as reading in Nehemiah 8 – although, absent the precise date, it nevertheless seems to be the passage referred to in Ezra 3.

Sukkot in Deuteronomy

Deuteronomy refers to a festival of 'booths', *Sūkkôt,* by name (Deut. 16.13, 16; 31.10). According to Deuteronomy 16:

> [13]You shall observe the festival of booths (*Sūkkôt*) seven days, when you have gathered in the produce from your threshing floor and your wine press. [14] You shall rejoice during your festival, you and your son and your daughter, your male and female slave, as well as the Levite, the alien, the orphan, and the widow who live within the gates [of your towns]. [15] Seven days you shall celebrate [the festival for] Yhwh your god at the place that Yhwh will choose; for Yhwh your god will bless you in all your produce and in all the works of your hands, and you shall surely be joyous.

Although the holiday is called 'booths' (*Sūkkôt*) here, there is nothing about gathering branches of leafy trees, of building booths, or of living in them. Indeed, there are no instructions at all for observing the festival, nor is a specific date set beyond 'when you gather in your produce' (Ulfgard 1998: 92). It should be noted that the 'gathering' is no longer from the fields, but rather from the 'threshing floor and the wine press'. That is, it is to take place only after all the work of the harvest season, not just the gathering from the fields, is completed (Gesundheit 2012: 156).

The text in Deuteronomy could not be the text that Ezra read, therefore. It would not be possible to learn from this text that the people should gather branches, build booths on their courtyards and rooftops, and dwell in them.

Sukkot in Leviticus

Leviticus refers to the festival of *Sūkkôt,* 'Booths', by name as well as to the seven days of 'Yhwh's offerings by fire' (23.33-36), summarizing the prescriptions found in Numbers 29 discussed above:

> [33]Yhwh spoke to Moses, saying: [34] Speak to the people of Israel, saying: On the fifteenth day of this seventh month, and lasting seven days, there shall be the festival of booths to Yhwh. [35] The first day shall be a holy convocation; you shall not work at your occupations. [36] Seven days you shall present Yhwh's offerings by fire; on the eighth day you shall observe a holy convocation and present Yhwh's offerings by fire; it is a solemn assembly; you shall not work at your occupations.

This command in Leviticus is followed immediately by a statement which appears to be a summary of all the instructions for all the festivals and holy days listed previously in that chapter:

> [37]These are the designated times of Yhwh, which you shall celebrate as sacred times, for presenting to Yhwh offerings by fire – burnt offerings and grain offerings, sacrifices and drink offerings, each on its proper day – [38] apart from the

Sabbaths of Yhwh, and apart from your gifts, and apart from all your votive offerings, and apart from all your freewill offerings, which you give to Yhwh. (Lev. 23.37-38)

Then, curiously, it immediately supplies an addendum:

³⁹Now, the fifteenth day of the seventh month, when you have gathered in the produce of the land, you shall keep the festival of Yhwh for seven days; a complete rest on the first day, and a complete rest on the eighth day. ⁴⁰ On the first day you shall take the fruit of majestic trees, branches of palm trees, boughs of leafy trees, and willows of the brook; and you shall rejoice before Yhwh your God for seven days. ⁴¹ You shall keep it as a festival to Yhwh seven days in the year; you shall keep it in the seventh month as a statute forever throughout your generations. ⁴² You shall live in booths for seven days; all who are citizens in Israel shall live in booths, ⁴³ so that your generations may know that I made the people of Israel live in booths when I brought them out of the land of Egypt: I am Yhwh your God. (Lev. 23.39-43)

Only this addendum could be the passage referred to in Nehemiah, since this alone refers to dwelling in booths and gathering branches (vss. 40, 42). The command to 'rejoice before Yhwh' suggests a celebration in Jerusalem or at a local shrine, however, whereas the passage in Nehemiah commands people to celebrate in their own homes. Nevertheless, Leviticus 23.40 is the only place in our present Torah where the people are told not only what to procure when they go out to the hills, but also what to do with the branches they bring back. If so, if this is the passage that Ezra read, then it is evident that the wording of the passage in Leviticus has changed between the time when Nehemiah 8.15 was written and now:

Leviticus 23.40	Nehemiah 8.15-16
ולקחתם לכם פרי עץ הדר כפת תמרים וענף עץ עבת וערבי נחל ושמחתם לפני יהוה אלהיכם שבעת ימים	צאו ההר והביאו עלי זית ועלי עץ שמן ועלי הדס ועלי תמרים ועלי עץ עבת לעשות סכות ככתוב
You shall take for yourselves fruit of majestic trees, branches of palm trees, boughs of leafy trees, willows of the brook; you shall rejoice before Yhwh your God for seven days.	Go out to the hills and gather foliage of the olive tree, foliage of the commiphora bush, foliage of myrtle, foliage of palm, foliage of large trees, to make booths, as it is written.

The lack of correspondence, moreover, between the types of trees listed in Nehemiah and Leviticus, and the fact that Leviticus nowhere mentions what to do with the branches, militates against the likelihood that the present text of Leviticus provided the command in Nehemiah 8. Indeed, the reference in Lev. 23.40 to 'taking fruit' makes it clear that in contrast to Nehemiah, the Leviticus passage excludes using the material gathered to construct a booth (Eerdmans 1910: 308; Rudolph 1949: 151).

Sukkot in Second Temple Texts

The fruit and the leafy branches described in Leviticus refer much more to a bouquet which one holds in one's hand for a festal procession rather than to building a booth. Indeed, this is how the holiday was celebrated during the Hellenistic and Roman periods, as can be seen from numerous Second Temple texts.

2 Maccabees

The celebration of the holiday of Sukkot is described in 2 Maccabees (10.5-7; likely written in the late second century BCE: Doran 2012: 3, 35; Goldstein 1983: 53). According to the text, the cleansing and rededication of the temple was celebrated in the manner of the Sukkot celebration:

> [5]The purification of the temple occurred on the very same day as the one on which the Temple was defiled by foreigners, the twenty-fifth of Kislev. [6]For eight days they observed tent-living, as they recalled how, a little time before at the festival of Tents, they had been living like wild animals in the mountains and in the caves. [7]Therefore, holding ivy-wreathed wands and harvest branches as well as palm fronds, they offered up hymns to him who succeeded in having his own place be purified. (Tr. Doron, 2012: 199).

There is no mention of making or living in tents or booths, however, only of using the branches to process in Jerusalem, probably around the altar, as described in Leviticus. The important part of the holiday as described here seems to be processing around the altar while carrying the ivy-wreathed wands, branches and palm fronds.

Jubilees

The holiday of Sukkot is also described in Jubilees, a first-person account of God's revelation disclosed on Sinai to Moses as told by the 'Angel of the Presence'. The original Hebrew text is dated to about 170–140 BCE (VanderKam 2004: 1030). Besides emphasizing a 364-day yearly calendar, a purpose of the text was to show that the patriarchs observed all the commandments and celebrated all the holidays (Rubenstein 1995: 51).

We read about Abraham's celebration of the holiday in Jubilees 16.30-31:

> ³⁰This has no temporal limit because it is ordained forever regarding Israel that they should celebrate it, live in tents, place wreaths on their heads, and take leafy branches and willow branches from the stream. ³¹ Abraham took palm branches and the fruit of good trees, and each and every day he would go around the altar with the branches – seven times per day. In the morning he would give praise and joyfully offer humble thanks to his God for everything.(Tr. VanderKam and White Crawford, 2018: 528)

Although the Jubilees text states that the people Israel are commanded to live in tents [booths], there is no mention here of Abraham doing so. Rather, he is described using the branches, plants and fruit that he had gathered to parade with them around the altar. The branches are not used to build a booth or a dwelling; rather, they are used simply to be carried in procession. Most notable as well is the command that the holiday be celebrated by their 'setting wreaths upon their heads, while carrying leafy boughs and willows'. Wearing wreaths seems to have been a major custom for the holiday, and Rubenstein sees evidence for it in the paintings of the Dura Europa synagogue (Rubenstein 1995: 53, n48).

Josephus

Josephus, writing in the late first century CE, describes the holiday of Sukkot similarly to that in Jubilees:

> They should celebrate a festival for eight days and at that time offer whole burnt-offerings and sacrifices of thanksgiving to God, bearing in their hands a bouquet made up of myrtle and willow-branch together with a branch of palm, with the fruit of the persea [avocado?, citron?] being present. (Tr. Feldman 1999: 3.245)

He also describes one occurrence of the holiday's celebration:

> As to Alexander, his own people were seditious against him; for at a festival which was then celebrated, when he stood upon the altar, and was going to sacrifice, the nation rose upon him, and pelted him with citrons [which they then had in their hands, because] the law of the Jews required that at the feast of tents, everyone should hold wands (*thyrsous*) made of the palm tree and citrons; which thing we have elsewhere related [i.e., in *Ant.* 3.245]. (*Ant.* 13.372; Tr. Whiston, 1828)

According to Josephus, the festival primarily included thank offerings at the temple, plus a procession in Jerusalem in which various objects were carried.

Josephus refers to the branches being carried as *thyrsoi,* the very wands used in Greek harvest festivals. This wand is defined as a 'wand of long fennel stems, wound in ivy and vine-leaves with a pine cone at the top' (Liddell and Scott 1996: 812). It is clear that the booths are not the main point of the holiday, but are simply lean-tos or tents in which to reside in temporarily while celebrating in Jerusalem.

Sukkot in Nehemiah

Why is Sukkot presented so differently in Nehemiah from other Second Temple texts? The description of the holiday in other Second Temple texts emphasizes parading around the altar in Jerusalem carrying leafy branches and decorated wands of olive branches, while wearing wreathes on one's hair. In contrast, the main point of the holiday according to Nehemiah is to use the branches gathered not to carry in procession, but to build a booth or hut. Moreover, the hut is not to be used to live in while celebrating in Jerusalem, but rather the celebrants are to stay at home and build these huts on the roof of their own houses and in their own courtyards in all the cities of Judah.

The Political Situation at the Time of Nehemiah's Writing

Lipschits (2019) suggests that the way of celebrating Sukkot described in Nehemiah goes back to ancient, pre-exilic customs in Judah that were preserved by the people who remained in the land during the exile. These did not become part of the holiday's customs, traditions or ceremonies in second-temple Jerusalem until it was resurrected by the author of Nehemiah 8 in the late fourth century. I propose instead that Nehemiah's unique proposal of a home holiday had to do with the political circumstances taking place during the time of Nehemiah's writing. It was likely written later than Lipschits proposes but much earlier than the late second temple texts referred to above. Josephus of course was written under Roman occupation, while 2 Maccabees and Jubilees were written under the Maccabees or the Seleucids. It is likely that this passage in Nehemiah 8, in which Ezra reads the law to the assembled populace, was written a little earlier than those other late second temple texts and under the Ptolemies. We know that the story of rebuilding both the second temple (now told in Ezra 1–6) and the story of rebuilding Jerusalem's city wall (now told in Nehemiah 2-4, 6, 12.27-43) were known to Ben Sira (49.11-13), a contemporary of the High Priest Simon II (ca. 221–204 BCE; VanderKam 2004: 491; *pace* VanderKam 2004: 147–57). It is well known that Ben Sira did not know the story of Ezra, however, either of his bringing the law to Jerusalem (Ezra 7) or of his reading it to the assembled populace (Neh. 8.1-8). Had he known it, he certainly would not have omitted Ezra from his praise of famous men. (For a discussion of Ben Sira's silence regarding Ezra see Piwowar 2011 and articles cited therein). The story of Ezra's reading the Law in Nehemiah 8 therefore must have been written after Ben Sira, in the last quarter of the third century BCE at the earliest. Thus, it was likely written under the Ptolemies, before the Seleucid conquest of Judea in 198 BCE by Antiochus III. When we realize that the story of Ezra's reading the law and the subsequent celebration of Sukkot was written under the Ptolemies, we can understand the reason behind the unique peculiarities of the holiday's description in Nehemiah 8.

The Ptolemies

The Macedonian rulers, being conquerors and invaders, required legitimation through a divine pedigree and so portrayed themselves as descended from the gods. The Seleucids claimed descent from Apollo, the Attalids from Athena, the Antigonids from Heracles, and the Ptolemies from Dionysus (Green 1990: 397). The importance of Dionysus to the ruler cult of the Ptolemies cannot be overstated. That Dionysus was upheld as the Ptolemies' divine ancestor is visible in the poems of Theocritus, a poet at the court of Ptolemy II Philadelphus (309–246 BCE). Theocritus not only celebrated the king's descent from Dionysus in his poems (17.13-33: Friesen 2013: 67), but also transformed Euripides' description of Dionysus' followers in his play *The Bacchae* from political subversives who kill the monarch into submissive imperial subjects (Friesen 2013: 57). Most startling is the line: 'I do not care; nor should anyone give a thought to one who is an enemy of Dionysus', that is, one who is an enemy of the king who embodies the god (Idyll 24:27, *apud* Friesen 2013: 68).

The Procession to Dionysus

The descriptions of Sukkot in the books of the Maccabees, in Jubilees, and in Josephus all agree in describing a holiday very similar to the way the holiday of Dionysus was celebrated under the Ptolemies. Although it was Ptolemy IV Philopator (244–204 BCE) who had been the first to be given the name 'The New Dionysus', it was Ptolemy II Philadelphus who instituted the great annual procession to Dionysus in Alexandria (Nilsson 1957: 60). A giant statue of Dionysus was paraded, his image housed in a booth or under a canopy decorated with vines of ivy and festooned with ribbons and fruits of every kind. The wagon on which it was carried was followed by priests and priestesses, Bacchants and Maenads: all beating on tambourines, all wearing wreathes in their hair and carrying *thyrsa* (i.e., wands of long fennel stems, wound in ivy and vine-leaves with a pine cone at the top). This procession was brought up by a huge statue of a phallus, the symbol of fertility (Nilsson 1957: 11).

Except for carrying a phallus and a statue of Dionysus in procession, celebrations of the Dionysia and of Sukkot were very similar. They were both celebrated by a procession, and in both, those in the procession wore wreathes in their hair, carried wands and *thyrsoi* of various plant material; and celebrants of both built tents, booths, or canopies decorated with all manner of vines and fruit. Indeed, it was because of the holiday of Sukkot that non-Jews assumed that the Jews worshipped Dionysus. Plutarch, a Greek historian (45–127 CE), spent the last thirty years of his life as a priest of Delphi. Besides writing his more famous *Lives*, he wrote a work,

Questiones Convivivales, which contains a discussion about the god of the Jews. Symmachus, one of the characters in this work, asserts that the Jews worship Dionysus:

> When all the company requested and earnestly begged it of him; first of all (says he), the time and manner of the greatest and most holy solemnity of the Jews is exactly agreeable to the holy rites of Bacchus; for that which they call the Fast they celebrate in the midst of the vintage, furnishing their tables with all sorts of fruits, while they sit under tents made of vines and ivy. The day which immediately goes after this they call the day of Tents. Within a few days after they celebrate another feast, not darkly but openly, dedicated to Bacchus, for they have a feast amongst them called Procession of Thyrsos, from carrying palm-trees, and *Thyrsoi*, when they enter into the temple carrying *thyrsoi* (wands). What they do within I know not; but it is very probable that they perform the rites of Bacchus. First they have little trumpets, such as the Grecians used to have at their Bacchanalia to call upon their Gods withal. (Plutarch, *Quaestiones Convivales*, 6.1, trans. William W. Goodwin, Perseus Project)

Although there is confusion here with Yom Kippur, the day of fasting, the description of the holiday is that of Sukkot, a holiday which follows three days after the fast.

Sukkot in Nehemiah – A Holiday of Resistance

According to the text in Nehemiah, however, there was to be no procession around the altar in Jerusalem, no carrying of wands or *thyrsoi*, no wearing of wreathes on the heads. Rather the people were to use the boughs they gathered not to wave them in procession, but to build booths. Moreover, the booths were not simply a temporary place to live in while celebrating the holiday in Jerusalem. Rather, they were to build the booths on the roofs of their own houses and in their own courtyards. If they lived in Jerusalem, they could build them there, but otherwise they should stay at home. There was to be no pilgrimage to Jerusalem and no procession around the altar:

> **8.16.** So the people went out and brought [them] and they made for themselves booths *each on his own roof, in their own courtyards*, as well as in the temple courtyards, in the square of the Water Gate, and in the square of the Gate of Ephraim.

The author of the Nehemiah text was proclaiming a holiday of Sukkot that was in direct contrast to the laws of the torah and to the Dionysia with which it was compared. Rather than processing publicly in Jerusalem, as was customary, people were to stay quietly at home, in a holiday of quiet resistance against the Ptolemaic rulers of Judah and against their god, Dionysus.

Lessons for Today?

It is clear that the way of celebrating the holiday proposed in the book of Nehemiah was not followed by celebrants during the days of the second temple. It is only now, after the fall of that temple, that Jews around the world take up Nehemiah's suggestion and build *sukkot* on the roofs of their own homes and in their own courtyards. Indeed, I have celebrated sukkot in a sukkah on the roof of a house in Damascus, carefully hidden from the watchful eyes of the police who were everywhere.

Nehemiah's injunction is clear: Do not give even the appearance of celebrating the rites of other gods; observe your own traditions to your own god, and if you must, do it hidden away. My grandmother's family was wiped out in the holocaust. I remember her sitting in a chair by the window and weeping for close cousins, aunts, and uncles, whom she had frequently visited in Germany during her youth. Now they were all gone. The lesson my mother seemed to have learned from this was that we must keep our identity secret. She would host Passover *seder*s and Shabbat dinners, always with the curtains closed, and she never served red wine, only white. I never knew why, until a friend told me it was to avoid the blood libel.

Bibliography

Ayali-Darshan, Noga (2015), 'The Seventy Bulls Sacrificed at Sukkot (Num 29:12-34) in Light of a Ritual Text from Emar (Emar 6, 373)', *VT* 65: 9–19.

Baltzer, Klaus (1971), *The Covenant Formulary in Old Testament, Jewish, and Early Christian Writings*, trans. D. Green; Philadelphia: Fortress Press.

Duggan, Michael W. (2001) *The Covenant Renewal in Ezra-Nehemiah (Neh 7:72b–10:40): An Exegetical, Literary, and Theological Study*; SBL Dissertation Series 164; Atlanta: Society of Biblical Literature.

Doran, Robert (2012), *2 Maccabees: A Critical Commentary*. Hermenia – A Critical and Historical Commentary on the Bible; Minneapolis: Fortress.

Eerdmans, B. D. (1910), 'Ezra and the Priestly Code'. 306–26 in *The Expositor*, edited by William Robertson Nicoll, Sr, seventh series, vol. 10. London: Hodder and Stoughton.

Feldman, Louis H. (1999), *Flavius Josephus: Translation and Commentary*, Volume 3: Judean Antiquities, Leiden: BrillOnline.

Friesen, Courtney Jade (2013), 'Reading Dionysus: Euripides' Bacchae Among Jews and Christians in the Greco-Roman World'. PhD diss., University of Minnesota.

Gesundheit, Shimon (2012), *Three Times a Year: Studies on Festival Legislation in the Pentateuch*, Tübingen: Mohr Siebeck.

Goldstein, Jonathan A. (1983), *II Maccabees*, AB 41A, New York: Doubleday.

Green, Peter (1990), *Alexander to Actium: The Historical Evolution of the Hellenistic Age*, Hellenistic Culture and Society 1, Berkeley, CA: University of California Press.

Liddell, Henry George, and Robert Scott (1996), *A Greek-English Lexicon. Revised and Augmented Throughout by Sir Henry Stuart Jones with the Assistance of. Roderick McKenzie, with a Revised Supplement*. Oxford: Clarendon Press.

Lipschits, Oded (2019), 'Questions of the Times, the Processes, and the Design of the Customs of the Holiday of Sukkot at the End of the Persian and the Beginning of the Hellenistic Periods', *Beth Miqra*, 64.2: 286–310 [Heb.].

Nilsson, Martin P. (1957), *The Dionysiac Mysteries of the Hellenistic and Roman Age*, Lund: C W K Gleerup.
Piwowar, Andrzej (2011), 'Dlaczego Syrach Pominal Ezdrasza w Pochwale Ojców (Syr 44–50)?', *The Biblical Annals* 1: 105–31.
Rubenstein, Jeffrey L. (1995), *The History of Sukkot in the Second Temple and Rabbinic Periods*, Brown Judaic Studies 302, Atlanta: Scholars Press.
Rudolph, Wilhelm (1949), *Esra und Nehemia Samt 3. Esra*, Tübingen: Mohr.
Ulfgard, Håkan (1998), *The Story of Sukkot: The Setting, Shaping, and Sequel of the Biblical Feast of Tabernacles*, Beiträge Zur Geschicte der Biblischen Exegese 34. Tübingen: Mohr Siebeck.
VanderKam, James C. (2004), *From Joshua to Caiaphas: High Priests After the Exile*, Minneapolis: Fortress Press.
VanderKam, James C. (1992), 'Ezra-Nehemiah or Ezra and Nehemiah?', 55–75 in *Priests, Prophets and Scribes: Essays on the Formation and Heritage of Second Temple Judaism in Honour of Joseph Blenkinsopp*, edited by J. W. Wright E. Ulrich and R. P. Carroll. JSOTSup 149, Sheffield: Sheffield Academic Press.
VanderKam, James C., and Sidnie White Crawford, *Jubilees: A Commentary in Two Volumes*. Augsburg Fortress Publishers, 2018. Project MUSE.muse.jhu.edu/book/61964

READING THE BIBLE REPATRIATELY:
EZRA-NEHEMIAH, A CASE STUDY

Roger S. Nam

Introduction

The apropos call for biblical scholars to reflect on the task of 'Reading in These Times' carries significance beyond our academic field.[1] I received the generous invitation to contribute to this volume while on year-long sabbatical as a visiting Professor at Sogang University in Seoul, Korea.[2] The importance of the question playfully emerged in an interaction with my then-six-year-old son, just a few weeks into his own journey as a third-generation child returning to Korea. After playing at the apartment playground with other neighbourhood kids, he returned home and asked, 'Am I Korean, or am I American?' Even a six-year-old had the sense to know that there was something different about his identity from the other children, despite having a common ethnic origin. How does one respond to a child, knowing that his own perceived identity is a totalizing aspect of his personhood and his perceived places of access?

In many ways, this simple conversation with a child signifies a wider societal phenomenon. Today's unparallelled ethnic heterogeneity forces new understandings of identity with concomitant power struggles and marginalization. Accordingly,

---

1. This article was originally presented in the 'Minoritized Criticism and Biblical Interpretation' Section at the 2014 Society of Biblical Literature (SBL) Annual Meeting in San Diego. It will also appear in a forthcoming volume of collected papers from this section. I am grateful for the faculty of the Sogang University Graduate School of Theology for hosting me for the sabbatical year 2014–15 and for an initial forum to share my ideas of repatriation as a reading lens. My return to South Korea in 2014 marked forty-seven years since my mother and father first left their country in 1967, following the passage of the Immigration-Nationality Act of 1965. Serendipitously, the passage of forty-seven years also spans the purported exile (586 BCE) and return under Persian rule (539 BCE).

2. In naming Korea, I specifically refer to South Korea, while recognizing the artificial nature of the border between North and South Korea.

minoritized critics must form reading strategies that align to this reality. In this article, I present a brief chronological review of the biblical studies guild in relation to the prospects of minoritized criticism. I contend that perceptions of minoritized biblical criticism have threatened traditional historical critical approaches. But at the present moment, the ethnic diversity of 'these times' gives more legitimacy for minoritized readings. Drawing on the seminal addresses of Vincent Wimbush, Fernando Segovia, and Gale Yee as the first African American, Latinx American, and Asian American to have ever occupied the Society of Biblical Literature's presidential position, I propose broad constructs for moving forward in minoritized readings (Wimbush 2011; Segovia 2015; Yee 2020).[3] I advocate for repatriation as an effective 'prefigurative' reading strategy alongside the many rich expressions of minoritized approaches.[4] A 'prefigurative' strategy rejects a singular current reading, but rather catalyzes a broader imagination for interpretive options. Accordingly, a repatriate reading takes seriously the multivalent cultural expressions within North America and has direct repercussions on present issues that we must face as biblical critics. The final section will present some of the themes that emerge from a repatriate reading of Ezra-Nehemiah as a second-generation Korean American.

Where We Have Been

Minoritized Bible scholars stand as members of an academic guild with roots in the Enlightenment and the alleged autonomy of the historian.[5] From the turn of the eighteenth century, Bible scholarship has relied heavily on historical critical methods, an umbrella term that covers a variety of diachronic exegetical approaches such as source criticism, form criticism, redaction criticism, etc. These approaches emerged and reached relative prominence at different points in the last two centuries. All of these different critical methods share an emphasis on reconstruction of historical contexts and textual developments in the spirit of Wellhausen's Source Criticism of the Pentateuch. Throughout this period of historical critical scholarship, biblical scholars pursued truth on terms that were considered objective and scientific. The aim of scholarship was to recapture 'original' meanings through skilled philology and reconstruction of ancient

---

3. Other SBL presidential appointments have continued these conversations on contextual readings in Athalya Brenner-Idan (2015) and Brian Blount (2019).

4. Tat-Siong Benny Liew (2008: 2) distinguishes the terms of 'prefigurative' and 'prescriptive,' by drawing on Hom (2001); the prefigurative approach does not claim exclusivity, but rather intends to function as a complementary option. For Liew, the priority to a 'prefigurative' reading does not result in any singular conclusion, but gives space to the possibility of Asian American hermeneutical activity, and concomitant recognition and agency.

5. For a review of the historical critical method in the context of intellectual history, see Legaspi 2010: 27–78.

contexts. The historical studies or biblical contexts were the centre of interpretation, via the principle of analogy. The context of the interpreter was not merely secondary; it was rarely even acknowledged. Rather, scholars pursued scientific reconstructions, assigning dates and strata to textual units with the vigor of an archaeologist excavating a *tel* (mound). Theoretically, proper application of historical critical methods assured reliable results.

The fruits of these historical critical pursuits were quite remarkable, as critical studies opened up an enormous amount of data to illuminate biblical texts and correct previously erroneous interpretations. Textual discoveries, such as Ras Shamra and the Dead Sea Scrolls, as well as the maturing field of Assyriology, brought forth an abundant data set for Bible scholars. New genres were acknowledged. Ancient Near Eastern religions gave a broader context for Israelite religion and muddied the uniqueness of biblical texts. The nature of historiography shifted, from the perceived von Rankean approach of objectivity to one that recognized the politicized nature of ancient Near Eastern scribal cultures. Textual studies underwent a lengthy shift from the pursuit of an assumed scientific reconstruction of the *urtext*, replete with emendations, to a gradual acknowledgement of the multiple textual traditions of antiquity that represented biblical texts. Most significantly, historical critical studies demonstrated the composite nature of biblical texts and the multiple accretions over different phases of ancient Israel. Two centuries of historical critical study resulted in a more sophisticated understanding of the nature of the biblical text.

But on the very principle of criticism, as articulated by Ernst Troeltsch, historical criticism requires continued review and revision of new data and new conclusions (Troeltsch 1991: 12).[6] Inevitably, historical critical scholarship questioned the allure of reader objectivity as the limitations of diachronic methods opened the door for synchronic approaches. The 1980s saw the beginnings of the decline of Wellhausen's JEDP paradigm for the Pentateuch, after a century of its axiomatic dominance. On a broader scale, the intellectual climate of postmodernity had cut into some of the bravado of the idea of 'objective' interpretation. John Collins (2005: 12–17) argues that postmodernity's critique of a unilateral reading was actually an inevitable result of the historical critical enterprise. The historical focus freed the text from so-called objective approaches and allowed the fluidity of the text to emerge. This fluidity was already a phenomenon during the actual textualization of the Bible based on the pattern of appropriating traditions for present contexts, such as the Pauline usage of Hab. 2.4, or the Chronicler's retelling of the history of the Davidic monarchy. Historical critical methods explained that new social contexts, whether the Persian Empire or the nascent Christian Church, warranted new interpretations of received traditions. But the natural progression of this line of thought opened the door for more explicit reference to the modern reader's social context. Texts have meaning only with readers, and said readers have assumptions and political agendas that influence interpretations.

6. For a summation on the influence of Troeltsch on historical criticism, see Chapman 2001: 45–74.

Alongside the attack of history and the newly emerging recognition of the importance of reader context, the demography of the biblical studies field began to shift. Up to the 1980s, the field of biblical studies largely consisted of white, male, Protestant scholars. But recent times have seen the addition of more ethnic minorities.[7] The growing recognition of the importance of multiple perspectives has led to an improvement in nurturing such voices, whether through monograph series for minoritized readings, or more dedicated sessions in the Society of Biblical Literature meeting for minoritized scholars. Higher education accrediting bodies and nonprofit groups, like the Forum for Theological Exploration, pressure theological institutions to embrace greater ethnic diversity in scholarship. More recently, the financial crises in theological education have created more expansive recruiting efforts towards a more diverse pool of applicants. As a result, institutions are more conscientious about hiring people of color.[8] More than ever before, minoritized biblical critics may find themselves in tenured or tenure-track spaces, which afford a privilege more elusive to the minoritized critics of earlier generations.

Despite these positive movements, the spaces for minoritized criticism still do not commensurately reflect the diverse realities of North America. Regardless, I hope that minoritized critics can appreciate an unprecedented opportunity to define ways in which we read biblical texts for the academy and the broader society. Although the concept of minoritized criticism is still theoretically nascent, our unique voices can potentially reverse marginalizing approaches, and open new vistas of biblical interpretation.[9] In the next section, I argue that contextualized approaches need not be ahistorical, but that historical critical tradition and contextualized synchronic approaches are deeply complementary, particularly in reading the Bible in a fruitful way for both our minoritized communities and the broader society in which we dwell.

Where We Can Go

Before suggesting a path for the future of minoritized biblical studies, I must explain my own social location. Academically, I am formally trained in traditional historical critical methods of the Hebrew Bible. I attended a doctoral programme in Near Eastern Languages and Cultures with emphases on traditional fields like Semitics and archaeology. My graduate reading lists contained authors like William Albright and Frank Moore Cross, with little from authors like Homi Bhabha and

---

7. In addition, the field of biblical studies saw increased numbers of Catholic, Jewish and atheist scholars as well as more diversity in gender and sexuality.

8. For a snapshot, the Association of Theological Schools stated that in 1991, the non-White faculty was slightly less than 10%, a percentage which had grown to about 19% in 2012; see Association of Theological Schools (n.d.).

9. Despite advances in the work of minoritized criticism, Segovia (2009: 386) notices the lack of explicit theoretical foundation.

Jacques Derrida. Ethnically, I am a second-generation Korean American but, of course, that answer is distressingly simplistic. I have lived in Korea for a total of five years during adulthood, including a recent sabbatical year. Much of my life in America has been in communities with strong Korean American populations (San Francisco, Los Angeles), but I am raising my young family in a significantly less-diverse suburb near Portland, Oregon. I was raised in a Protestant household, and my interest in biblical texts was initially nurtured within faith contexts. To date, almost exclusively, my scholarship has drawn on ideas extrinsically distinct from my own persona. At the same time, I am aware that I have my biases, assumptions and agendas, like every other scholar.

With that said, it will come as no surprise that I largely object to the bifurcation between historical critical and minoritized approaches. Many of the scholars who work exclusively in the historical critical tradition perceive that minoritized readers have little interest in ancient contexts.[10] This assumption is false and does a tremendous disservice to those working along the lines of minoritized approaches. Since the beginning stage of post-critical scholarship, many traditional scholars considered the notion of reader bias as an attack on their own rigorous training in languages and exegetical methods. Several of these scholars rejected notions of reader-centred interpretations, decrying them as a freefall into relativism. But in fact, many minoritized critics are well trained in historical methods, apply them, and even come to similar results as historical critical approaches. Historical criticism and minoritized approaches need not be adversarial. In fact, the intersection of historical context and reader context can preserve an ideal theoretical platform for minoritized criticism.

Furthermore, the very concept of a clear divide between original and reader contexts is problematic. Historical criticism clearly teaches that biblical texts are composite, the result of continuous redaction of received traditions. For example, 1 and 2 Chronicles take earlier traditions from Samuel and Kings and rework and supplement the material to match the concerns of the Persian period. But in actuality, such editorial activity essentially replicates the actual work of Samuel and Kings, the rest of the deuteronomistic History, the Torah, etc. Each of these sections of the Hebrew Bible underwent formation and reformation during pre-exilic, exilic and post-exilic periods before crystallization into the Hebrew Bible. These biblical narratives were written down precisely because they were presumed to have value for future generations who received and adapted those traditions. Consequently, Bible scholars must reconsider the supposed bifurcation between text and readers.

To this problem, Brennan Breed proposes that this fuzzy boundary between text and reader can actually provide a way forward through the concept of a 'nomadic' text (Breed 2014: 131–41).[11] Because of the lack of any singular context,

---

10. In particular, see the assumptions of John Barton's passionate defence of historical criticism (Barton 1998: 9–20).

11. See the expanded theoretical basis in Breed's monograph (2014: 15–51); also a concise summary with insightful responses by Nyasha Junior, Jeremy Schipper and William Brown in *At This Point* (Breed 2015).

Breed suggests an avoidance of any direct questions regarding a purported original, but rather encourages the alternate question of 'What Can This Text Do?'(Breed 2015). He argues that this question can still account for contextual origins but can more productively examine the function of texts within communities across spatial and temporal boundaries. Breed proposes that intentional attention to the life of the text will catalyze new dialectic approaches in scholarship, ultimately widening the possibilities for biblical theology. For him, these spaces include 'learning across those borders, from other communities, about their versions and meanings and contexts for sacred scripture' (Breed 2015). He argues that historical contexts can offer a starting point in the discussion of texts, but that the social locations of readers can then extend these discussions in directions most meaningful for those particular locations.

Many questions remain as to how to regulate dialectical work that takes these three worlds in place. How do readings co-exist with paradoxical, even contrarian readings? Of course, the tendencies to prioritize certain readings, without some methodological control, may merely result in reinforcing interpretive hegemonies that have been plaguing biblical studies since its inception. For minoritized critics, questions of textual authority are particularly significant, as assimilation is an immigration strategy. Thus, readings of biblical texts are often tied to our own communities of faith; and when such readings subvert traditional notions of authority, minoritized critics find themselves excluded from their own social group.

It is in response to this question that I draw on three landmark Society of Biblical Literature presidential addresses: by Vincent L. Wimbush, the first African American to hold the position (2010); Fernando F. Segovia, the first Latinx American from the global south (2014); and Gale A. Yee, the first Asian American and first woman of colour (2019). Each of these addresses gives a distinct contribution to the place of minoritized criticism. All three presidential addresses have different perspectives and unique callings to the biblical studies guild. But areas of convergence arise, and these convergences may serve to guide us in claiming our own place as minoritized critics.

First, minoritized criticism must claim relevance beyond the academy. Wimbush confronts the painful racial history of the Society of Biblical Literature, particularly in the absence of intentional spaces for minoritized critics, citing the late 1980s as a key moment of change with the publication of Cain Hope Felder's *Stony the Road We Trod* (1991) at the initiative of Thomas Hoyt Jr and John W. Waters (Wimbush 2011: 7). Wimbush uses the categories of 'enslaving', 'enslaved' and 'runagates' from Frederick Douglass' *Narrative of the Life of Frederick Douglass, an American Slave, Written by Himself* (1845). For Wimbush, the key figure was the 'runagate' as a runaway in both body and consciousness. As an analogy of the Society of Biblical Literature, Wimbush was arguing that the critical interpreter 'must seek to escape, must run, must be oriented "outside the circle"' (Wimbush 2011: 20). The 'circle' stands for traditional historical critical studies, which had erroneously connected the ancient Near Eastern world to the modern White world (2011: 12). But the double-consciousness of the runagate led to a certain clairvoyance in interpretation.

The call for a runagate is not restricted to black interpreters, but is for all who can recognize ways in which biblical texts have been harnessed and used as an instrument of oppression. For Wimbush, the experiences of the minoritized critic can potentially occupy a unique vantage point in biblical readings to impact broader society.

Similarly, Segovia draws on earlier Society of Biblical Literature presidential addresses to argue that, historically, the biblical studies guild has called for societal impact during critical times. The place of intellectualism as a positive force on a wider society is neither assumed, nor self-evident. Segovia builds on Edward Said and argues for a formative place of intellectual spaces to influence and challenge trends in the general populace (Segovia 2015: 26). He describes the present age as a period with multiple crises. Biblical readings must 'bring the field to bear upon the major crises of our post-Cold war times, in both individual and converging fashion' (2015: 26). Segovia calls for a biblical criticism that will bridge these worlds of text, interpretations and interpreters. This relevance seems magnified for those Bible scholars who find themselves primarily in positions of relative privilege as professors and administrators at institutions of higher education. Segovia then argues that an impactful political discourse can address three primary issues of importance for these times: global economics, climatological problems and worldwide migration.

Second, minoritized criticism must be dialectical in order to achieve societal relevance. A dialectical approach can allow for greater access to speak and represent multiple readings of a biblical text. Such scholarship must create methodological entry points for sharing concerns and readings. Of course, the danger of emphasizing the interpreter's context may result in forms of relativism or chaos. Because readings of the Bible often tie to faith communities, a methodological frame must guide the readings. Herein lies a critical way forward and crucial task for minoritized scholars. In accord with our given space in academic circles, we must strive to engage in dialogues not just among other minoritized biblical scholars, but for all those who engage with the thematic elements within biblical texts. For example, Breed's question of 'What Can the Text Do?' can extend dialogue beyond scholars to broader reading communities.[12] Accordingly, minoritized scholars must read the Bible in a way that empowers moral and ethical directives for our world. Our readings should connect communities and help people come to a better understanding of the religious dimensions of our texts.

Gale Yee's presidential address provides an example on the fecundity of such dialectical interpretations. As the first woman of colour and the first Asian American to be elected as the president of the Society of Biblical Literature, Yee (2020) connects her own personal narrative identity to her interpretive lens. In approaching biblical texts, Yee recognizes, 'Depending on one's social location as a

---

12. One must be aware of the tensions between the issues of inclusion and exclusion under the rubric of 'biblical scholars'; Schipper (2015) argues that the dialectic must cross the disciplinary silos and engage those outside of academic fields, broadening access to the dialogue.

gendered, raced, classed and etcetera'd individual, one must recognize that she could simultaneously be both oppressor and oppressed, powerful and powerless, because of her different and shifting locations in a matrix of domination' (Yee 2020:16). She then presents an intersectional study of the impoverished widow of 2 Kgs 4.1-7 as a demonstration of the ways that different components of one's identity will overlap and even contradict. The analysis is a rich invitation to a broadly dialogical interpretation.

Third, minoritized criticism must be interdisciplinary. Because minoritized critics represent such a broad swath of humanity, diverse theoretical approaches must frame the dialogue. Social models often set delimiters in categories such as ethnicity, gender and class; thus, these models can incorporate perspectives outside of the traditional majority readers and connect overarching themes across different minoritized groups. Since the onset of sociological approaches in the 1980s, biblical scholars have been better equipped to apply such models judiciously.[13] Nowadays, we are more aware of the dangers of anachronism or the temptation to let social models straitjacket readings of texts. Instead, we recognize that the best sociological readings catalyze our imaginations and help us understand new ways of reading.[14] These interdisciplinary approaches allow for input from those not trained in the historical critical field; one can think of the impact in biblical studies of literary scholar Robert Alter or anthropologist Mary Douglas. Such interdisciplinary dialogue must be nurtured further, as the current modus operandi is actually more fractionalization and insular work.

Thankfully, many of the approaches towards minoritized biblical criticism already seek to be broadly impactful, dialogical and interdisciplinary. With the loosened hegemony of historical critical methods, a minoritized criticism in this spirit may contribute to reinvigorate biblical scholarship. For much of modern critical study, biblical criticism has been sterile, with formulaic approaches such as text criticism to source criticism to redactional criticism and so on. I wish to present repatriation as a reading strategy for minoritized criticism. In line with previous musings on minoritized criticism, repatriation readings need not serve as 'prescriptive,' but rather, 'prefigurative' (Liew 2008: 2). My 'prefigurative' approach interprets Ezra-Nehemiah through the experience of repatriating back to Korea as a second-generation Korean American. Consequently, development of prominent Ezra-Nehemiah themes, such as identity, coalesce around the interplay between the text and my lived reality of speaking Korean, and relationships with my Korean extended family. More specific examples appear below. For now, suffice it to say

---

13. For a recent review of social scientific approaches, see Chalcraft, Uhlenbruch and Watson 2014.

14. In my own specialty of ancient economies, economic anthropological theories have helped Bible scholars think of non-capitalist settings without modern equivalents of money, inflation, and unemployment. More than give us new terms, sociological models allow us to enter ancient Near Eastern contexts so different from our natural intrinsic modes of life. Such economic paradigms place high value on social relations, kinship and land, values associated with Asia and Africa more than with North America; see Nam 2012: 29–69.

that this reading strategy makes no claim to interpretive exclusivity; rather, this particular lens is intended to open up complementary visions of the text and how it can richly articulate the minoritized contexts of today's readers in line with the ancient contexts of the repatriate Judeans of the Persian Empire.

Reading Repatriately

In the early twentieth century, the social sciences established immigration studies as an academic field, in response to the massive influx of Europeans to the United States and the accompanying controversies resulting from this demographic shift.[15] Immigration research was extraordinarily interdisciplinary in its approach, with contributions from history, sociology, anthropology, linguistics, even archaeology. But despite the relative longevity of immigration studies as a field of research, it is only very recently that repatriate studies have emerged as a distinct subdiscipline, and it is still in very nascent stages.[16] Scholars often assumed that returning home was a relatively straightforward phenomenon. To complicate matters, countries typically did not collect data on repatriation as they did not consider their own returning citizens as 'immigrants' (Koser 2000: 57–67). But with the rapidity of globalization, along with the sheer number of migrants, scholars have appropriately realized the unique experience of return to a country of origin. Repatriation pervades all geographic and temporal boundaries. One recognizes repatriation during every period of recorded history. Presently, the study of repatriation has become both humanistic and humanitarian. It is humanistic in that repatriation concerns itself with the real struggle regarding identity issues of displaced peoples. It is humanitarian in that political freedom and economic survival often motivate the repatriation.

With repatriation studies as a relatively new field, scholars have yet to find consensus on a singular definition of repatriation, though most adopt George Gmelc's definition of repatriation as 'any movement of emigrants back to their homeland to resettle' (Gmelc 1980: 136).[17] The reasons for initial emigration are varied: long term study abroad, political and religious refugees, mail order brides, long-term migrant workers, forcibly abducted slaves, etc. Gabriel Scheffer (2006: 143-5) distinguishes between 'repatriation' which he declares as 'forced', against more neutral and voluntary movements back to the homeland due to pragmatic economic and social pressures. Francesco Cerase (1974) identifies four types of repatriates: retirement, failure, conservatism (never intended to integrate), or

---

15. For a broad review of the intellectual history of immigration studies, see Foner, Rumbaut and Gold 2003.

16. See Rumbaut 2003; the first focused study on the phenomenon of repatriation developed from a working group in the American Anthropological Association under Robert Rhodes (1979).

17. The publication of Gmelc's article on repatriation marked the legitimization of repatriation as a subdiscipline within immigration studies.

innovation (returns with innovation). Michael Piore (1979: 60–1) simplifies Cerase's model into two main, self-explanatory types: success and failure, with parameters for judgment primarily economic. Some even dispute the term repatriation, preferring 'transnationalism', to emphasize the liminality between two political and cultural identities, or even 'circular migration,' emphasizing the temporal nature of multiple repatriations. The latter term is apt as the return to a country of origin is often a single step from a continuous migration pattern (Bartram, Poros and Monforte 2014: 121–4).

Despite the formidable role of the post-exilic repatriation for the development of the Hebrew Bible, repatriate studies have not received much coverage in biblical studies. Admittedly, we have little reliable data on the Judean repatriation of the sixth and fifth centuries BCE. Though it contains historically dubious data, Ezra-Nehemiah does recount a rich report of a repatriate existence. The report can take priority over any Von Rankean historical construction, particularly if read through the lens of social memory. As Bible scholars have demonstrated, it is often the memory of the event that is more informative than the actual historical event.[18] This social memory within Ezra-Nehemiah will help to consolidate into a portrayal of repatriate life in Yehud. This self-identity in narrative and labels provides a meaningful paradigm to understand the place of the remnant in the greater Persian world. To this end a theology that encapsulates this complexity is long warranted.

The Judean return as articulated in Ezra-Nehemiah offers an opportunity to reflect on modern Korean repatriation for two primary reasons. First, for Koreans, the historical construction of Korea is deeply tied to blood purity, almost obsessively so (Shin 2006: 2–6). Ethnic purity reflecting national ideology often reaches official policy, such as in president Park Chun Hee's declaration to Koreanize the national language, thus temporarily eliminating Chinese characters from the writing systems. Nationality and ethnicity can be synonymous. Japanese colonial policies of forced assimilation in the twentieth century ironically strengthened Korean nationalism. The end of Japanese colonization in 1945 did not slow down this emphasis on blood purity; rather, the Korean War and subsequent American military occupation continued to bring issues of purity and emphasis on racial homogeny to the forefront. These issues continue to manifest themselves in different ways: explicit parental distrust of marrying foreigners, resistance over adoption, negative attitudes towards multi-racial children, renaming of lexical items, insistence on domestic rice – all stemming from a sometimes illogical commitment to nationalism and ethnic purity.

---

18. Bible scholars see the post-exilic period as a defining vantage point for the Israel narrative, thus the recollection includes many of their own projections; consequently, the usage of social memory in Hebrew Bible studies has exploded of recent years. Prominent examples includes Davies 2008; Edelman and Ben Zvi 2014; Edelman and Ben Zvi 2013; Zerubavel 1995. Much present research draws on Jan Assmann's seminal work on cultural memory as a tool for forging identity for ancient Egypt (1992).

Second, Korean American repatriation comes after a much more long-term displacement. Helpful for discussion of a repatriate theology in Ezra-Nehemiah, some studies focus on the experience of second-generation peoples on return to their country of origin.¹⁹ Not surprisingly, many of these repatriates have great hope at their return, but often are shocked to find a very different place. Still others are disappointed that their homes remained static and did not change at all. Oftentimes, such returns result in conflict with original peoples. For others, repatriation does not close the migration loop, as further disenchantment leads to additional migration. Many second-generation repatriates arrive in Korea with cultural ties more tuned to America. Most have limited Korean language skills. Because of the long period of expatriation, Korea has changed dramatically since the family of origin's period. During the 1960s, when my parents emigrated from Korea to the United States, Korea had an economy comparable to poorer Asian and African countries. It is now the world's thirteenth-largest economy, according to the 2014 Gross Domestic Product. Associated with this long-term repatriation is the voluntary nature of the migration. Despite Cyrus' magnanimous edict, some of the diaspora Judeans freely chose to remain in their new countries. Similarly, the movement of Korean Americans back to Korea is almost always voluntary and not life dependent. These Korean Americans return with social capital from their roots and try to form their place in a very different land. There are many divergences between the Korean American and the Judean returnee, but these points of contact encourage a dialogical investigation of those repatriate journeys.

The Korean American repatriation is merely one example across the world. Yet within such diversity of repatriate experiences, it is striking to observe broad commonalities that all of these disparate experiences share. Whether the repatriation is in the East or the West, whether after forty-seven weeks or even forty-seven years, whether the repatriates are self-perceived as rich or poor, or whether coerced politically or voluntary, repatriates share a common experience. The period of expatriation changes both the migrant as well as the mother country, sometimes in extreme ways. If such commonality can expand across social scientific studies of repatriation, then I suggest that these modern repatriate experiences may integrate our experiences as minoritized critics in a way that centers on the repatriate experience in biblical texts.

A Repatriate Reading of Ezra-Nehemiah

A full repatriate reading of Ezra-Nehemiah cannot be done here and will be reserved for a future work (Nam 2021). But I will briefly offer how a repatriate lens can enhance an imaginative reading behind some of these texts. Of course, the Judean repatriation heavily influenced much of the Hebrew Bible, especially books like Chronicles, Esther, Ruth and Daniel. But I wish to focus on four themes that

---

19. See Mandel 2008, Christou 2015; for a recent Korean American repatriation perspective, see Kim 2008.

emerge in Ezra-Nehemiah, as they explicitly focus on the return and resettling in Judah. These themes are neither exclusive to nor comprehensive of the theology within Ezra-Nehemiah; but I will contend that they may potentially capture the repatriate experience as contained in the biblical texts, as well as parallel migrations of today. I contend that a repatriate theology can provide a framework to allow us to articulate the uniqueness of our repatriate experiences with each other and with the experience of the Judean returnees as portrayed in Ezra-Nehemiah. Such a dialogue can serve the stated mandate of minoritized criticism.

Trauma

Although the exile experience has driven much of trauma scholarship in biblical texts, social displacement theories suggest that the repatriation event was similarly traumatic.[20] Repatriates often hold a utopian vision of a return. But multigenerational returns to a homeland reveal the brokenness of such utopian visions. Instead of belonging and security, repatriates often face immediate crises both pragmatic, such as economic hardship, as well as existential, such as questioned identity. Such confrontation between perception and lived reality generates trauma in the repatriation. Cathy Caruth describes trauma as an event and continuing memory, which 'registers the force of an experience that is not yet fully owned' (Caruth 1995: 151). In this regard, Ezra-Nehemiah forms a type of trauma literature, as articulated by Caruth, which calls for both recognition and continued expression of the traumatic event. Whereas Chronicles and much of the prophetic literature present the return to Jerusalem as the triumphant restoration of Israel, in Ezra-Nehemiah the returnees meet immediate conflict and their hopeful return quickly digresses into an unsettled homecoming. Ezra shatters the optimism of the Cyrus Edict (Ezra 1.1-4) with reports of verbal and political struggles with surrounding adversaries. In the Nehemiah Memoir, the trauma of repatriation figures prominently at the outset, with the battered state of the city walls and gates (1.3) leading to Nehemiah's response of weeping, fasting and penitential prayer (1.4-11). The rest of Ezra-Nehemiah follows a similar movement of crisis in the midst of the struggle to re-establish religious practices. This paradoxical movement of trauma throughout restoration is particularly evident in divergent responses to the completion of the temple, as most of the people respond with joyful praise, but the older ones 'wept with a loud noise' (Ezra 3.12). This remembrance of the earlier temple stymies the celebration with overtones of nostalgic longing for the past glories of the monarchic era.

Power

Like all social displacements, repatriation necessitates adjustments to new positions of power. As a starting point, repatriation can utilize Hannah Arendt's

20. Some of the important works on trauma studies include Carr 2014; O'Connor 2001; and Smith-Christopher 2002.

definition of power, which draws on classical Weberian notions of domination but also recognizes how the actions of community can negotiate power in subversive ways (Arendt 1969: 43). This understanding of power works well for Ezra-Nehemiah, as the community navigates power relations with both the local groups who stayed in the land and the Persian overlords. But whereas Ezra-Nehemiah recognizes their subservience to the Persian overlords, the texts clearly present the muted yet pervasive power of God as ultimately authoritative, as evident from the opening verse in which the 'Lord moves the heart of Cyrus, King of Persia' (Ezra 1.1). Throughout the narrative, Judeans subversively negotiate their place within the empire through local and imperial instruments of power, namely taxation and textuality. Ezra-Nehemiah generally gives a positive portrayal of taxation, in that it supports the temple and those who service its cultic practices (Ezra 6.3-10, 7.15-24; Neh. 10.32-39, 13.10-14). By pledging continued tribute, the returnees demonstrate their loyalty to the Persian leaders, who replaced the defunct Davidic line. This loyalty empowers the returnees against their adversaries, resulting in the completion of the temple and the city walls, two tangible expressions of restoration.

In addition to taxation, Ezra-Nehemiah prominently features the role of textuality, another instrument of ancient Near Eastern power, which is adopted by the returnees to leverage their own authority. Written texts form the major blocks of Ezra-Nehemiah. The two nearly identical lists of returnees (Ezra 2.1-70; Neh. 7.6-72) surround the activities of rebuilding the temple and the wall. Ezra-Nehemiah employs code switching to Imperial Aramaic in integrating the royal epistles to navigate the conflict between the returnees against the various adversaries. Ezra-Nehemiah presents written Torah as divinely authoritative even against imperial taxation in Neh. 5.1-13.[21] The public reading of the text spurs reconstruction of the temple and repair of the wall. Even the physical scroll features prominently in the dedicatory ceremony (Neh. 8.5). Although Ezra-Nehemiah accepts colonized status for the Judeans, the strategic adoption of taxation and textuality along with their respective reformulation for the Judean interests brings power to the *golah* against their adversaries.

Identity

The repatriate struggle within the Persian orbit of power propels new expressions of their identity, a crucial marker for Ezra-Nehemiah as evidenced by the flurry of recent scholarship on Second Temple identity.[22] Richard Jenkins provides a suitable understanding of identity as 'ways in which groups and individuals define themselves and are defined by others on the basis of race, religion, ethnicity,

---

21. See Frei 2006: 4–50, and rebuttal in Ska 2006: 161–182.

22. One of the foundational aspects of this repatriate self-understanding is terms that the repatriates use to refer to themselves. Notably, Ahn 2011: 27–34; 40–66 uses migration studies; also consider Becking 2011: 43–57, Jonkers 2011: 11–28 and articles in Knoppers and Ristau (eds) 2009.

language, and culture' (Jenkins 2008: 4). This definition emphasizes differentiation, a crucial part of the identity negotiation in the repatriation of Ezra-Nehemiah. Throughout the history of interpretation, scholars have not sufficiently recognized the repatriate context of identity in Ezra-Nehemiah, resulting in mischaracterizations of exclusionism and xenophobia. For example, some of the theologically challenging passages, such as on the mixed marriage crisis, must be interpreted in light of the challenge of forging identity in repatriation. The Judeans, as a subjected group within the Persian Empire, face a real danger of ethnic extinction from assimilation. The multiple exiles and contention with local groups makes identity formation immensely crucial for the repatriates. Consequently, Ezra-Nehemiah constructs an identity based on the community's own chosen standing before God, sustained through the exile experience. The shared exile forces a binary view of identity, isolating Judeans against all other local groups. The text primarily refers to the returnees as the 'children of exile' (Ezra 4.1; 6.19; 8.35; 10.6; 10.16) or 'the exile' (Ezra 1.11; 9.4; 10. 6, 8), in addition to other exclusive labels such as the 'holy seed' (Ezra 9.2), the 'remnant' (Ezra 9.13, 14-15; Neh. 1.3), 'assembly of the exile' (Ezra 10.8), 'returnees of exile' (Neh. 7.6), and 'assembly of God' (Neh. 13.1). These terms of self-identity contrast against competing groups, such as the now maligned 'people of the land' (Ezra 4.4, 9.1,2,11, 10.11; Neh. 9.10, 24, 10.30). Furthermore, Ezra-Nehemiah omits any mention of the diaspora Judeans in Egypt (cf. Elephantine papyri; Jer. 44.26-27). The multiple census lists rigidly define this strict identity by naming the returnees (Ezra 2, Nehemiah 7), as well as the constructors of the wall (Neh. 3.1-32), the signatories of the pact (Neh. 10.1-28), resettlers (Nehemiah 11), and priests and Levites (Neh. 12.1-26). The Jerusalem wall has a similar function of identity demarcation, but the exclusivity is more pronounced, with a physical barrier that separates the *golah* from the rest of the world (Oeming 2012). The Levitical prayer of Nehemiah 9 shapes the internal character of this repatriate identity, moving beyond mere separation to Torah obedience and exclusive worship through a fiercely monotheistic view of Yhwh.

Hope

Within the successive generations of repatriation, the *golah* communities face trauma, power struggle and continued quests for identity. Despite these difficulties, the very movement of repatriation implies an underlying hope, and that a difficult journey will culminate in the fulfillment of a better existence. Ezra-Nehemiah expresses such hope in different forms throughout the narrative. At strategic points, hope comes in the form of the Persian rulers, who act favorably towards the returnees (Ezra 1.1-14; 6.3-12). In other places, the object of hope moves to Yhwh through penitential prayers (Ezra 9.6-15; Neh. 1.5-11, 9.5-37), which unabashedly express struggle, but end in confidence in divine restoration. The weaving themes of trauma, power, and identity necessitate dependence on God to bring hope to the *golah* in the midst of their repatriation struggles. The Nehemiah Memoir closes in turmoil. In the midst of proclamations of joy, the last chapter of Ezra-Nehemiah speaks of the ongoing issues of mixed marriages, discord, the need for Levites to work, Shabbath violation, and continuous encroachment from foreigners. Yet, the book still closes with the hopeful plea to 'Remember me, my God, for good' (Neh. 13.31).

Conclusions: Still Far from Home

These themes of trauma, power, identity, and hope emerge in the rich repatriate experiences of both the Judean returnees and the Korean diaspora. Social reality creates an opportunity for those who find themselves in repatriate spaces to provide readings for the distinct community who returned to Judea under the Persian Empire. These readings emphasize the crucial aspect of negotiating identity across borders and emerging with new complex understandings of the self. As with my child, this understanding arises most explicitly when confronted with a new social context.

Is our child Korean? Is he American? How do we address a child who is, at least for a moment, navigating his own identity? Perhaps the repatriation experience contributes to our parenting strategy. The question, raw and honest, from the voice of child was filled with complexity. The innocence of the child refracted a complex cultural experience of a Korean American child, born in LA, moved to Lake Oswego, Oregon, then repatriated back to Korea. Of course, his question was not simple to answer. As his parents, we turned back to the child as a fallback strategy, perhaps to mask our own lack of confidence in addressing the question:

'What do you think?'
He answered, 'I think that I am both Korean AND American'
(emphasis exaggerated, as befitting a six-year-old child.)
'You are absolutely right,' I replied.

And so he is.

Bibliography

Ahn, John (2011), *Exile as Forced Migrations: A Sociological, Literary and Historical Approach on the Displacement and Resettlement of the Southern Kingdom of Judah*, BZAW, 417, Berlin: DeGruyter.
Arendt, Hannah (1969), *On Violence*, New York: Harcourt, Brace & World.
Assman, Jan (1992), *Das kulturelle Gedächtnis. Schrift, Erinnerung und politische Identität in frühen Hochkulturen*, Munich: Beck.
Association of Theological Schools (n.d.), 'Racial Ethnic Students Represent Largest Growth Area for Theological Schools', http://www.ats.edu/uploads/resources/publications-presentations/documents/racial-ethnic-growth.pdf accessed 28 March 2018.
Barton, John (1998), *The Cambridge Companion to Biblical Interpretation*, Cambridge: Cambridge University Press.

Bartram, David, Maritsa Poros and Pierre Monforte (2014), *Key Concepts in Migration*, London: Sage.
Becking, Bob (2011), *Ezra, Nehemiah, and the Construction of Early Jewish Identity*, Tübingen: Mohr Siebeck.
Blount, Brian (2019), 'The Souls of Biblical Folks and the Potential for Meaning', *JBL* 138: 6–21.
Breed, Brennan (2012), 'Nomadology of the Bible: A Processual Approach to Biblical Reception History', *Biblical Reception* 1: 299–322.
Breed, Brennan (2014), *Nomadic Texts: A Theory of Biblical Reception History*, Bloomington: Indiana University Press.
Breed, Brennan (2015), 'What Can Texts Do?: A Proposal for Biblical Studies', *At This Point*, https://www.ctsnet.edu/at-this-point/can-texts-proposal-biblical-studies/
Brenner-Idan, Athalya (2016), 'On Scholarship and Related Animals: A Personal View from and for the Here and Now', *JBL* 135: 6–17.
Carr, David M. (2014), *Holy Resilience: The Bible's Traumatic Origins*, New Haven, CT: Yale University Press.
Caruth, Cathy (1995), *Trauma: Explorations in Memory*, Baltimore: Johns Hopkins University Press.
Cerase, Fernando (1974), 'Expectations and Reality: A Case Study of Return Migration from the United States to Southern Italy', *International Migration Review* 8: 245–62.
Chalcraft, David J., Frauke Uhlenbruch and Rebecca Watson (eds) (2014), *Methods, Theories, Imagination: Social Scientific Approaches in Biblical Studies*, Sheffield: Sheffield Academic.
Chapman, Mark (2001), *Ernst Troeltsch and Liberal Theology: Religion and Cultural Synthesis in Wilhelmine Germany*, Oxford: Oxford University Press.
Christou, Anastasia (2015), *Counter-Diaspora: The Greek Second Generation Returns 'Home'*, Cambridge, MA: Harvard University Press.
Collins, John (2005), *The Bible after Babel: Historical Criticism in a Postmodern Age*, Grand Rapids: Eerdmans.
Davies, Philip R. (2008), *Memories of Ancient Israel: An Introduction to Biblical History*, Louisville, KY: Westminster John Knox.
Douglass, Frederick (1845), *Narrative of the Life of Frederick Douglass, an American Slave, Written by Himself*, Boston: Anti Slavery Office.
Drescher, Hans-Georg (1993), *Ernst Troeltsch: His Life and Work*, Minneapolis: Fortress.
Edelman, Diana V., and Ehud Ben Zvi (eds) (2013), *Remembering Biblical Figures in the Late Persian & Early Hellenistic Period*, Oxford: Oxford University Press.
Edelman, Diana V., and Ehud Ben Zvi (eds) (2014), *Memory in the City in Ancient Israel*, Winona Lake: Eisenbrauns.
Felder, Cain Hope (ed) (1991), *Stony the Road We Trod: African American Biblical Interpretation*, Minneapolis: Fortress.
Foner, Nancy, Ruben G. Rumbaut and Steven J. Gold (eds) (2003), *Immigration and Immigration Research for a New Century: Multidisciplinary Perspectives*, New York: Russell Sage Foundation.
Frei, Peter (2006), 'Persian Imperial Authorization of the Pentateuch', 4–50 in *Persia and Torah: The Theory of Imperial Organization of the Pentateuch*, ed. J. W. Watts; SBLSymS, 17; Atlanta: Society of Biblical Literature.
Gmelc, George (1980), 'Return Migration', *Annual Review of Anthropology* 9: 135–59.
Hom, Sharon K. (2001), 'Cross-Discipline Trafficking: What's Justice Got to Do with It?', 76–103 in *Orientations: Mapping Studies in the Asian Diaspora*, edited by K. Chuh and K. Shimakawa, Durham: Duke University Press.

Jenkins, Richard (2008), *Social Identity*, 3rd ed., London: Routledge.
Jonkers, Louis (2011), *Texts, Contexts and Readings in Postexilic Literature Explorations into Historiography and Identity Negotiation in Hebrew Bible and Related Texts*; FAT II, 53, Tübingen: Mohr Siebeck.
Kim, Nadia Y. (2008), *Imperial Citizens: Koreans and Race from Seoul to LA,* Stanford, CT: Stanford University Press.
Knoppers, Gary, and Kenneth A. Ristau (eds) (2009), *Community Identity in Judean Historiography: Biblical and Comparative Perspectives,* Winona Lake: Eisenbrauns.
Koser, Khalid. (2000), 'Return, Readmission and Reintegration: Changing Agendas, Policy Frameworks and Operational Programmes', 57–99 in *Return Migration: Journey of Hope or Despair?* edited by B. Ghosh, Geneva: International Organization for Migration.
Legaspi, Michael (2010), *The Death of Scripture and the Rise of Biblical Studies,* Oxford: Oxford University Press.
Liew, Tat-Siong Benny (2008), *What is Asian American Biblical Hermeneutics? Reading the New Testament,* Honolulu: University of Hawaii Press.
Mandel, Ruth (2008), *Cosmopolitan Anxieties: Turkish Challenges to Citizenship and Belonging in Germany,* Durham: Duke University Press.
Nam, Roger (2012), *Portrayals of Economic Exchange in the Book of Kings;* Biblical Interpretation Series, 112, Leiden: Brill.
Nam, Roger (2021), *Theology of the Books of Ezra and Nehemiah,* Cambridge: Cambridge University Press.
O'Connor, Kathleen (2001), *Jeremiah: Pain and Promise,* Minneapolis: Fortress.
Oeming, Manfred (2012), 'The Real History: Theological Ideal behind Nehemiah's Wall', 131–50 in *New Perspectives on Ezra-Nehemiah: History, Historiography, Text, Literature, and Interpretation,* edited by I. Kalimi, Winona Lake: Eisenbrauns.
Piore, Michael J. (1979), *Birds of Passage: Migrant Labour and Industrial Societies* Cambridge: Cambridge University Press.
Rhodes, Robert (ed.) (1979), *The Anthropology of Return Migration,* Norman: University of Oklahoma Press.
Rumbaut, Ruben (2003), 'Immigration Research in the United States: Social Origins and Future Orientations', 23–43 in *Immigration Research for a New Century: Multidisciplinary Perspectives,* edited by N. Foner, R. Rumbaut and S. Gold, New York: Russell Sage Foundation.
Said, Edward (1996), *Representations of the Intellectual: The 1993 Roth Lectures,* New York: Vintage Books.
Scheffer, Gabriel (2006), *Diaspora Politics: At Home Abroad,* Cambridge: Cambridge University Press.
Schipper, Jeremy (2015), 'Do Biblical Scholars Make Ideal Nomadologists?', *At This Point.* https://www.ctsnet.edu/at-this-point/biblical-scholars-make-ideal-nomadologists/
Segovia, Fernando (2009), 'Towards Minority Biblical Criticism: A Reflection on the Achievements and Lacunae', 365–94 in *They Were All Together in One Place? Towards Minority Biblical Criticism,* edited by R. Bailey, B. Liew and F. Segovia; *Semeia*, 57, Atlanta: Society of Biblical Literature.
Segovia, Fernando (2015), 'Criticism in Critical Times: Reflections on Vision and Task', *JBL* 134: 6–29.
Shin, Gi-Wook (2006), *Ethnic Nationalism in Korea: Genealogy, Politics, and Legacy,* Stanford: Stanford University Press.

Ska, Jean-Louise (2006), 'Persian Imperial Authorization: Some Question Marks', 161–82 in *Persia and Torah: The Theory of Imperial Organization of the Pentateuch*, edited by J. W. Watts; SBLSymS, 17; Atlanta: Society of Biblical Literature.

Smith-Christopher, Daniel (2002), *A Biblical Theology of Exile*, Minneapolis: Fortress.

Troeltsch, Ernst (1991), *Religion in History*, trans. J. Adams and W. Bense, Edinburgh: T & T Clark.

Wimbush, Vincent L. (2011), 'Interpreters – Enslaved, Enslaving, Runagate', *JBL* 130: 5–24.

Yee, Gale A. (2020), 'Thinking Intersectionally: Gender, Race, Class, and the Etceteras of Our Discipline', *JBL* 139: 7–26.

Zerubavel, Yael (1995), *Recovered Roots: Collective Memory and the Making of Israeli National Tradition*, Chicago: University of Chicago Press.

INDEX OF BIBLICAL REFERENCES

Hebrew Bible		23.39-43	193	15.10	46
		23.40	194, 195	15.63	12, 23
Genesis		27.16	22	19.38	46
1–2	49			19.41	46
1.24	49	*Numbers*		24.11	23
1.25	49	25.1-3	141		
1.26	49	25.4	47	*Judges*	
1.28	49	25.15-18	141	1.8	12
1.30	49	29	192	1.21	12
2.5	50	29.12	192	2.10	57
2.19-20	49	29.12-38	192		
3.19	57	35.33-34	44	*1 Samuel*	
4.10	44			10.1	144
8.9	50	*Deuteronomy*		10.25	144
8.22	50	7.1	12, 23	14.49	45
15.18	151	7.1-3	178	14.50	36
22.12	52	12.2-4	165	15.27-28	146
25.8	57	12.29-30	165	16	11
36.24	48	14.13	48	16.13	144
49.29	57	16	193	17	16, 17
49.29-33	57	16.13	193	17.54	16
49.33	57	16.16	193	18.19	45
		16.21	165	22.17	145
Exodus		17.3	165	25.2-44	36
3.8	12	17.15	144	25.16	101, 102
13.5	12	19.10	165	25.36	36
17	12	19.19-14	165	25.43	36
22.1	153	20.16-17	45		
23	192	20.17	12	*2 Samuel*	
23.16	192	23.4	179	2–3	60
23.23	12, 23	23.8-9	179	3.7	60
33.2	12, 23	31.10	193	3.13-16	37
34	192	32.4	51	5	16, 17
34.11	23	32.8	192	5.3c	20
34.14	12			5.6	12, 13
34.22	192	*Joshua*		5.6-9	1, 9, 11, 18
		3.10	23	5.7	13
Leviticus		9–10	60	5.8	10
11.14	48	9.3-27	45	5.9	13
23.33-36	193	10.12-13	46	5.13	34
23.37-38	194	15.7	46	5.14-16	20

2 Samuel (cont.)		23.13-17	14	22.4	140
6.23	38, 45	23.34	35	29–31	146
8.18	145	24	16, 17		
9	60	24.16	16, 21	*2 Kings*	
11–20	34	24.18	22	1	124, 130
11.1-2	35	24.18-25	20	1–2	120, 132
11.3	35	24.21-24	23	1.8	125, 127
12.8	36	41	10	2.1-18	124
12.11	35			2.11	124
13.15	10	*1 Kings*		3.7	140
15–20	39	1.5	145	4.1-7	210
15.1	145	1.7	145	8.18	140, 141
15.6	2, 35	1.8	145	8.24-25	141
15.16	32, 38, 39	1.15-31	142	8.26	140
15.16-17a	38	1.19	145	9.7–10	142
15.19-22	36	1.25	145	9.24	140
16.4	60	1.26	145	9.25-26	128
16.7	37	1.32	145	9.27	140
16.8	37	1.34	144, 145	9.27-28	141
16.20-23	32	1.38	145	9.29	141
16.21-22	2, 32, 35, 39	1.39	144	9.33	140
16.22	36	1.42	145	10.13-14	141
17.27-29	37	1.44-45	145	10.25	145
18.33	39	1.45	144	11.2-3	143
19.7	10	2.11	20	11.4	143, 144, 145
19.25-31	60	3	60, 114		
19.30	37, 38	3.4-5	46	11.11	145
20.1-3	35	3.16-28	3, 109	11.13–16	3, 139, 146
20.3	2, 32, 35, 38, 39	3.24-25	113	11.14	146
		4.13	166	11.16	141
20.11	37	8.53	46	11.18	146
20.23	145	9	50	11.19	146
21	62	9.1-3	46	11.20	141, 146
21.1-14	2, 43, 44, 46, 51, 60, 61	11.1-10	141	12.10	143
		14.27-28	145	12.21	140, 155
21.3-6	45	15.27-8	140	15.5	146
21.6	47	15.31	142	15.14	140
21.7	60	16.15-20	142	15.30	140
21.8	45	16.31	141	17.14	44
21.9	46, 47	16.32	141	21	168
21.9-10	67	17–19	120, 124, 130, 131	21.1-9	166
21.10	48, 49, 50, 51, 52, 53, 66	17.17-24	128	21.1-18	3, 165
		21	120, 124, 127, 128, 130	21.2	165
				21.3	165
21.14	53			21.6	165, 171
22	10	21.1-19	126	21.10-17	166
22.3	51	21.8-14	142	21.16	165
22.8-14	52	21.19	126	21.23	140
22.18	10	21.21–23	142	21.24	146
22.32	51	21.29	52	22.4	143
23.1-7	53			23.4	143

Index of Biblical References

2 Kings (cont.)
23.30	146
24	143
24.8	142
24.12	142
25.18	143
25.25	140

Isaiah
6.6	50, 69
40.22	51
51.13	51

Jeremiah
5.24	44
7.20	52
13.18	142
29.2	142
31.14	67
42.18	52
44.6	51
44.26-7	216

Ezekiel
5.5	11
13	50
24.8-7	52
29.5	50
31.6	50
31.13	50
32.4	50
38.20	50
40.18	50
42.3	71

Hosea
2.20	50
4.2	50

Jonah
3.10	52

Nahum
1.6	51

Habakkuk
2.4	205

Zechariah
10.1	44
13.4	127

Malachi
3.23-24	120, 122, 124

Psalms
95.1	51
104.2	51

Job
16.8	52
28.7	48

Esther
1.6	50
3.1	165
3.8-9	164
6.11	164
7.7	164
7.8	164
7.9-10	164

Daniel
9.11	52

Ezra
1–6	197
1.1	215
1.1-4	214
1.1-14	216
1.3	214
1.4-11	214
1.8	178
1.11	216
2	216
2.1-70	215
3	192
3.12	214
4.1	216
4.4	216
6.3-10	215
6.3-12	216
6.19	216
7	197
7.5	143
7.10	176
7.15-24	215
7.25	177
8.24	178
8.35	216
9.1	19, 216
9.1-2	178
9.2	216
9.4	178, 216
9.6-15	217
9.11	216
9.13	216
9.14-15	216
10.2	180
10.2-5	179
10.6	216
10.8	216
10.11	216
10.16	216
10.26	180

Nehemiah
1.3	216
1.5-11	216
3.1-32	216
3.7	60
5.1-13	215
7	216
7.6	216
7.6-72	215
8	191, 192, 197–8
8–10	191
8.1-8	197
8.5	215
8.13	191
8.14	191
8.15	191
8.15-16	194
8.16	191–2, 199
8.17	192
9	191, 216
9.5-37	216
9.8	19
9.10	216
9.24	216
10	191
10.1-28	216
10.30	216
10.32-39	215
11	216
12.1-26	216
12.27-43	197
13.1	216
13.10-14	215
13.31	217

1 Chronicles
1.40	48
11.4-9	19

Index of Biblical References

1 Chronicles (cont.)		24.20-25	155	Acts	
11.5	12	26.20	143	7.56	85
17.11-15	147	31.10	143		
29.27	20	33	168	Revelation	
		33.1-9	166	1.8	92
2 Chronicles		33.1-20	3, 165	3.7-13	98, 102
7.3	50, 71	33.2	165	3.10	98
8.7	19	33.3	165	3.12	98
12.10-11	145	33.5	165	4–5	93, 97
18.1-3	140	33.6	165	4.3	93, 102
19.1	143	33.7	165	4.7	97, 102
20.35-36	140	33.11-12	171	5.12-13	93
21.4	141	33.14-16	166	8.7	95
21.6	140	36.22-23	170	8.8	95
21.12	120			8.10	95
21.16-17	141	New Testament		8.12	95
21.18	166			9.1	95
22.1	141	Matthew		9.13	95
22.2	140	28.1	65	11.15	95
22.3	141			11.15-19	95
22.8	141	Mark		20.11-15	94, 102
22.9	141	16.1	65	20.15	94
22.11-12	143			20.21	102
22.12–15	146	Luke		21	92–3, 94, 96
23.1	143	1.44-55	33	21.5	92
23.12–15	3, 139	9.62	33	21.5-7	92, 102
23.15	141	18.18-43	33	21.6	92
23.21	141	18.35-43	33	22.1-2	92
24	155	24.10	65	22.2	98
24.6	143			22.13	92
24.11	143	John		22.14	96, 98, 100, 102
24.17	155	20.1	65		

INDEX OF AUTHORS

Ahlström, G. W. 21
Ahn, J. 215
Aloni, N. 48, 129
Alter, R. 210
Alterman, N. 123
Amit, Y. 125, 127, 128
Amitai, O. 130
Amorai, Y. 124
Anderson, A. A. 11, 12, 13, 14, 19, 24, 34, 47
Anderson, J. 169–70
Andrews, S. J. 22
Angel, M. D. 187, 188
Appleton, N. 112
Aran, G. 152
Arbeiter, A. 91
Arendt, H. 40, 41, 214–15
Arnold, B. T. 11, 13, 14, 19
Ashman, A. 142
Assis, E. 124
Assmann, J. 212
Auld, A. G. 24, 35
Avioz, M. 19
Ayali-Darshan, N. 192

B. Michael 153
Bachrach, Y. 128
Bal, M. vii
Baltzer, K. 191
Banai, J. 127–8
Barron, R. 34
Barton, J. 15, 207
Bartram, D. 212
Becker, J. 167
Becking, B. 215
Bede, V. 99
Beilen, Y. 147
Bell, S. 84, 85
Ben Amos, A. 120
Ben-Barak, Z. 144, 146

Ben-Yashar, M. 44, 52
Ben Zvi, E. 212
Bergen, R. D. 22
Berger, R. 91
Berlin, A. 38
Berlovitz, Y. 123, 130
Bird, P. A. 114, 115
Birnbaum, P. 150
Blatman, D. 150
Bloch, M. 128, 129
Blount, B. 204
Boon, P. G. 164–5
Bourquin, Y. 33
Brecht, B. 115
Breed, B. 207–8
Brenner, A. x, 46, 54, 62, 114, 115, 116
Brenner-Idan, A. 2, 4, 5, 140, 141, 204
Brewster, P. G. 110
Brison, O. 3, 4, 5
Brooks, S. S. 46
Brown, B. 176, 181, 183, 189
Brueggemann, W. 11
Bryant, W. C. 67, 70, 76–8
Buber, M. 128
Buchanan, A. S. 147
Buchanan, R. W. 65–6, 70, 71–2
Buchner, D. 168
Burney, C. F. 46
Butler, A. 99

Campbell, A. F. 10, 19
Capdevilla, L. 84, 85
Caro, J. 188
Carpenter, S. S. 84
Carr, D. M. 214
Carson, D. A. viii
Caruth, C. 214
Carvalho, C. L. 15
Cazelles, H. 47
Cerase, F. 211–12

Chafin, K. 11, 12, 13
Chalcroft, D. J. 210
Chang, T. 111
Chapman, M. 205
Chavel, S. 44, 45, 48, 50
Christou, A. 213
Cogan, M. 124, 126, 128, 145, 146, 147
Cohen, S. A. 140, 146, 153
Cohen-Levinovsky, N. 123
Collins, J. 205
Connor, C. 94
Cook, S. E. 16
Cowell, E. B. 112, 114
Crabtree, J. 9
Cutler, A. 91, 94

Davies, P. R. 170, 212
DiAngelo, R. 164
Dor, Y. 180
Doran, R. 195
Dossin, G. 49
Douglas, M. 210
Douglass, F. 208
Driessche, T. Van 86, 87, 88, 89, 90, 91, 95, 96, 97, 98
Driver, S. R. 45
Dror, Y. 126, 127
Du, W. 112, 114
du Plessis, T. (M.J.) 165
Due, M. W. ix
Duggan, M. W. 191
Duran, N. x
Dus, J. 46, 47
Dutcher-Walls, P. 141, 142, 144, 146

Echternkamp, J. 84, 87
Edelman, D. V. 49, 61, 212
Eerdmans, B. D. 195
Egan, R. 110, 111
Eiserer, H. 185
Elior, R. 149, 150, 152, 153
Ephron, D. 147
Eran, O. 147
Erisman, A. R. 14
Eskenazi, T. C. 178
Esler, P. F. 14
Euripides 198
Evans, K. 148
Evans, S. 85

Fanon, F. 41
Fausbøll, V. 112
Felder, C. H. 208
Feldman, L. H. 167, 196
Feng, X. 113
Fichman, J. 124
Filkins, D. 155
Fischer, S. 152, 153, 154
Fokkelman, J. 51
Foner, N. 211
Fontaine, C. R. 113, 114
Frayne, D. 49
Freedman, R. O. 140, 147, 149
Frei, P. 215
Freytag, A. 86, 87, 88, 89, 90, 91, 95, 96, 97, 98
Fried, L. S. 4, 180
Friedman, I. 140, 153
Friesen, C. J. 198
Frolov, S. 46, 47, 48
Frye, S. 113

Garsiel, M. 48, 126
Gaster, T. H. 110
Gavrieli, N. 129
Gesundheit, S. 193
Gevaryahu, H. 124, 128
Gilsdorf, S. 91, 94
Gilson, E. 164
Ginzberg, L. 124
Glück, J. J. 13
Gmelc, G. 211
Goebel, S. 84
Gold, S. J. 211
Goldstein, J. 148,
Goldstein, J. A. 195
Gordon, R. P. 11, 12, 13
Goren, Z. 125
Grabbe, L. 21
Gray, J. 141, 143
Green, B. 36
Green, P. 198
Greenwald, I. 124
Gressmann, H. 109
Griffith, M. 63
Grimshaw, J. x
Grossman, H. 123
Gudenberg, E. von 88
Guo, L. 112

Ha-Levi, B. 127, 129
Hackett, J. A. 36
Hacohen, E. 122
Hadari, A. 4, 6
Halpern, B. L. 36, 166
Handy, L. K. 166, 167
Haran, M. 124, 128
Harper, F. E. W. 65
Havea, J. ix
Hayes, E. 65
Hays, J. D. viii
Heller, J. 46
Hemans, F. D. 65
Hens-Piazza, G. 14, 15
Henten, J. W. van 2, 5, 83, 85, 87, 93
Hentschel, G. 20, 34
Hertzberg, H. W. 20, 34, 44, 47, 48, 49
Hettling, M. 84, 87
Hill, A. E. 20, 34
Holm-Nielsen, S. 12
Hom, S. K. 204
Hoshen, D. 124
Huang, B. 112
Huang, W. 3
Hye-Jin 40

Inbari, M. 140, 153, 154
Irudayaraj, D. S. 1–2, 5, 14
Israel, C. E. 65

Jaishankar, K. 10
Japhet, S. 166, 167
Jastrow, M. 177
Jenkins, R. 215–16
Ji, X. 112
Jones, G. H. 12, 14, 20, 21, 24, 25
Jonkers, L. 215

Karchevsky, H. 123
Karpin, M. 140, 153
Katz, J. 150
Katzenstein, J. H. 140
Katznelson, I. 150
Kaufmann, Y. 124, 126, 127
Kegler, J. 13
Kelly, B. 166
Kendall, H. 66–7, 70, 75–6
Ketelsen, U.-K. 87
Kim, N. Y. 213

Kim, U. Y. 35
King, A. M. 85
Kipnis, L. 122, 125
Kirchmeier, F. 88
Kirsch, J. 10
Klausner, J. 128
Knechtges, D. R. 111
Knoppers, G. 215
Kochman, M. 142, 156
Kohlberg, E. 86
Koser, K. 211
Küppers, B. 89, 97

Lammfromm, T. 3, 4, 71
Lammfromm Lederson, T. 120, 130
Landay, J. M. 11, 21
Lasine, S. 114, 166, 167
Lau, B. 182, 183
Lau, P. H. W. ix,
Lee, A. C. C. x, 111
Legaspi, M. 204
Levenson, J.D. 11, 36
Levinas, E. 164
Li Q. 111–12
Liddell, H. G. 197
Liew, T.-B. 10, 204, 210
Lindbeck, K. H. 124
Lipschits, O. 197
Liss, H. 167
Liver, J. 144
Loewenshtamm, E. 145, 146
Lurz, M. 88, 95

McCarter, P. K., Jr. 11, 34, 39, 45, 49
Mair, V. H. 112
Mandel, R. 213
Marguerat, D. 33
Markus, K. 93
Martinez, F. G. 183
Mathias, Y. 120
Mbuvi, A. M. ix
Mbuwayesango, D. R. ix
Meer, F. van der 91
Meier, E. 99, 100
Merrill, E. 19
Meyers, C. L. 146
Miller, D.M. 124
Miller, R. D. 113
Monforte, P. 212

Montgomery, J. A. 46, 141, 143
Morgenstern, J. 141, 142
Morrison, C. E. 11, 13, 14, 16, 18, 19, 23, 36, 37, 38
Morrow, W. S. 168
Mosse, G. 87
Mossinson, B. 126, 127
Muraoka, T. 52

Nam, R. 4, 5, 210, 213
Naor, A. 124
Neff, A. 91, 93, 94
Nelson, W. B., Jr. 11, 21
Newsom, C. A. ix
Nicholson, E. W. 146
Nilsson, M. P. 198
Nir, R. 124
Nodet, E. 167
Noga-Banai, G. 91, 92
Noth, M. 48, 50

O'Connor, K. 214
Oeming, M. 216
Ofek 120
Ohm, A. T. 165
Okure, T. x
Onasch, K. 91
O'Neill, P. 93
Orel, V. 46, 47, 48
Oryanowski, A. 129

Page, H. 167
Paniyadi, G. A. 25
Park, H. H. 2, 5
Patte, D. viii, x
Payne, D. F. 11
Peli, P. 124
Penner, T. viii
Peretz, I. L. 131
Peri, Y. 147
Persico, T. 150
Piore, M. J. 212
Pisano, S. 20
Piwowar, A. 197
Plutarch 198–9
Poilpret, A.-O. 91
Poirier, J. C. 14
Polak, F. A. 64
Polzin, R. 36–7, 47

Poros, M. 212
Poulssen, N. 47, 50
Powell, M. A. 48, 49, 50
Prawer, M. 182, 183

Qian, Z. 110–11

Rabinovich, I. 148, 149
Ravitzky, A. 140, 152, 154
Raz, H. 123
Reshef, S. 130
Reviv 142
Rhoads, D. viii, x
Rietz, H. W. M. 41
Ringe, S. H. ix
Ristau, K. A. 215
Roberts, H. 92
Robinson, G. 13
Rofé, A. 124, 126, 128
Römer, T. 165, 168, 169
Rosnak, A. 153, 154
Roth, M. T. 49
Rouse, W. H. D. 112, 114
Rozowsky, S. 122
Rubenstein, J. L. 196
Rudolph, W. 195
Rumbaut, R. 211

Sagi, R. 140, 152
Said, E. 33–4
Saloul, I 83
Scheffer, G. 211
Schiller, G. 91, 93
Schipper, J. 209
Schmelkes, Y. 187
Schoneveld, J. 126, 127
Scott, R. 197
Seeligmann, I. L. 126, 128
Segovia, F. F. viii, 10, 204, 209
Seng, Y. 112
Shaked, M. 120
Shapira, A. 122, 128, 133, 150
Sharpe, C. J. 15
Sheinfeld, A. 185
Shemesh, Y. 124, 126
Sherman, A. 185, 186, 187
Sherwood, Y. 14, 15
Shin, G.-W. 212
Shinan, A. 120

Shir, M. 125
Shneur, Z. 122
Shua, Z. 125
Simon, U. 120, 128, 133, 150
Sister, M. 126, 127, 128
Ska, J.-L. 215
Smart, C. 65
Smith, H. P. 44, 45
Smith, J. 99
Smith, J. Z. 22
Smith, M. 143
Smith-Christopher, D. 214
Snape, M. 84
Snyman, G. F. 3-4, 5, 164
Soggin, A. J. 146
Soltau, H. 88
Spera, L. 91
Spronk, K. 2
Stravakopoulou, F. 165, 166
Supercic, I. 93
Sutskover, T. 2, 4, 5, 57
Sweeney, M. A. 143, 144, 169

Tadmor, H. 124, 145, 146, 147
Talmon, S. 145, 146
Tchernichovsky, S. 5
Tennyson, A. Lord 66, 67, 70, 72-4
Theocritus 198
Thrall, M. E. 124
Tigchelaar, E. J. C. 183
Tolbert, M. A. viii
Troeltsch, E. 205
Tsevat, M. 146
Tsumura, D. T. 16

Uffenheimer, B. 124
Uhlenbruch, F. 210
Ulfgard, H. 192, 193

Vaka'uta, N. ix
van Keulen, P. S. F. 166
Van Seters, J. 145-6
Vancoillie, J. 89, 95
Vander Stichele, C. viii
VanderKam, J. C. 195, 196, 197
Vaux, R. de 146
Voldman, D. 84, 85

Waal, H. van de 93
Walter, C. 91, 94
Walters, S. D. 45, 47
Watson, R. 210
Welscher, L. 89, 94, 96
Wensinck, A. J. 124
Whiston, W. 196
White Crawford, S. 196
Wiener, A. 124
Wimbush, V. 204, 208
Winnington-Ingram, A. 84-6, 101
Winter, J. 84
Wolffe, J. 84, 85
Woodfin, W. T. 94
Wright, J, L. 2

Yadin 141
Yalan-Shteklis, M. 133
Yamada, F. M. 10, 41
Yee, G. x, 204, 209-10
Ying S. 111, 116, 117
Yoon, S.-H. 11
Young 99
Youngblood, R. F. 12

Zang, M. 111-12
Zer-Kavod, M. 180
Zerubavel, Y. 120, 212
Zimmerman, J. D. 150
Zuta, H. A. 129

www.ingramcontent.com/pod-product-compliance
Lightning Source LLC
Chambersburg PA
CBHW062148300426
44115CB00012BA/2045